THE SOCIAL BIOME

THE
SOCIAL BIOME

How Everyday Communication
Connects and Shapes Us

Andy J. Merolla and
Jeffrey A. Hall

Yale

UNIVERSITY PRESS

NEW HAVEN & LONDON

Published with assistance from the foundation established in memory of
Calvin Chapin of the Class of 1788, Yale College.

Yale University Press books may be purchased in quantity for educational,
business, or promotional use. For information, please e-mail sales.press@yale.edu
(U.S. office) or sales@yaleup.co.uk (U.K. office).

Set in Yale type by IDS Infotech Ltd.
Printed in the United States of America.

Library of Congress Control Number: 2024937390
ISBN 978-0-300-27214-7 (hardcover : alk. paper)

A catalogue record for this book is available from the British Library.

This paper meets the requirements of ANSI/NISO Z39.48-1992
(Permanence of Paper).

10 9 8 7 6 5 4 3 2 1

CONTENTS

PREFACE

Despite abundant technological tools to build and maintain relationships, it seems that people are feeling ever more disconnected from one another. Keeping in touch, making time for friends, and prioritizing connection require work. And right now, for so many of us, the social energy required to stay connected is in short supply.

That's not to say we've stopped communicating. Hardly. Best estimates suggest we speak, on average, sixteen thousand words per day. Add in texts, direct messages (DMs), emails, social media, and mobile notifications, and it's clear that we're awash in messages demanding our attention. But what are we getting out of all this communication? Perhaps more important, what are we contributing? Even if our quantity of communication hasn't necessarily waned, the nature and types of communication we're prioritizing seem all too often ill-suited to our social needs. We've found ourselves in an age of interiority marked by an individual and collective sense of inertia that stops us from creating the kinds of connections we need to flourish.

Relationships and the communication that builds them are hard and always have been hard, marked by paradoxes and disappointments. The fundamental need to belong that we all have necessitates mutual obligation, a condition that generates friction that humans are naturally equipped to manage. To do so, we need a balance of connection and solitude, but there are many interpersonal and societal barriers that make connection feel difficult to achieve. Furthermore, many of us seem to have become less accustomed to, and perhaps less capable of dealing with, the stressors that allow us to live fulfilling social lives. This situation matters because the less familiar we are with social stress, the more energy intensive it is to deal with. This leaves us in a state of social inertia. We feel stuck, which can lead to greater loneliness on the personal level and mistrust on a societal level. Because mustering enough energy to leave a state of inertia can be the most difficult stage of enacting change, we should look to moments of seemingly insignificant everyday interactions as starting points to catalyze us out of isolation and help us become more connected.

To cope with, if not reverse, ongoing trends toward disconnection, we must embrace the struggles inherent in interpersonal communication. Moving us into a world of greater sociability—a goal that we share with many practitioners, government officials, and academics—requires an appreciation of the tendencies that steer people away from it. We must understand why *not being social* sometimes makes a lot of sense and can be a safer choice. To that end, this book frames precisely why communication, relationships, and social life in general, despite their importance to our well-being, can feel so frustrating and complicated. We also explain why the rising disconnection people feel is not solely attributable to personal choices and priorities—the social world controls us as much as we control it. Social structures and institutions that govern our day-to-day lives often impede, if not outright antagonize, connection, thwarting even our best intentions to build positive relationships with others.

We wrote this book, though, not just to describe the cooling of our social climate and why this is a problem, but also to offer a hopeful vision of how people can create connections with one another in their daily lives. Informed by decades of research, we offer readers ways to think about everyday social life from a *communication perspective.* Such a perspective holds that we can better understand ourselves, our relationships, and the world around us by zeroing in on the complexities of, and opportunities within, moments of everyday social interaction. When we recognize just how consequential our day-to-day moments of interaction are, including the mundane ones, we can begin to scrutinize how we spend our days and the changes we might make to strengthen our relationships with others. Establishing and building meaningful relationships is hard work. But it's work worth doing.

To conceptualize that work, we're guided by the idea that we all inhabit unique communication environments that fundamentally shape our moments of social interaction. We call these communication environments *social biomes* — complex ecosystems or interconnected communities of relationships and interactions. We can think about our social biomes as consisting of all our individual moments of interaction — in-person and digital — with significant others, people at work, neighbors, store clerks, and complete strangers whom we just happen to come across. The types and diversity of our interactions and communication partners play critical roles in the health of our social biome and, by extension, our well-being. As we'll demonstrate, our daily social interactions are so important because as they accumulate, they shape, reflect, and reinforce our self-concepts and worldviews. Everyday moments of interaction provide opportunities to connect with others, and, as we argue throughout the book, we must take advantage of these moments.

A hopeful vision, of course, is not necessarily an easy one. We don't have the option of sidestepping the stress of social life if we want to build the kinds of connections that give meaning to our lives. We have to optimize *good* social stress by building routines of connection, all the while recognizing the inherent barriers to, and necessity of, our effort. Many of the healthiest habits, such as those involving diet and exercise, are notoriously difficult to maintain. Although we often admit—sometimes reluctantly—that doing the "healthy thing" feels good afterward, we still struggle to continue doing it. But the more we commit to it, the easier it gets. It's our hope that by exploring the evidence regarding the benefits (and limits) of connection and communication, while also envisioning your life as embedded within a social biome composed of all your moments of interaction, you'll think about your everyday communication and the possibilities for belonging and hope for yourself and others in new ways.

Chapter 1

COMMUNICATING TO BELONG

In a landmark study published in 2010, Dr. Julianne Holt-Lunstad, a Brigham Young University professor of psychology and neuroscience, and her colleagues discovered that social relationships have greater implications for mortality than physical activity, body mass index, and alcohol consumption do. Having high-quality social support and a rich social life are as predictive of longevity as smoking fifteen cigarettes a day is predictive of premature death.[1]

The evidence across a vast array of studies is remarkable:

- Social support, time spent socializing, and good relationships cause people to live longer, healthier lives.
- Spending time with friends and family predicts long-term happiness and life satisfaction.
- Social relationships can change over time, and when the change is positive, it can promote longevity.[2]

And you don't have to wait a lifetime to realize the value of human connection. A socially connected day is a better day.[3] Jeff and

---

1

his colleagues conducted an experiment over three years, with nearly a thousand participants across five college campuses, before, during, and after the initial outbreak of the COVID-19 pandemic. Student volunteers were randomly assigned to engage in one of seven different communication behaviors, including joking around with, being a good listener to, or complimenting a friend. Other volunteers were asked to carry out their day normally. These seven ways of being friendly mattered — even one conversation was enough for the participant to experience the benefits. Some of the volunteers took it upon themselves to be more social that day, and when they did, they felt more connected and less stressed.

You're welcome to leave it at that; the evidence is clear that having a good social life is beneficial.[4] But, for the curious, this chapter will answer a variety of questions about this fact. Why is a rich social life so important to our health? What is it about being human that makes social relationships so crucial? Are social needs like other needs, and how do they work? What's the role of everyday communication in meeting our social needs? The answers to these questions can help us understand, appreciate, and perhaps reconsider our obligations to one another.

Need, Nourishment, and Hope — Now and Later

Nearly all explanations about why social relationships matter start with the bond between an infant and its caregivers.[5] To survive and flourish, babies must form nonverbal connections with the adults who care for them.[6] Neuroscience tells us that two-week-old babies' brains are already active in areas associated with social cognition.[7] These physical connections and neural pathways help establish babies' secure attachments, which will go on to affect their sense of self-worth and trust in others throughout their lives.[8]

We need one another—from day one—not only to meet basic needs, but also to feel emboldened to pursue our passions. Early experiences of connection reverberate, shaping our capacity to hope across the life span. As the late psychologist and preeminent researcher of hope C. R. Snyder once put it, "To not connect with others, in many ways, is not to hope."[9] Although some people are predisposed to optimistic outlooks, research—including Andy's—has demonstrated that hope is best understood as created *between people* in moments of social interaction—from childhood onward.[10] Hope is as much about the *we* as the *me*.[11] Throughout this chapter, then, as we discuss the *need to belong* and its role in our everyday communication, it's critical to keep in mind that our day-to-day sense of belonging throughout our lives is foundational not just to good overall health, but also to our ability to achieve the hopes and dreams we have for ourselves and the people we care about most.

Communication and the Need to Belong

People love to talk. As the psychologists William von Hippel and Nicholas Smith observed, "Humans appear to be the only species on the planet that continually seeks opportunities to share the contents of their minds with each other, even when there is no immediate benefit from doing so."[12] Much of the content of our day-to-day talk is observational in nature, rather than purposeful or transactional.[13] Conversation also exceeds our typical limits of attention. Whether it's about sports, celebrity scandals, or the nuances of office politics, many of us can sustain a point of view and agree with or object to another's viewpoint for hours. If we include written and mediated communication along with face-to-face conversation, it's clear that we ceaselessly consume and produce communication.[14] Given how much energy and time communication occupies, it must serve a purpose.

In the early twentieth century, conversing sociably with others was identified as a fundamental human need.[15] This was an important shift from the idea that communication is merely a tool for achieving various other goals. Although several relationship scientists laid the foundation for these ideas, the need to belong gained its full articulation by a pair of psychologists, Roy Baumeister and Mark Leary, in the summer of 1993.[16] As Leary recounted, the big shift they were making from previous ways of thinking was considering belongingness to be "a master motive" in how we live out our daily lives.[17] At that time in his career, Leary was examining the ways we manage the impressions that others have of us. He argued that people don't attempt to look good just to look good — they do it in service of connection.[18] Connection with others, he recognized, was a primary drive.

Leary would later propose the concept of the *sociometer*, which is essentially an acceptance thermostat.[19] This mechanism attends to whether "I" am valued by others. When we sense that we're not accepted, we're motivated to rectify it by seeking approval. A successful self-presentation in times of embarrassment, for example, through apologizing or laughing off a mistake, can restore feelings of acceptance. Clearly, communication is an essential part of meeting the need to belong. The need to belong, however, doesn't lead people to communicate in any specific way per se. Rather, the need to belong exists — in a more general sense — to *keep us accepted by and in the good graces of other people.* Good thing, too. As we all know, people are fickle, relationships break up, and new friends are hard to make and keep. Every Tinder match doesn't end in marriage, and casual friends don't often become lifelong companions. We make mistakes and hurt one another. Against these headwinds, the need to belong creates an enduring motivation to keep us trying to connect. This innate drive, which evolved long ago, is both an animating force and a cementing glue.

Belonging and Mutual Obligation

In the remote valley of Lake Turkana in Kenya, the 1.7-million-year-old remains of a young female *Homo erectus* were discovered. The woman's bones were deformed by a disease called hypervitaminosis A, which comes from eating the liver of a carnivore. This painful disease makes it impossible to survive without help. Archeologists who studied the bones of our ancestor were surprised to learn she survived for weeks if not months with the disease. They concluded that "it was the first sign of tenderness in hominid evolution."[20] Once upon a time, isolation was a death sentence. Our social processes — the need to belong included — evolved in a time when the costs of isolation were extremely severe.

Forged in times long past, our neural structures prompt us to care about others. Even when we're alone, we spend a great deal of time thinking social thoughts. *What did they think of me? Did they like what I said? When am I going to see them again?* Social thinking is our default, which suggests that it's natural for us to feel obliged to others, to care about them.[21] Such obligation is evidenced by the fact that reciprocity norms are upheld in cultures across the world and mentioned in the writings of the ancients.[22] It's a fact of relational life, then, that as relationships develop, the people in them become increasingly inclined to act on behalf of each other.[23] Reflecting on the evolution of the need to belong, Leary told an interviewer that he "can't escape the conclusion that nature wanted to be certain that human beings paid adequate attention to potential and actual rejection" because "being valued and accepted was exceptionally important."[24]

Meeting the need to belong is an inherently interdependent process that spans *relationship types* (from strangers to spouses), *contexts* (from home to the workplace), and *time* (from birth to death).[25] That's one of the most fascinating aspects of belonging: it's not just about our close circle of family and friends. Consider that the majority of our daily interactions, and most of our waking hours for that matter, are shared with strangers and *weak ties* — people we don't know especially well.[26] We're all in this process of belonging together. Simply no alternative exists. And although the word *obligation* can evoke thoughts of duty and effort that might inspire dread, being obliged to others can be simpler and subtler than we might think. Belongingness is often communicated in small moments of day-to-day life with rather minimal effort. It happens, for instance, when we choose to text an old friend just to say "Hi," or to greet a stranger or coworker with dignity through a flash of acknowledgment and maybe even a smile.[27] Moving society at large toward greater inclusivity and connection requires us to appreciate and take seriously our social obligations. We must accept our interdependence — *what I do matters to those around me and what others do matters to me* — and recognize how that interdependence shapes our everyday communication.

Getting Your Social Calories through Communication

But what patterns of everyday communication are most supportive of belonging? The answer is complex. Why? Because human communication is, in a word, messy. The very definition of communication, in fact, has been disputed for decades. What counts? Is a passing glance or smile enough? Is it what you said or what you meant to say? Or is it what the other person heard or perceived? Maybe it's all those things. If so, what behavior isn't communication? To top it off, we use communication to describe communication, which adds another layer of muddle and mystery.[28]

For pioneering social scientists aiming to understand the general types of everyday interpersonal communication that build connection, simply asking people what they do and say during their daily social interactions presented a promising way forward. But how do you measure a conversation? Which characteristics matter? And how can you collect this kind of data soon after conversations occur? Relationship researchers arrived at a solution. Lad Wheeler, Harry Reis, and John Nezlek from the University of Rochester in New York and Steve Duck from the University of Iowa independently developed social interaction diaries. Volunteers carried these diaries to describe their conversations right after they occurred — with classmates, friends, strangers, partners, and family. Was the interaction pleasant? Was it formal? Was it meaningful? How well did you know the person you were talking to? And so on. The researchers found that certain characteristics of social interactions, such as whether they're generally positive or negative and whether a conversation partner is supportive, were linked to feeling more connected and less lonely. These approaches laid the foundation for methods social scientists commonly use today to understand moments of day-to-day communication.[29]

As anyone could tell you, communication, in addition to being pleasant, accepting, and meaningful, can also be hostile, dismissive, and dull. Sometimes it's rewarding and invigorating, and other times it makes you sick and tired. Interaction diaries capture this variability and suggest it's the nature of our day-to-day interaction that ultimately determines our *social nutrition*. The social nutrition concept was proposed by the psychologists Shawn O'Connor and Lorne Rosenblood from the University of Victoria in British Columbia in 1996. "Like the different foods we eat," wrote O'Connor and Rosenblood, "[social interactions] may provide us with different amounts of 'social calories' or 'social interaction units,' which correspond to the quality of an interaction."[30] The idea that social interactions, depending on their nature, can be nourishing suggests that interactions have some sort of calorie-like quality. Intriguingly, this idea also suggests that social interaction can be healthy for everyone, regardless of their inclination for interaction. Adopting both ideas nearly twenty years later, the psychologist Mike Prentice and his co-authors likened social interaction to oranges. Prentice and his colleagues tell the story of a woman who loves oranges so much that "she walks next door and enthusiastically asks that her neighbor try them. The neighbor, not much for oranges but agreeable, obliges and chokes one down. Although the neighbors diverge greatly in their wanting and liking of the oranges, the nutritive benefits won't be appreciably different between them."[31] This view suggests that engaging in conversation is like getting your five-a-day of fruits and vegetables.

Given that our communication appears to be linked to our health, the most basic question researchers from various fields have set out to answer is whether it's the quality or the quantity of communication that matters most. According to the social nutrition concept, it's reasonable to assume that quality is king. Ultimately, when quality and quantity are compared side by side, research supports that assumption.[32] But research shows that quantity still matters — that is, interaction quantity uniquely contributes to outcomes, including longevity. This makes sense. Just as we need healthy food *and* a sufficient amount of food, we need both quality and quantity in our interactions to thrive. One of the reasons people might be inclined to dismiss the value of interaction quantity is that so much of their day-to-day talk tends to consist of small talk and chitchat—what communication scholars have long referred to as *phatic communication*.[33] Although such talk is largely superficial and forgettable, it still has critical functions and social consequences. Phatic communication, irrespective of topic, can represent a choice to acknowledge another person as worthy of attention and time. It can instantiate a moment of joint orientation that implicitly communicates, "I see you, and value you, in this moment."[34] Speaking to the importance of interaction quantity, a study of nearly half a million people found that the frequency of social contact positively predicts the length of people's lives.[35] The healthiest communication pattern found in that study was having frequent conversations with a wide variety of people, including friends, family members, neighbors, workmates, and acquaintances. Frequent interaction, in sum, does appear to contribute uniquely and positively to health and well-being.

Yet high-quality, more "nutritious" talk, the complexities of which we explore in chapter 2, is most predictive of a longer life, less loneliness, and greater well-being.[36] The benefits of higher-quality talk have been found, for instance, in studies that digitally record little snippets of talk as participants go about their days.[37] We typically think of high-quality talk as occurring within close relationships, and that's often the case. Interaction within close, stable relationships is, after all, one of the most essential components of belonging.[38] But it's not the whole story. What we talk about and how we communicate matter independent of whom we talk to. Simply put, we can benefit by having a good conversation with strangers and close relational partners alike.[39] And, in what will be a theme throughout this book, high-quality talk doesn't always have to be a major commitment of time or energy to be beneficial.

To Want and To Have

Overall, then, sufficient amounts of high-quality communication, preferably at least some of which is with close relational partners, is crucial to meeting our need to belong. In general, when it comes to needs, there are two ways that researchers conceptualize them. In one sense, needs are a motivating force, moment by moment, as in "I'm hungry, I need to eat." In another sense, needs are a long-term requirement for survival, as in "people need food to live."[40] The need to belong functions in both ways. It manifests as a motivating force in day-to-day life when we long for company and companionship. In response to the feeling *I feel disconnected,* we're motivated to act to address that feeling by, for example, reaching out to a friend. When we find ourselves lacking connection, the need to belong prompts us to act, just as hunger prompts us to eat. Using fMRI and a clever research design, a group of researchers at MIT demonstrated just how similar our hunger for the company of others is to our hunger for food. After depriving volunteers of either social contact (both in person and online) or food for ten hours, the researchers scanned volunteers' brains. Neural activity in the midbrain and striatum, the areas associated with wanting or craving, was heightened for the socially deprived when they were shown photos of social activity and for the hungry when they were shown pictures of food.[41] Of course, we don't need to endure ten hours of social isolation to feel the need to belong. It's a common daily experience – more common, for instance, than a desire for coffee or alcohol.[42]

Baumeister and Leary contend that, because the need to belong is a fundamental part of the human experience, it's as powerful a drive today as it ever was. But they also believe that the widespread availability of communication technology in contemporary life represents a dramatic change in how people pursue belongingness.[43] There's widespread evidence that face-to-face communication plays a special role in fostering feelings of connection for adolescents, young adults, and older adults alike.[44] For socially isolated individuals, communicating through online channels can mitigate the harms of lost face-to-face contact, but it doesn't seem to fully replace it. In chapter 7 we propose a research-based hierarchy of mediated forms of communication. According to the hierarchy, telephone calls are probably the most connecting. Texting or DMs are less so, but still valuable, especially compared to no contact at all.[45] All these channels are better than browsing on social media, which research suggests might be better than no contact whatsoever—but might be worse.[46]

The hierarchy of channels is most important to remember in times when we're really hungry for connection. When we're experiencing a high need to belong in a day, or during a particularly tough time of life, online contact is likely at its most helpful, but it still is no substitute for in-person company.[47] This ranking of channels assumes, though, that the interactions available to us are at least somewhat pleasant; hurtful and mean-spirited communication is typically harmful no matter the channel. Overall, the literature supports the following conclusion: although some mediated communication is truly amazing and some in-person companionship is detrimental, the need to belong can't be fully satisfied in the long-term physical absence of other people. Some social interaction and at least one close relationship partner appear to be bare minimum requirements for us to get our need to belong met, which is consistent with Baumeister and Leary's original arguments. Yet at those minimal levels, few people would say they're socially thriving.

Why Do Quality Social Interactions Promote Well-Being and Longevity?

Since Holt-Lunstad and her colleagues' landmark study over a decade ago, research from across the world keeps piling up on the benefits of social interaction and strong relationships. It's worth pausing for a moment, however, to consider what this research isn't saying. It isn't saying that *everyone* who has reliably enriching interactions and high-quality relationships is going to live the longest or be among the happiest of people. There's a huge degree of luck or misfortune (not to mention genetics) that shapes our lives.[48] It isn't saying that structural inequities aren't crucial factors in understanding mental and physical health outcomes; they clearly are (see chapter 6).[49]

What the research does tell us is that prioritizing relationships on any given day is one of the best things we can do in efforts to make our days better. Time spent socializing, particularly face-to-face, is, on average, more rewarding, enjoyable, and connecting than nearly any other activity we can engage in.[50] By contrast, time spent alone is typically rated as being less enjoyable than time spent communicating with others, especially when that communication is face-to-face and with friends.[51] Research indicates that just acting extraverted—that is, trying to be more social—tends to improve the quality of our days and enhance our well-being, whatever our personality.[52]

It doesn't seem to be the case that we're confusing cause with consequence. A study of three thousand adults over twenty years revealed that people who were socially integrated and felt valued and understood were more likely to be satisfied with their lives decades later.[53] Other studies that have tracked people over a lifetime show that establishing strong, healthy relationships by middle age forecasts a healthier, happier life down the road.[54] And the importance of connection holds true all over the world. In an enormous study of happiness across 123 countries, feeling respected and loved by others was the key predictor of happiness.[55] Supporting the idea of belongingness as a master motive, being loved was found in that study to be more consequential to happiness than feeling accomplished, independent, or powerful. This further establishes the crucial importance of getting the need to belong met. It's a precondition of living well.[56] But that doesn't explain how relationships and social interaction promote physical and mental health. How exactly do relationships and social interaction — the high-quality ones, in particular — benefit us?

According to a University of North Carolina psychologist, Barbara Fredrickson, positive moments of interaction resonate throughout our entire bodies, all the way down to the cellular level. As communicators connect, they become attuned to one another, syncing up their nonverbal behaviors, including body orientations and eye contact. These micro signals of attunement, says Fredrickson, facilitate belonging and underpin our most complex emotions, including love. And this isn't just between intimate relational partners. It even happens in interactions between complete strangers. Fredrickson hypothesizes that as we accumulate moments of positivity resonance with others through our communication, this positivity "alters gene expression in ways that fortify disease resistance and in turn keep people in good health."[57]

Yet we know that not all relationships and interpersonal encounters are positive. Both the best and the worst parts of life are connected to our relationships and interactions. Research backs this up; relationship struggles can cause pain as real as physical pain. Long ago in evolutionary history, the physical pain system developed to protect organisms. It sends the message "Stop! Prevent further damage!" The social-psychological pain system may have adopted this mechanism to alert the individual that there's a risk of loss of inclusion and acceptance; the system may function much like Leary's sociometer.[58] Breakups and relational transgressions hurt, in part, because they threaten our sense of acceptance and value. People are motivated to heal such wounds by repairing their strained relationships, seeking support from people they love, or finding new friends and partners. These forms of interaction are particularly important for how we manage stress.

Indeed, a crucial biological pathway through which social interaction and relationships can affect health involves reduced inflammation by means of stress management. When people express and receive affection and love, those feelings buffer the negative effects of, and improve recovery from, stress. When people aren't acutely stressed, supportive relationships promote relaxation through lower blood pressure and resting heart rate. People with high-quality relationships are therefore less susceptible to disease because relationships lessen stress responses, enable speedy recovery from stressful events, and reduce baseline inflammation. Relationships, in this way, bolster the body's ability to be healthy. Through the processes of stress recovery, prevention, or deactivation, moments of positive social interaction can extend life and boost well-being.[59]

The researchers Jos Brosschot, Bart Verkuil, and Julian Thayer further clarify the nature of the links between social experiences and stress in their groundbreaking work on the *generalized unsafety theory of stress* (GUTS). This theory proposes that positive social interaction and relationships benefit our physical health because they make us feel safe, which is essential for our bodies to turn off the stress response. Brosschot and his colleagues contend that our stress response is always active unless we sense sufficient safety in the social environment to deactivate it. The reason negative experiences, such as loneliness, isolation, and hurtful communication, contribute to disease, then, is that they lead people to feel a chronic and largely unconscious sense of unsafety that lingers long after acute stressors are present in their environments. This explains why negative everyday moments of communication that threaten belonging can harm us repeatedly – that is, in the moment and over time as we ruminate about them. When people feel excluded, ostracized, or discriminated against during social interaction, they feel unsafe, which puts their brain on high alert for further danger. This ongoing surveillance of the world is a byproduct of our brain's effort to protect us. As Brosschot and his colleagues put it, "It is better to play it safe and to flee 10 times too often than once too few."[60] Thus, whereas positive moments of interaction fortify us and foster the requisite sense of safety to turn off the stress response, everyday slights and indignities, which signal danger, keep the stress response activated, sometimes for extended periods, which exacts a significant toll on the body.

Relationships Are Good for Managing Life's Struggles and Maximizing Life's Joys

Koreans have a delightful greeting – "Bap meogeosseoyo?" – which literally translates to "Have you eaten?" In the United States, a common greeting is "How are you doing?" Neither is a literal question. Neither requires an honest response. Rather, both are

---

15

ways to show concern. Beyond the benefits regarding, for instance, stress and inflammation reduction, socially connected people tend to live longer because they have people looking out for them. Are they eating well, taking care of themselves, and doing okay? Close partners can promote negative behaviors too, but social relationships are, on balance, more positive than negative. Some of the benefits of relationships are quite practical – lending money, helping get jobs, sharing work, offering a hand, encouraging doctor visits.[61]

Supportive friends and family can assist us in reframing life's challenges and making sense of our struggles in ways that enhance our resilience.[62] Our friends and family members can also help us develop our abilities or see the strengths we already have.[63] And although social relationships can't prevent bad luck or hardship, they can neutralize – or at least take the edge off – life's disappointments and help us make better decisions when we find ourselves at crossroads. Let's also not forget that our friends and family members promote our well-being through what researchers call *capitalization*, which is when the people around us celebrate our achievements with us, thus intensifying the positive emotions we draw from the happy moments in life.[64] Fun activities and experiences are, quite simply, more enjoyable with good company.

This chapter has made the case that social interaction, whether it is chitchat or deep conversation, can make us feel relevant, that our very existence is important to others – that we belong. Given our innate drive to connect with others, no social experience is likely more destructive than the feeling of irrelevance. A study of loneliness among Londoners from lower socioeconomic status backgrounds emphasizes this point, finding that the sense of not mattering was a core component of their enduring sense of isolation.[65] Believing that you're important to the people around you is the exact purpose of the need to belong, and small moments of connection with others in day-to-day life are essential to the process of belonging. These moments can benefit us right when they occur and over a lifetime. They can even alter how we see the world; they enable us, for instance, to perceive that we have people in our corner whom we can call on anytime we need them. Research shows that this perception alone promotes well-being.[66]

So far this is a good news/good news story. Social relationships are key determinants of the best things in life, and we've evolved an adaptive set of mechanisms that push us toward repairing relationships, staying in touch with one another, and thinking about and caring for the people around us. We feel good when we have positive communication with others, and they benefit as well. Sure, there are challenges, but we can strengthen our own and promote others' sense of belonging by enacting the kinds of good communication strategies identified by researchers.

But what exactly does "good" communication entail? What strategies should we be using to build new connections and shore up our old ones? What's the secret formula for communication success?

This is where things start to get really tricky.

Chapter 2

COMMUNICATION IS HARD AND ALWAYS HAS BEEN

Ask U.S. parents which life skills they believe are essential for their children to thrive, and at least 90 percent will say good communication skills. Compare this to the percentage citing math skills (79 percent) and science skills (58 percent).[1] Why do parents place so much value on their children having good communication skills? Because parents worry that without good communication skills, their kids won't achieve the goals they want most for them, such as loving relationships and rewarding careers. Roy Baumeister and his collaborator, Davina Robson, agree, arguing that communication skills help children develop the two most critical social competencies of all — social connection and self-promotion. At first blush, these competencies seem at odds with one another. After all, isn't connection about building bridges with others, while self-promotion is about standing out from the crowd? In fact, these competencies work together, primarily in service of the need to belong that we discussed in the last chapter. To see why, let's compare our modern lives with the lives of our distant ancestors. "During a one-hour student assembly in a modern school," Baumeister and Robson remind us, "each student may see more other human beings than their hunter-gather ancestors encountered in an entire lifetime."[2] Because our ancestors interacted primarily in small groups, encounters with strangers were a rarity. This meant that in just about every interaction they had, existing relationships were a given.

Today, in contrast, we're surrounded by people throughout our days, if not physically then virtually, and relationships are rarely a given. We have to actively build relational identity with others, and our ability to do so directly rests on our ability to communicate well. This brings us to the importance of self-promotion. We have to demonstrate to people that they should be friends with us. We have to make a good impression, put our best foot forward, and spend the necessary energy to promote ourselves. But valuing good communication — that is, the communication that builds rewarding relationships and satisfies the need to belong — and defining it are two very different things. Research is far less clear than you might imagine on what constitutes good communication across the many contexts of our lives. This chapter examines why the communication that fosters connection is often so contradictory, confusing, and uncertain. Yet we also explore why a messier view of good communication is actually far preferable to a tidy one as we endeavor to build and strengthen our connection with others.

The Realities of Relational Life

Right from the start of our lives, we learn that relationships, while essential, are also complex, volatile, and difficult — even the good ones. In early adolescence, roughly half of best friendships don't last more than a single school year.[3] As we move into adulthood, most of us find it difficult to build new friendships and keep old ones alive. Families are no cakewalk either. Estrangement in parent-child and sibling relationships is common, and research suggests alienated family members often prefer to keep it that way.[4] At work, negative relationships with coworkers are a perennial drain on workers' mental health and job satisfaction, not to mention employers' bottom lines.[5] In our neighborhoods and buildings, neighbor disputes are reportedly growing more common and vitriolic.[6] If you ask people why these various types of relationships are so difficult, they invariably point to communication. For the same reasons we want our kids to have good communication skills, we assume that if we could just communicate better, we would build stronger bonds and ease strife. But what specific types of communication build strong relationships and heal wounded ones?

There's the rub.

Consider those moments in life when you said something you felt was competent, well crafted, even charming, only to have the other person respond with irritation or indifference, leaving you thinking, What just happened? Maybe you used a communication strategy you read about in a book or learned about in a class, and it didn't work out as promised. Any parent who's tried to use communication strategies recommended in parenting advice books knows this kind of outcome all too well.

In everyday life, we often try to say the "right thing" to someone, depending on our goals and perceptions of the situation. But our perceptions are just that: ours. Determining what our communication means during any given social interaction is ultimately a joint affair, contingent on the perspectives of everyone involved.[7] Scholars commonly refer to this as the co-construction of meaning.[8] In many situations, two people in the same interaction interpret things in wildly different ways, which is why some experts recommend that we assume *mis*communication is occurring whenever we're interacting with others, even the people we're closest to.[9] It's fair to say, then, there's no one right way to communicate.[10] Every time we enter a conversation, we bring with us a lot of baggage. And so does the other person. This includes our identities, our relational histories, our understandings of relationships, and our cultures.[11] These are prisms through which meaning is filtered. Two people can even inhabit microcultures unto themselves, which explains why close friends can say things to one another that, to the outside observer, sound nonsensical or even downright mean.[12] Because of the unique speech codes the friends have built over time within their relational microcultures, however, such comments are just fun, lighthearted banter.[13]

Further complicating things, our interpretations of interactions are shaped by ephemeral and subconscious factors. Consider those days you brought your work stress home with you, only to find yourself irritated by things that you wouldn't normally give a second thought to.[14] Feeling drained after a long day can erode the quality of our communication as a result of distraction and inattention.[15] And it doesn't take much to throw things off. Research indicates that the slightest delays in responding to someone who's sharing information with us — which often happens when we're distracted by our own thoughts — can derail a conversation and make someone feel unsupported.[16] But all this information about difficulty isn't reason to lose hope.

The Communication That Connects Us

There are some clear ideas in the literature about the types of communication that build positive relationships. A good example is social support. We often turn to our friends and family members, for instance, when we're feeling stressed or hurt, hoping they'll lend an ear and help us work through our problems. Extensive research suggests that social support yields positive outcomes when it's *person-centered*—that is, the communication acknowledges people's feelings in a nonjudgmental way and helps recipients gain perspective on what they're going through.[17]

Yet people often fall short of enacting this type of high-quality support. Why? One reason is that it's really hard work. To express and receive effective support, people have to be emotionally available, present in the moment, and motivated to really listen. It can be exhausting. The odds that two people in a close relationship will both be sufficiently available, present, and motivated at the same time are astonishingly low—by one estimate, it happens only about 9 percent of the time.[18] Thus, people often aren't necessarily in the right headspace to be as supportive as they want to be. All the knowledge of interpersonal communication in the world can't overcome that fact. Because communication is an energy-intensive activity, we fly on autopilot whenever possible. We have no choice but to conserve our energy for the most demanding moments each day, and often those moments come from requirements, especially from our jobs, that don't directly involve our close relationships.

Even in social situations when we *are* in the right mental place to use widely accepted "good" communication strategies, conversations won't always go as planned. Consider a specific example straight out of the good-communication playbook: active listening. Active listening occurs when we use strategies such as paraphrasing, subtle encouragements (head nods), follow-up questions (*How did you feel when that happened?*), and "I language" (*What I heard you say is . . .*) when others are speaking to us.[19] Many researchers and practitioners will tell you that if you could improve just one feature of

your day-to-day communication to enhance the quality of your relationships and moment-to-moment connection with others, it would
be to become a more active listener. We agree. People want to feel
heard, and active listening can signal that we're there for them.
Given that we're constantly pushed and pulled by so many responsibilities, vices, and devices, it's increasingly hard to give our undi-
vided attention to others.[20]

So what's wrong with active listening? Nothing per se, but listening behaviors are just one piece of a larger relational and communicative puzzle. After carefully listening to someone, we still need to
respond to them verbally, and what we say matters quite a bit.[21] But
before we even get to verbal communication, we should pause and
ask a critical question: What exactly is good listening behavior?
According to the best available research, it's more complicated than
you might think.[22] In studies in which researchers ask respondents
what they believe good listening entails, responses are quite varied.
Some respondents point to general behaviors (keeps eye contact;
asks questions), some identify states of being (compassionate; caring; confident), and others point to global goals (don't dominate the
conversation; speak knowledgeably).[23] In studies of actual recorded
dialogue between people in relationships, active-listening behaviors
don't always align with the ones that researchers and therapists
describe.[24]

And in laboratory studies that train people to engage in active-
listening behaviors with strangers, the results can be surprising.
Harry Weger, a communication researcher, and his research team,
for example, randomly sorted participants into three groups. In each
group, participants answered requests such as "Please describe
your plans for the weekend," asked by a stranger who was trained to
use specific listening behaviors. In the first group, the listener used

23

active-listening techniques (paraphrasing, elaborating). In the second group, the listener merely acknowledged what the other person was saying (*Okay; I see*). In the third group, listeners gave advice in response to what was shared. Unsolicited advice, mind you, is often offered in the absence of good listening; a course of action is recommended before sufficiently acknowledging the other person's emotions and concerns.[25]

Which was best? That is, which group made participants feel the most understood, the most satisfied with the interaction, and most approving of the listener? As expected, active listening (on average) led to a greater perception of understanding than did mere acknowledgment or advice. And, in general, active listening yielded better outcomes than simple acknowledgment. But when it came to satisfaction with the interaction and approval of the listener, active listening was rated as being no better than giving advice. This is just one study, of course, and we don't want to extrapolate too much from it. But the results remind us that there are multiple routes to social approval and, ultimately, connection. It's not that carefully listening to people is bad. Obviously not. Rather, simple formulas or recipes for good communication are tough to find.[26] There's just too much contextual, relational, and cultural variability for simplistic descriptions of good communication.[27] Consider, too, just how messy our actual speech is. Unlike the polished, well-defined dialogue between movie characters, most of our everyday face-to-face communication is incoherent, filled with starts and stops, self-corrections, rapid topic changes, and interruptions.[28] We often speak in no more than six-word chunks, with fillers such as "um" or "uh" representing one out of every sixty words we utter.[29] Good interpersonal communication — including the kinds that foster rewarding connections and fulfill the need to belong in our everyday lives — exists within all this mess.

According to researchers, the top indicators of whether someone is deemed a good listener include the extent to which they are
perceived as trying hard and willing to understand another person.[30]
These findings speak directly to the idea that connection is often
linked to the effort we are *perceived* as putting into our communication. Some researchers have gone so far as to say that the secret to
strong relationships, including long-term relationships such as marriages, is less about specific communication behaviors partners use,
such as particular eye behaviors, facial expressions, and phrases, and
more about the extent to which they, across all their moments together, try hard to demonstrate that they have each other's best interests at heart.[31] We see this most clearly in research on long-term
romantic relationships. Reflecting on his decades-long research program on marital communication and conflict management, John
Gottman, along with Nan Silver, once wrote that "one of the most
startling findings of our research is that most couples who have
maintained happy marriages rarely do anything that even partly re-
sembles active listening when they are upset."[32] Gottman contends
that many of the communication strategies we stereotypically think
of as good listening initially emerged from work on therapist-client
interaction in the 1950s, which is why some of these tactics don't
come naturally to people, especially when they're upset or hurt. Day-
to-day relational life bears little resemblance to the intentional se-
renity of the therapist's office, and thus seemingly helpful questions
(*How did that make you feel?*) can prove helpful *or* can sound clunky
(maybe even condescending) in talk with friends, colleagues, and
family members. The most complex and sophisticated communication research to date on supportive interactions has begun to show
just how nuanced social support can be: the same interaction patterns reduce people's distress in some situations but not in others.[33]

Gottman, over time, softened his perspective, acknowledging that relational interventions focused on increasing active listening can be quite effective for strengthening relationships.[34] Carefully listening to people, after all, is foundational to conveying respect and building connection. This is true not only between spouses, but in various types of relationships; research shows that training workers to be better listeners can improve their perceptions of workplace climate over time.[35] But Gottman remains adamant that what often differentiates positive from negative communication is the underlying trust that exists between people, which becomes a filter through which communication is interpreted and meaning co-constructed. Trust shapes how words and nonverbal cues are understood. Trust opens us up to appreciate another person's point of view (even if it differs from ours), attend to their needs, and think beyond present-moment desires, all of which are necessary for building and sustaining relationships over time.[36] The secret to interpersonal success, then, isn't so much a specific set of communication behaviors as it is the generalized meanings people draw from our efforts toward "good" communication.[37] Thus, the key question we need to ask ourselves is this: Does our communication explicitly and implicitly make the case that we're worthy of trust?[38] We have to show we're doing the work for our communicative efforts toward connection to be taken in good faith.

When trust is low, any good deed can be interpreted as suspicious and any bad deed as further confirmation of someone's deficiencies. Without trust, ostensibly positive turns of talk—*How are you doing? You look nice today. How did that make you feel?* Even *I love you*—come across more like mere platitudes than rewarding or skillful communication. When relational partners do genuinely trust one another, they are, as researchers describe, communally oriented toward one another.[39] They view themselves as teammates, "in it together." When communal orientation is low, however, people view themselves as separate entities, fending off life's hassles on their own. This is true at work, in our friendships, and at home. The exact same verbal and nonverbal cues from a teammate and a rival will probably be interpreted differently. And we often fail to appreciate just how much of being a good (trusted) relational teammate to our friends, colleagues, and romantic partners is about perceptions of accountability. Warm communication doesn't amount to much if we habitually cancel plans at the last minute or never unload the dishwasher. Brad Stulberg, opining in the *New York Times,* made this same point about accountability and obligation to others: "By definition, obligation is not optional. And therein lies its power: It makes you think twice before opting out. In the moment, canceling plans in the name of boundaries, wanting to be more efficient or take better care of yourself might feel great. But in the long run, the communities and people to whom we commit ourselves play a central role in what gives our lives joy and meaning."[40]

That last word in the Stulberg's quote — *meaning* — is critical. Meaning is formed by what we do as much as it is by what we say. This is, in fact, specifically recognized in research on relationship maintenance, which examines the behaviors that keep various types of relationships healthy, whether they're close friendships or neighborhood, family, or work relationships.[41] The most commonly used measures of relationship maintenance specify "tasks" as an essential dimension, assessed by items such as my partner/friend/roommate/sibling/coworker . . . shares in the joint responsibilities that face us, . . . does not shirk their duties, . . . performs their household/work responsibilities, and . . . does their fair share of the work we have to do. Studies show that regularly pulling one's weight regarding tasks is often as strongly associated with people's relationship and communication satisfaction ratings as is the frequency of their positive communication, such as expressions of affection or compliments.[42] This is actually really good news. It suggests that building strong relationships isn't about getting our communication "just right," which, as we've discussed, is quite difficult in practice. Even deeper appreciation for this fact emerges when we recognize that our basic understandings of communication itself can be fundamentally different from those of the people around us.

Different Logics of Communication

We typically think of and talk about communication as if it's a singular entity. It's not. We all differ in what we think communication is for and what it should be like. And this affects how we understand and relate to one another in profound ways. Think about clothing. You know folks who care very little about what they wear each day. For them, clothes address basic needs — nothing more — and overthinking one's choices is not only unnecessary but a nuisance. You know other people who care *a lot* about their clothes. Their chief goal is for their clothes to "get things right" in terms of whatever situation they're entering. Then there's the fashionista, who takes things to the next level. Why simply meet expectations for appropriateness when your sartorial flair can transcend norms and expectations? Are any of these views about clothes right or wrong? Of course not. They're just different understandings of what clothes are for and can (even should) do.

Everything we just said about clothing is also true about communication. As the communication researcher Barbara O'Keefe put it, the "facts about how communication works [are] systematically different for different people." O'Keefe's research captured these systematic differences in the form of three unique *message design logics* — expressive, conventional, and rhetorical.[43] Although we communicate differently across situations, we typically default to a preferred logic that reflects how we relate to others. A person with the expressive message design logic is the proverbial straight shooter. Communication is all about transferring thoughts and feelings in direct ways. Say what you mean — no more, no less. For the person with the conventional logic, communication is about more than just information transfer; it's about properly managing norms and expectations for any situation. They want their communication to be "by the book," which is why they usually prize politeness. For the person with the rhetorical logic — the most sophisticated of them all — communication enables people to shape social reality. It can be creatively used, for instance, to show how two opposing viewpoints are actually completely aligned or how ostensibly negative events are actually quite positive. Words and actions for the rhetorical message designer, like clothes for the fashionista, are for creating new and nuanced portrayals of the world.

These different understandings and preferences are common, yet often hidden, sources of miscommunication in daily life.[44] That coworker with an expressive message design logic, who "tells it like it is," can be perceived as rude and uncooperative by colleagues with conventional or rhetorical logic. This can be true even if both people generally agree about the content of the communication. Similarly, that rhetorically minded brother-in-law, whose long explanations about the subtleties and gradations of, well, everything, might be considered overly wordy and attention-seeking by those with expressive and conventional logics. Again, keep in mind that message design logics are operating separately from whatever topics people

---

might be talking about, offering us layers upon layers of potential misunderstanding. Considering that people communicate on the basis of unique understandings of communication – and the social world more broadly – is it any wonder that relationships of all kinds can, at times, be so confusing?[45] Or, for that matter, that some people might find advice offered in a given social interaction supportive, while others find it unsupportive?

We don't, however, have to lapse into complete relativism about the types of communication that bring and keep people together. The same is true of harmful communication. Conversational narcissists who regularly dominate conversations and make everything about them will predictably repel others.[46] Physical violence and verbal abuse are destructive forms of communication with clear adverse effects across situations. But let's get back to the communication that brings people together, which research indicates we need to look at through a *holistic lens*.[47]

Good Lies in the Gestalt

Researchers have proposed very specific and often minute neural, physiological, and communication-based indicators of emotional connection.[48] These include the degree to which communicators are, for example, synchronized in their moment-to-moment nonverbal behavior during conversations.[49] This is fascinating and important research, to be sure, but there's also value in not getting too far down into the weeds when thinking about forms of communication that foster belonging. As we have discussed with regard to good listening, which researchers often conceptualize at a higher-order level (as opposed to the granularity of individual verbal or nonverbal cues), the categories of communication that foster connection are often best conceived as generalized in scope.[50] Ultimately, when it comes to building relational connection, the most important thing is that we demonstrate genuine effort to respect, care for, and validate people.[51] This is the exact same conclusion Harry Weger and his colleagues drew from their lab study on active listening that we described earlier. "Research," they said, "is beginning to suggest that people respond to listeners' overall level of responsiveness regardless of the form it takes."[52]

This is why the concept of *perceived partner responsiveness* is such an important one for defining the communicative experience of belonging and connection. Fundamentally, responsiveness is the perception that another person acknowledges, respects, and cares for us as unique individuals. When we aim for responsive communication, we're essentially promoting the best version of ourselves to others, convincing them that they matter—right here, right now. The psychologist Harry Reis, mentioned earlier, proposed the perceived partner responsiveness concept as a "core organizing principle" for the study of social interaction and positive communication.[53] Scanning the social scientific literature, Reis saw numerous concepts revolving around similar themes. Perceived partner responsiveness brought that work together. Since then, study after study—using lab experiments, observational methods, and surveys of everyday life— has shown that perceptions of responsiveness contribute to relational, psychological, and mental well-being during moments of social interaction. This is true with intimate partners, acquaintances, work associates, and strangers.

So, what is responsiveness? Simply put, responsiveness is communication that conveys the messages "I'm open to connecting with you" and "I'm willing to spend my finite energy on you." Responsiveness typically isn't about the communication content

31

that's being discussed during a conversation. Although we can directly say to someone, "I respect you," in service of conveying responsiveness, we're much more likely to *show* someone that we respect them through our conversational presence, and this can take many forms. Holistic or "gestalt" impressions of responsiveness seem to be what really matter. Whereas communication behaviors are individual notes, responsiveness is the melody composed of all the notes together.[54] During an interaction, did a person seem interested? Did they try to see where I was coming from? Focus, care, and interest are telltale signs of someone investing their energy during a moment of social interaction. And this is critical: we want people to be responsive in whatever ways seem authentic to them and map onto their unique understandings of how these types of goals are (and should be) accomplished through communication.[55]

The focus on holistic perceptions is true of other forms of connection-enhancing communication. Earlier we described relational maintenance behaviors. When measuring relational maintenance behaviors, researchers don't tally the amount of eye contact and number of head nods or chart the specific amount of paraphrasing and number of kind words used during interactions. Instead, they ask generalized questions, usually in surveys, about how often people are perceived as acting positively, kindly, and equitably toward one another. Each person must decide what positivity or assurances of commitment mean to them in the context of their relationship.[56] There's good reason to think about positive forms of communication, such as responsiveness, in this generalized and subjective way, as it reflects how people actually experience interpersonal communication. People typically remember their impressions of others and moments of interaction in general terms. The brain isn't built to focus solely on individual words and actions in conversation. And this fact has important implications for trust—it's the melody, not the notes. Researchers contend that we're more likely to trust others when there's a perception of consistency in cues.[57] This suggests that the trust that scholars like John Gottman argue is so essential to meaning construction stems in part from the consistency of treatment people receive during and across social interactions. It comes from efforts to repeatedly, rather than intermittently, communicate responsively with one another. Consistent treatment builds predictability, and we want—better yet, *need*—ample moments of interaction with predictably responsive people.

Subjectivity, Inevitable Failure, and Why Failure's Okay

This insight about responsiveness as a subjective evaluation of others can be freeing, because it loosens restrictions on what good communication needs to look and sound like in our day-to-day interaction. The experts plainly state that no behavior or phrase is inherently responsive, and the behaviors we perceive as responsive are partly rooted in mental projections based on contextual factors and generalized feelings toward another person.[58] Dev Crasta and his colleagues put it this way: "The same behavior (e.g., partner leaving the room) can be interpreted as responsive (e.g., 'giving me space') or insensitive (e.g., 'abandoning me') based on context."[59] There's a troubling part of all this, too. We have to accept that failure and miscommunication are normal and to be expected. As we noted earlier, the reality is that we're often unmotivated to be responsive to others—it can be exhausting, and there's only so much attention to go around. Giving our attention and care to others, moreover, often comes with inherent trade-offs. Consider, for instance, that carefully listening to and supporting others often helps reduce other people's distress but can simultaneously heighten our own.[60] We don't have endless wells of supportiveness to draw from. There's no getting around the give-and-take, contradictory reality of social life.[61] Or, as the communication scholar William Wilmot once noted: "Relationships are problematic — if we don't do anything about their natural dynamic, they may atrophy. If we try to force them, to 'make them happen,' we may destroy their essential nature."[62]

Situations can also change the costs and benefits of our communication, including responsive communication. This is especially apparent in situations where responsiveness is expected of us — not in service of our family or friends, but of our jobs. Many jobs, especially those in customer service or emergency care, require that employees maintain high levels of responsiveness with customers and strangers throughout the day. Mandated "emotional labor" of this sort can be taxing on people's well-being and a common source of burnout. Working environments that negate people's full identities by framing any displays of pain or distress as unprofessional or "needy" have the veneer of positivity, but such demands can take a significant toll on mental health, while also reducing the energy people have left for friends and loved ones.[63]

There will also be times when we try to be responsive, but we won't be perceived that way by other people. This could be due to passing circumstances or more enduring differences in people's communication logics. Imagine a situation when you hold the door open for someone at a grocery store and the person suddenly feels compelled to move more quickly than they might prefer to accept your gesture. Behind their smile of appreciation might be a bit of annoyance at your "kindness." Failure and disappointment are baked-in features of interpersonal communication. But it's hard to keep that in mind. And it's often our intolerance for our own and other people's communicative failures and disappointments that impedes connection. Often, we fear getting things wrong and are overly critical of ourselves. Such fear can lead us to avoid trying to connect with people altogether. This is actually one of the paradoxical effects of loneliness. Although loneliness, by its evolutionary design, is intended to guide us back into social interaction in service of belonging, it often corrupts our expectations and evaluations of communication (ours and other people's).[64] It reduces our comfort in "putting ourselves out there" and increases our fear of failure. This combination of discomfort and fear is part of the reason why heightened loneliness across populations can fuel the kinds of societal shifts toward interiority that we discuss later in the book.

Lonely or not, people often leave conversations ruminating about what was said.[65] This is quite common in difficult moments, such as conflict episodes, but it also happens in the moments that are supposed to be positive. Consider, for example, an evening spent with friends. Along with the fun we might experience, we sometimes can't avoid feeling uncertainty and regret about things said or unsaid throughout the night: "I should have said *this*. I shouldn't have said *that*. What did they mean when they made that comment?"[66] We worry that our good faith efforts to be responsive may not have been taken that way. It can be tempting to conclude from these experiences that maintaining relationships is just too hard and that nobody will ever truly "get us." But if we recast communication challenges, misunderstandings, and differences in people's communication styles as unavoidable and necessary facts of our messy social lives, we can evaluate ourselves and others with requisite mercy. This is an important realization because compassion for self and empathy for others are inextricably interwoven.[67]

Given communication scholars' assumption that the meaning of communication is always filtered through layers of interpretation, we can say that people build strong relationships with others by learning how they understand the world. This takes time and patience. Good communication in relationships, argues the communication scholar Steve Duck, is a matter of people's personal meaning systems, which are revealed to us over multiple interactions, often implicitly. This explains why one person wants a friend to be brutally honest, while another wants a friend who always takes their side no matter what. Even if two people in a relationship share their communication preferences with one another, Duck reminds us, this is "only a first crude layer of meaning."[68] Relational connection and long-term relational success lie in how well we're able to tailor our communication to others—often through trial and error—in ways that align with their personal meaning systems and logics.[69] This suggests it's best to think of communication strategies, such as active-listening techniques, as important and instructive starting points and targets for us to consider. The specific ways we enact these and other forms of communication, however, should be responsive to people's unique needs, as we come to learn them—in good times and bad.[70]

When Values (Inevitably) Clash

But we don't always want to connect with and be responsive to other people's ideas. Sometimes we want to, and should, express disagreement, if not rejection. This is often the case when someone expresses views or acts in ways we find distasteful or harmful. Intentional rejection and dissent are necessary in well-functioning relationships and societies more broadly.[71] People who assume others will always be responsive to them no matter what they do or say undermine the very accountability that we said earlier was so important for strong relationships. Sometimes we're conflicted. We disapprove of what someone is saying, but we still want to be responsive to them as a person. In social interactions, we usually have multiple goals, and these goals can be at odds with one another.[72] Consider interactions among family members who love one another yet vehemently disagree about politics. Clashes over differing values are a staple of family life and the most common reason that parents and adult children give for why they chose to sever their ties.[73] It's possible, however, to be responsive without agreeing. Challenging people, in fact, can be part of what it means to care for them.[74] Keep in mind, too, that communicating responsively with people, even when we're critical of their viewpoints, can be an important step toward eventually changing their minds. Essentially, if we want to persuade someone to adopt a different viewpoint or ideology, we have to reflect the same type of openness we ultimately want from them.[75] But even if we can't change their minds—which is probably an uphill battle at best—we should consider how much we want to prioritize connection versus ideological alignment. In a perfect world, we would find both in our closest relationships. In the world we actually have, communication is hard and people are imperfect.

In any communication situation in which conflicting goals are present, such as when we want to maintain a positive relationship with someone while also calling them out for their viewpoints, the probability that the interaction will quickly spiral into heated conflict or icy standoff dramatically increases. This is a clear reminder of why apologies and forgiveness (of self and other) are among the most important forms of communication in our lives.[76] If we first accept that we often fall short of expectations, we can be more accepting of others' missteps.

Take Off Your Jacket

Maybe we can all benefit from releasing some of the pressure we put on ourselves. Maybe we could use some advice from Andy's mom. When Andy was in grade school, he took school a little too seriously. He *still* takes school a little too seriously. As a kid, he would come through the back door of his house, head straight to the dining room table, unzip his bookbag, and start working on his home-work—coat invariably still on. This behavior was rooted less in love of learning than in fear of failure. Fortunately, he was blessed with a loving mom, who would routinely come over to him and gently re-quest that he take a few deep breaths and remove his coat before hitting the books. To this day, if Andy chats with his mom and his stress levels seem to be running too high, his mom will calmly re-mind him, "Take off your jacket," by which she means, "Relax a little bit, take the pressure off. Do the small things first."

We can apply this same advice to social interaction and our ex-pectations of ourselves and others. Despite the inherent miscommu-nication that we're bound to encounter in day-to-day life, things often aren't as bad as they seem. We just need a moment to put things in perspective. Consider research on the liking gap, which shows that we tend to chronically underestimate how much people, including complete strangers, enjoy interacting with us.[77] The up-shot of this research is that we're often much harder on ourselves than we need to be.[78] Research in labs and naturalistic environments reveals that our conversation partners tend to evaluate us more fa-vorably than we think they will and that they rate our conversations more positively than we expect them to. Interestingly, this isn't just an adult thing—research suggests that the liking gap emerges as early as five years old.[79]

Normalizing missteps and miscommunication, and eschewing any notions of getting things perfect, better calibrates our expectations of others and ourselves. It can help us overcome any defeatism we might be prone to. It can ensure that our tendencies toward harsh self-evaluation and fear don't get turned around and directed at others, ratcheting up what we expect of them. This doesn't mean we should automatically give people a pass, or expect people to give us a pass, on offensive or hurtful behavior. Rather, it means taking a deep breath and adopting a more realistic and humane view of the realities of sociality. More skill is not always better, and overthinking our communication can get in the way of doing it competently.[80] We have to battle our communication perfectionism and cringe impulses. Communication and connection are difficult for many of us – unavoidably so. We aren't going to please everyone with how we interact, regardless of our intentions (*but that's not what I meant!*) or how much we work at it (*but I tried so hard!*). Things will be a bit awkward at times. To be awkward is to be human.

When we feel disconnected and worried about trying to build new relationships, it's easy to feel stuck. We stress over getting things wrong, craving an easy-to-follow recipe for good communication. In those moments, take off your jacket. Give yourself a chance at a fresh start. Focus on the little things – the "layups of relational life." If a basketball player is struggling to hit three-pointers, it can be helpful for their confidence to move closer to the basket and put in a few easy buckets near the rim. Just seeing the ball go through the hoop can be uplifting. Similarly, if connecting with others is difficult, focus on the easier moments and build up from there. Giving our attention to others through a little extra eye contact, trying extra hard to leave our phones in our pockets, asking them a few more questions about themselves (their likes, dislikes, etc.), and sprinkling in expressions of gratitude are a lot easier in the humdrum "nice to meet you," "how was your day," and "what groceries do we need" moments of life. These moments, as we discuss later, are actually the bulk of our social experiences. Take advantage of the mundane moments, when the shooting percentage is highest. They add up, accumulating the consistency and confidence needed for our efforts at good communication to have their desired effects. Are these moments without stress? Absolutely not. But, as we explore next, there are some very real costs of avoiding social stress.

Chapter 3

TOWARD OPTIMAL SOCIAL STRESS

Since 1998, the tutors of the Experience Corps have been improving the literacy skills of the children of Baltimore City Public
Schools. People from all walks of life, many who've never worked
with children, provide one-on-one or small-group tutoring to improve students' reading ability. Volunteers must be over fifty years
old, but many are considerably older, and some are socially isolated.
The Experience Corps clearly benefits the children: the reading levels
of 50 percent of students increased by one grade level or more from
the beginning to the end of the school year. But what the Experience
Corps does for the older adult volunteers is truly incredible – being
a tutor delays memory declines and may increase brain volume.[1]
With these rewards, however, come significant stressors. Working
with the children can be difficult and frustrating. Volunteers saw
firsthand children's disruptive behavior, their conflicts with classmates, and the lack of much-needed resources. Yet they also experienced a sense of purpose and meaning in caring for and bonding
with the children.[2]

The Experience Corps is an obligation — one willingly taken — and not without significant hassles and invested time and energy. Sometimes volunteers felt hopeless, exhausted, and afraid for the future of the children they cared for. At the same time, they also reported that they got more out of that work than they put in. As one volunteer said, "To help others helps me."[3] Sometimes their weariness and worries for the children followed the volunteers home. Caring for other people is often tiring, and maintaining relationships can be inconvenient and stressful. People will often avoid that work if they can. But this gets it backward. We should care for others *because* of the energy it costs. Like many other biological systems, we thrive when we invest an optimal amount of energy in our social world. This includes voluntarily expanding our opportunities for connection, as the tutors in the Experience Corps have done. Just as a tree's root structure develops only when the tree is blown by the wind, we grow to our full potential through relational stress — but only to a point. Just as an oak will split in a storm, even the strongest relationships can break when the stress is too much.

This means not all social stress is bad for us. We just need the right amount of it. *Hormesis* is the concept that moderate doses of stress produce positive biological responses, whereas high doses of stress can be debilitating.[4] More isn't better. Whether we're talking about homeostasis in social interaction or our number of close relationships, it's both impractical and unhealthy to endlessly do more. When it comes to expending social energy, however, doing nothing is a bad idea. Without the stress inherent in being interdependent with other people, our social practices and relationships aren't sturdy enough to endure the strains of life. In overcoming challenges, relational and otherwise, we build our capacity to cope with future ones. Just like the volunteers for the Experience Corps, all of us need the stress that comes with the feeling of being valuable, meaningful, and obligated to others.[5]

Hormetic social stress is the stress needed to renew our social health. Hormetic stress builds vitality. When our relational challenges are a matter of choice and relationships strengthen our interdependence with others, they're good stressors. Ultimately, this type of stress ensures that our social needs are met in the long run. For those accustomed to giving less, some discomfort is necessary for growth. For other people, piling on stress is counterproductive and diminishing.

Let's begin by answering an important question: What, exactly, is social energy?

On Human Energy

A huge portion of the energy you burn on any given day is required to simply keep you alive. Thermal regulation, breathing, cellular growth and repair, blood flow, food digestion, and countless other internal processes account for most of human energy consumption. None of these are conscious processes. Try as we might, we can't observe them by thinking about them — energy is produced at the mitochondrial level.[6] An outlier among its peers, the brain is one costly organ. The brain uses 20 percent of a person's total caloric burn, despite accounting for 2 percent of a person's weight.[7] We can't observe or control what the brain does. The brain allocates energy so we can think about it. The energetic demands of our daily activities are in addition to this vast, integrated, and hidden machinery. One consequence of a lack of introspection about the brain's energy expenditure is that we tend to think of energy mainly in terms of caloric burn during physical activities.

Kinesiologists have developed remarkable tools for measuring human energy consumption. Both in laboratories and in studies of everyday life, a variety of physical activities have been quantified in terms of caloric burn. Scientists have estimated the energy demands of many exercise regimes and sports, both popular (walking) and niche (badminton and disco dancing).[8] Given that past research has focused mainly on fitness, one unmeasured activity is socializing. The activity in the research literature that's closest to socializing is "playing with children with moderate effort" — whatever that means. This activity, researchers tell us, burns more calories than taking a stroll but fewer than disco dancing.

Although there aren't any studies that specifically quantify how much energy it takes to socialize, there is research on the energy it takes to think.[9] Researchers are confident that mental work requires energy because certain areas of the brain consume glucose when engaged in complex cognitive tasks. For short periods of time, the difference between not thinking (staring blankly into space) and thinking hard (doing long division) is small — maybe only a 5–7 percent difference.[10] This is because so much of brain activity is nonconscious and taking place throughout the brain rather than in centralized regions associated with, say, doing math. As cognitive activities become longer and more difficult, the energy costs mount.[11] The brain can handle mental challenges in small doses, relying on available energy reserves, but the costs grow as time and complexity rise. Socializing involves thinking. No doubt, people vary in how much they think when they talk. There's a reason we cherish a well thought-out comment and honor the recommendation "think before you speak." This means the energy needed to socialize is difficult to quantify and varies quite a bit between social interactions. Conversation might also include standing, pacing, and expressing oneself nonverbally through hand gestures, head movements, and posture changes – sometimes while disco dancing.

Certain areas of the brain are associated with social cognition. A resting brain is not actually resting but, rather, is engaged in thinking about people and the self in relation to others.[12] Clearly, social interactions require cognitive energy – as they occur and after they're over. As anyone who's spent a wakeful night focused on what they should've said or anticipating tomorrow's big meeting knows, enduring social anxiety is an energy-intensive experience. One study of college men, for instance, found that participants who typically experienced high levels of anxiety expended more energy in the form of resting metabolic rate than those with low anxiety.[13]

The facts that our brains are dedicated to social cognition and that social interactions have psychological and physiological consequences before, during, and after interactions are two crucial clues in understanding why social interactions are energy intensive. We've studied social energy expenditure in regard to social interaction in our own research.[14] When we talk about social energy, we're referring to the behavioral, perceptional, emotional, and cognitive tasks required to engage in social interaction. This includes the energy costs of verbal and nonverbal communication during a conversation and of perceiving and understanding others' communication behaviors. Social energy also includes energy expenditure associated with the emotions that we feel and the effort we put into managing our own display of emotion. Social interaction is an energy-depleting process. "Energy," as Daniel Cochece Davis, a communication scholar and Jeff's research collaborator, once stated, is "a fundamental commodity of human interaction."[15]

Spending Energy and Gaining Vitality

Our perspective differs from the way people often think about energy and interaction. This popular account says that people get or increase energy from social interactions.[16] There's some truth to this. It's a universal and long-known phenomenon that just being around people is arousing—it piques our senses—often making us feel more alert and awake than being alone.[17] Long periods of forced solitude can leave people feeling lethargic.[18] Being around and interacting with people stokes our fires; it wakes us up, forcing energy expense. That's the point. It isn't energy gained, but rather energy being spent.

Another misunderstanding surrounds the feeling of being energized. This mixes the good feelings associated with social interaction, such as happiness, with the energy consumed by doing it. Think of it this way: if you have a heightened sense of taste in a given moment and then taste something delicious, it tastes even better. The same is true with social interaction. The arousal of being around other people can multiply the reward value of a moment of connection.[19] It can go the other way, too. Think of how upsetting an intense interpersonal conflict is—you vibrate with anger and frustration as you stew in it, all the while burning energy like a furnace.

The mechanism by which we gain energy is called vitality. Vitality concerns the degree to which our various needs are met.[20] When people are getting their needs met on a physical level—they're fed, hydrated, rested, and safe—they feel more vital. Anything interfering with our eating, drinking, sleeping, and safety zaps our vitality. The longer we go without getting our nutritional or recovery needs met, the more our vitality suffers.[21] We burn through our reserves, leaving nothing behind. Our social experiences also matter.[22] Our sense of belonging, for example, is part of vitality. We need to spend valuable energy on positive social interaction to enhance our vitality.[23] This is why time alone, rest, and positive social interaction are inextricably linked – the energy that positive interaction requires of us to get our needs met must then be replenished through time alone. There's evidence, moreover, that people with greater vitality tend to recover more quickly from social exhaustion.[24] From this perspective, the reason loneliness and social isolation are tiring physically and mentally is that they deplete us (interfere with energy recovery) much as poor nutrition and insufficient sleep do.[25]

What Makes Social Interactions Energy Intensive?

Some conversations and certain people are exhausting, and we have only so much social bandwidth to go around. What are the factors that matter for understanding and allocating that bandwidth? Here are the seven factors that we've discovered contribute to energy expenditure during social interaction:

1. How long you talk
2. Whom you're talking to
3. What you talk about
4. Interest and engagement levels of the conversation
5. Degree of unavoidable or forced socialization
6. Use of communication technology
7. Level of familiarity

Length. This is intuitive. Longer conversations require more energy than shorter ones. Quick hellos and small talk are at the low end of the spectrum, and major social events reside on the high end. When interactions are stacked one after another, the cumulative interaction time is draining. Whether chatting with different people at a party or enduring back-to-back meetings at work, the total amount of time in interaction plays a role in how taxing it is. Both how tired a person is afterward and how long they need to recover depend – almost as much as anything – on how long the event or conversation lasted.[26]

Whom you're talking to. All other factors being equal, talking with people we know requires less energy than talking with strangers. Considering the energy costs of internal thoughts and emotions, familiar others require less awareness than less-familiar others. We know who they are, what they think, and how they communicate. The theoretical framework that undergirds our approach assumes that this familiarity comes from a network of expectations and reference points. Essentially, we can fill in the blanks in meaning. In friendship, for example, people often talk about being able to just be themselves or letting their guard down – it takes less work to be social among friends.[27]

It's not as if talking to strangers is a huge energy cost. Most people can buy something at a store without needing a nap. A lot of the social energy expense comes down to people working hard to make a good impression. When we talk to strangers, we often don't think too much about what they think of us. We rely on mental shortcuts in small talk, customer service exchanges, and greetings and good-byes. By comparison, when we asked people in our research to describe their most energy-intensive interaction or event in the last month, they often described situations where they wanted to make a good impression with someone new, such as job interviews and meeting a romantic partner's family for the first time.[28] This doesn't mean that we put less energy in total into familiar relationships. Over a lifetime, our close family and friends get the lion's share of all our social energy. On any given day, however, a conversation with an established, familiar partner tends to require less social energy.

What you talk about. Over one-third of people in our research named a difficult, challenging, or conflicted conversation as the most energy-intensive conversation they had had in the last month.[29] Meaningful, but not antagonistic, conversations are energy intensive too. This means social energy comes in both good and bad forms. Both meaningful conversation and conflict are high in energy expense, but they're complete opposites in terms of resulting feelings of connection. Showing empathy and support for another person, which may be necessary both in conflict and in meaningful talk, is wearing and cognitively taxing. A difficult conversation, or a deep one, can lead people to want to be alone afterward.[30]

Energy-intensive interactions share another characteristic: they're relatively rare. Our research involving over twenty thousand observations, as well as two studies collected in Spain, indicates that meaningful conversation — that is, focused conversation about personally relevant and important topics — occurred in 6 percent of interactions. Conflict occurred in less than 2 percent of interactions.[31] This means people could go days without either. Consider that the third most energy-intensive conversation is talk at work.[32] For employed adults, workplace talk is 250 percent more common than meaningful conversation and conflict combined. Particularly in the service sector, employees have to be customer-oriented: pleasant, self-aware, and accommodating.[33] No doubt, directing so much attention to self-presentation, especially during a difficult or cognitively complex customer exchange, is exhausting.

Interest and engagement. Although we discovered that length and topic matter, the most crucial determinant of energy expenditure during social interaction was how interested the person was in it and how important it was to them.[34] People invest their energy in what they want or care about. They're willing to work for it. Choosing an interaction is a sign that people want to invest energy in a person, conversation, or situation. Take catching up with a friend as an example. In such moments, the two friends are locked in and engaged with one another. The interaction is something they want, find interesting, and deem important. The friends become animated and their responsiveness toward one another is likely to be high. As one of Andy's studies showed, people tend to report higher levels of responsiveness from their interaction partners in conversations they wanted to engage in.[35] The longer social interactions last, the more fatigued people feel afterward, which results in their needing longer periods of time alone to recover. Importantly, though, after a positive interaction, people are more likely to experience time alone as rewarding.[36]

Forced choice. People aren't passive when it comes to social interaction and energy depletion. Let's return to that energy-intensive customer service job. When people don't choose an interaction, our research suggests, they try to keep their energy expenditure low. An employee might not want to contribute to a mandatory meeting, so they choose to make a superficial remark or say nothing at all. The involuntary nature of the interaction implies that people can't just opt out of it. People therefore check out to avoid using up energy on something they don't care about.[37]

Not being able to escape a social interaction is taxing. People may work very hard to stay at a low level of attention, showing others they'd prefer not to be there. Despite their best efforts, it's still an energy-expending conversation. Even the disengaged person is affected by the basic arousal of being around others, not to mention the duration and self-presentational demands.[38] Acting fake or pretending to care is exhausting. Here are some examples of what people said about this in our research:

> "I am not the best at faking interest in people, so when I had to go to a wedding with people I do not care for, I had a very hard time and used a lot of energy to fake my way through the very long day."
> "We had a celebration gathering at work, which was a forced event. It took a lot of mental and emotional effort to get through it. Very boring and no one wanted to be there."[39]

Communication technology. The way you communicate makes a difference in the energy used. In Jeff's book *Relating through Technology,* he looked at five different forms of communication and found that voice calls and video chats are more energy intensive than face-to-face conversation.[40] There are often significant challenges involved in encoding and decoding meaning in voice and video calls. It's harder, for instance, to take turns properly without cutting someone off or talking over them. Zoom, in particular, results in subtle processing delays of communication that can make us feel out of sync with another person.[41] This helps explain the "Zoom fatigue" many remote workers endure. By contrast, texting and interacting through social media require considerably less social energy. The sheer number of words is vastly lower than in the other three forms of communication, there's little nonverbal communication to attend to, and there are no energy costs from arousal since the other person isn't nearby. Although the lack of cues can be confusing and lead to energy expense, less communication (that is, fewer verbal and nonverbal messages) expends less energy.

Familiarity. The human brain is a pattern-detecting and pattern-formulating machine. Its function is to recognize and predict patterns everywhere and in everything, to minimize surprises and interpret order in chaos. We crave patterns because they're energy efficient.[42] Familiarity is the brain's way of recognizing a pattern.[43] Many of the above characteristics overlap with familiarity — strangers are unfamiliar, rare conversation topics are unfamiliar, public speaking is unfamiliar. Becoming familiar with something tends to reduce its energy costs.

The Energy of Building a Relationship

The seven factors we just reviewed suggest that long face-to-face conversations with an unfamiliar person, especially conversations about meaningful issues that we want to share, are very energy-intensive interactions. We should avoid these, right? Wrong. In fact, this is exactly what it takes to make a new friend. If we don't know someone very well but want to get to know them, it takes energy and time. According to Jeff's research, it takes forty to sixty hours to make a casual friend and more than two hundred hours to make a close friend. Meaningful and affectionate conversations can speed that process up, but they're also among the most energy-expending types of conversations. Such conversations shave off hours of the time it takes to build a friendship — essentially conserving energy over time. This comes with risks, however, since not all relationships are going to work out. New relationships are a combination of something we want and something that is unfamiliar and risky, which is a costly combination in terms of energy.[44]

What about restarting old relationships? Energy must be invested there too. You have to reach out, risk rejection, and schedule a time to meet or talk (all while balancing other obligations). You then need to have a high-energy social interaction; otherwise, you risk seeming not to care about your friend, which would undermine the whole purpose of getting back in touch. The bottom line is this: relationships, particularly new ones, take energy. The greater the potential for the interaction to build a relationship, the more energy it's going to take. This means there are direct relational benefits — simultaneously occurring with inherent personal costs — from having energy-intensive interactions. There are other examples: empathy and social support are taxing, but they bond us to another person and we feel less lonely.[45] Making a good impression on a date is taxing, but romance might follow. Investing time in assisting children to conceptualize their goals and work through challenges helps them build the hope needed for them achieve to their goals.[46] But any parent knows that helping children with their homework when they're frustrated can be exceedingly tough. Or consider conflict. Although not all conflict is productive, it's sometimes necessary to iron out problems in a way that ultimately facilitates relationship growth. All these are examples of hormesis in social energy. Brief, intermittent, and low doses of stress can lead to positive biological responses. They create the conditions of future growth. Hormesis offers an adaptive evolutionary benefit because it enables organisms to thrive through renewal, especially when exposed to harsh circumstances.[47] So what are the social conditions of hormesis?

The Goldilocks of Stress

If we were to describe the least energy-depleting conditions imaginable, we might think of someone with zero daily interactions. From an evolutionary perspective, this situation is a total and utter disaster for the species. One step up from total isolation is someone who favors short conversations, avoids both challenging and meaningful conversations, rarely chooses to interact with another person, doesn't bother trying to present a favorable image when they do, and tries to communicate exclusively through online text. This isn't great either. It's hard to imagine them being accepted or trusted, and they certainly would be no prize for romance or parenting. In both ancestral and modern times, survival is higher for people who invest energy in other people.

Building relationships through the investment of social energy is an adaptive behavior. This is where things get interesting, because investing energy in others can be quite efficient. Whether we look toward social mammals or human ancestors, relationships are valuable because they *save energy* in the long run.[48] Many activities that can be done efficiently and effectively with several people can't be done at all by a single person. In societies the world over, friends share when they have abundance and come to one another's aid when they're in need.[49] A variety of resources, from food to knowledge, are made available to people who have a strong social network. Our human ancestors may have had to expend less energy on challenging tasks, particularly physical labor, because they had other people around with whom to share the load. And the very source of human energy—food—was probably more abundant when people worked together and had friends to share and trade with, especially when resources were scarce. This means the tiny amount of energy (compared to physical labor) spent on being a responsive friend can be incredibly energy efficient over time. Such social behavior can result in getting help from others to do big, necessary, and challenging tasks, such as getting water, shelter, and food.

—

In a basic sense, people can't have friends if they don't make them and keep them around. And this takes work. People are both wonderful and difficult. Conversations are both connecting and disjointed. Relationships aren't simple, nor can they endure without effort. We need to take on the stress of investing energy in other people to thrive. We need to create a life that can sustain hormetic conditions of survival and growth, because without doing so, we lack the vitality to accomplish life's tasks and get our social needs met. It's absolutely necessary to expend energy to have enough of it to keep on going. Too much social stress, however, is a terrible recipe for thriving. It's all in the balance. But the balance is getting harder to achieve.

Life Gets in the Way

Modern social conditions don't always favor relational investment. Nonetheless, the need to belong is one of the few needs in modern times that still require social interactions and relationships. In many places around the world, basic needs, like food, water, shelter, and the financial means to attain those resources, are becoming increasingly accessible, at least for part of the population, with very little human contact. Modern life seems to be constructed to free us from social obligation. Remote work and online services, for instance, have reduced the amount of necessary in-person contact closer and closer to zero. Higher-level needs like career achievement and personal autonomy can be satisfied without close relationships. In fact, meaningful relationships can be a barrier to career success. After all, time enjoying friends can't be spent working, and people often forgo job opportunities for the sake of keeping their family stable and connected. Work is the most consistent obstacle to social time; valuing work for what it produces (money, mainly) appears to diminish the value of sociability. Research suggests that individuals who prioritize time over money spend more time socializing and more time getting to know new people. Those who value money over time, in contrast, are less interested in social interactions inside and outside the workplace. Talking gets in the way of productivity.[50]

Furthermore, there's a strong, persistent pleasure associated with accomplishment, especially in the near term. Work can facilitate an enticing sense of immediate reward. Yet extensively focusing on achievement at work can jeopardize longer-term life satisfaction and happiness, which are often directly linked to relational investments. Unlike completing a task at work, committing time to supporting a friend in need doesn't allow us to check off something on our to-do list. But the energy invested in supporting someone can blossom into a sense of relational fulfillment over time. The Nobel Prize–winning economist Daniel Kahneman argues that many people prioritize paid work over time with friends, despite the fact that time with friends is more likely to maximize happiness in the long term. "Altogether," Kahneman said, "I don't think that people maximize happiness in that sense. . . . This doesn't seem to be what people want to do. They actually want to maximize their satisfaction with themselves and with their lives. And that leads in completely different directions than the maximization of happiness."[51] In other words, the tangible—and often more immediate and pressing—requirements of work take precedence over our relationships. Perhaps it's because the pleasures of work accomplishments are more palatable than the struggles we often face in relationships. Alternatively, social structures and conditions sometimes force people to prioritize their work just to survive, an idea that we'll return to. In any case, the people around us are unpredictable, can sometimes be disappointing, and will need things from us. Choosing the struggle necessary for hormetic social stress can be unappealing, frankly, in the context of more immediate, controllable tasks and pleasures, including those tied to our jobs.

For many people, being geographically mobile is necessary to find work or climb the career ladder. This leads to a disruptive churn in the composition of social networks. With every move to a new town, change of school, or start of a new job, a person loses members in their social network, and new relationships must be built from scratch.[52] Although romantic partners will sometimes relocate with each other, friends rarely do. Distance is the great friendship killer; young people throughout the world (fifteen to forty years old) say it's the number one reason (61 percent) they lose touch with their friends.[53] If Kahneman is right, a culture of work achievement becomes detrimental to building long-term life satisfaction.

How would we regard someone who valued their relationships over their success? Let's say a young person decides to forgo their educational or career opportunities to spend more time hanging out with their friends. How would we judge those choices? Would we believe they gave up on reaching their full potential for something of lesser value? Maybe even something frivolous? Or worse? Most likely. As Sheila Liming contends in her book *Hanging Out: The Radical Power of Killing Time*, our "production-obsessed society" not only has led us to devalue unplanned time with friends but has caused us to "look askance" at and be "suspicious of those who hang out when they ought to be working and producing."[54] It seems that we're living in a society that is increasingly tipping the scales toward personal achievement over social obligation.

Chapter 4

BALANCING CONNECTION AND SOLITUDE

For almost three decades, Christopher Thomas Knight did everything he could to avoid other people. Disconnection was his mission, so much so that he chose to make his home in a makeshift camp deep in the Maine woods completely alone. Knight, who became known as the Hermit of North Pond, had only two fleeting human interactions, one with a hiker and the other with some ice fishermen, in the twenty-seven years he spent in the woods.[1]

Few of us can relate to the degree of isolation that Knight sought and maintained. But we can probably appreciate it in less extreme manifestations. During the outbreak of the COVID-19 pandemic, people became increasingly reluctant to interact. Early in the lockdown, Jeff was texting with a friend about trying to have a social life while working from home—a challenge both faced. She wrote, "This speaks to exactly what I've been battling. People are exhausting. And some of them are also uninteresting. But if I don't socialize, I get stuck in my own head." In a study we conducted on day-to-day social experiences that helped inspire this book, we found that the best predictor of well-being wasn't how many conversations people had or how much time they spent alone. The best predictor was how people felt when they were alone, namely, the degree to which they felt (a) happy to be alone, (b) that their needs were met, and (c) that they didn't wish for further company or interaction.[2] This finding makes sense when we consider that solitude is not inherently good or bad. Rather, its perceived value is attached to its ability to nurture connection when we're around others.

This chapter will develop the idea that we have a homeostatic social system that balances solitude and social time. We explore the idea that interiority and sociability are in tension with each other. We shall see that the very social processes that keep us safe and socially regulated can become a chronic state that's bad for our health and well-being. When interiority and disconnection become mutually reinforcing, our social system becomes dysregulated and a barrier to socializing enough for our own good. By understanding the value of solitude, we can better understand how to avoid social dysregulation and how to enhance its value when we can find time to be alone.[3]

Solitude and Sociability

Ultimately, we need a balance of connection and solitude. And we need to find this balance in a time when many people's social time is declining and their loneliness is rising. Less social time and more loneliness are critical trends marking what we call the *age of interiority* we're living in. But there's more to it than that. The age of interiority is a historical shift that capitalizes on our natural tendencies as humans. It's a time of greater self-focus and, at times, even a celebration of disconnection. Because it exists at several levels at once, interiority has been, and always will be, part of society's makeup. It's not unique to this time and place in history; people have always had a drive toward interiority. This is part of the reason that addressing problems like loneliness is so difficult. But we're getting ahead of ourselves. Let's start with a historical perspective.

David Vincent's book *A History of Solitude* traces the 250-year intellectual history of being alone. Vincent reveals that there are periods of history in which solitude is condemned and isolation is pathologized. There are also periods in which solitude is celebrated and its virtues are applauded. At some points in history, both extremes — enduring isolation and unending sociability — have been identified as the fount of human suffering. In the Romantic era, monastic life was celebrated for its purity. Wandering alone like a cloud was a vision of good health. At that time, *oneliness* (the state of being alone) did not have the negative connotation we now associate with loneliness. Being contained within oneself was a necessary counterweight to crowded spaces. The purity attainable in isolation compensated for a lack of privacy at home and the oppression of urban crowds. Living required living close to other people, and interior solace was hard to find. Technology adapted to these social shifts, offering workarounds to the unrelenting presence of others. Posted letters and later in-home telephone calls carved out time for mediated sociability, but they couldn't meaningfully disrupt the necessity of being around others. For most people, there simply wasn't an alternative to the obligations of sociability because of household size, how people worked, the nature of commerce, and prevailing social structures. True solitude was reserved for the rich, the adventurous, the holy.[4]

Consider the cultural signs of interiority now regarding, for instance, self-care — a trend that has, in some ways, supplanted the decades-long trend of self-help. Self-care is accepting of and nurturing to the self, which, on the surface, are very good things. There are indeed many benefits to saying, "I'm okay as I am." But if we're not careful, we can take it too far and potentially limit opportunities to connect with others.[5] There's been an uptick, for example, in calls to cut out "toxic" people from our lives. What behavior or relationship, though, counts as toxic? Cleary, harmful or abusive behavior should be eliminated. But the "toxic" label can get applied to decidedly less serious matters, such as a minor argument, a slight, or the friend who monopolizes conversations.

None of these inclinations, to be clear, is necessarily wrong. Self-reflection and repose can be quite renewing, whether through a Romantic era country stroll or modern-day Goop and yoga. Both can make future social demands more tolerable and enjoyable. Removing toxic relationships, moreover, can presumably free up time for healthier ones, which could improve our well-being. Yet relational detoxing, if taken to the extreme, operates from the logic that people are an inherent barrier to self-preservation and happiness. They need to be cut out. This extreme perspective seems consistent with larger social trends regarding interiority. The reality is that we all experience an omnipresent tension between solitude and connection.[6] Interiority and sociability, in other words, are two parts of a whole, and this has always been true, so let's explore this tension in greater depth.

Interiority and Sociability Constitute a Homeostatic System of Belongingness

As a guest on *The Late Show with Stephen Colbert*, the comedian Jim Gaffigan joked that when the pandemic initially forced people to stay at home, he was good with that. "You want me to eat pizza, too?" he quipped.[7] Like many people, Gaffigan enjoyed the isolation. Once the pandemic was better managed through increasing vaccination rates, some people did, in fact, miss being forced to stay at home. In chapter 1 we showed how the need to belong is as fundamental as needs for food and water and that it compels people to build and maintain relationships. But there's another part to this process. When given a choice, people sometimes prefer to avoid social opportunities and obligations. This is the fundamental contradiction we confront: being social and being alone both feel good.

We can go a step further and assert that the very ability to connect with others is inherently linked to our ability to separate from them. Consider that children's construction of secure attachments with caregivers (which is the basis for building strong adult relationships) is rooted in their capacity to comfortably experience closeness *and* distance. In short, healthy attachment enables contented solitude.[8] Moreover, just as societal-level tensions shape interiority and sociability, as Vincent points out, distance from people can facilitate human connection.[9] People will find themselves in situations — whether as extreme as a global pandemic or as common as moving for a new job — where separation is unbearable, just as people will find themselves in conditions in which their daily life demands too much communication.[10] Interiority and sociability aren't opposites, and both are needed to attain hormesis.

Drawing on various theoretical perspectives, we describe this process in our research as *homeostatic*.[11] Shawn O'Connor and Lorne Rosenblood, who originally described the nature of social calories, were instrumental in demonstrating how and why people transitioned from moments of interaction to moments of time alone.[12] Interaction and time alone, as O'Connor and Rosenblood showed, work together. Longing for or missing people is unpleasant but necessary for a well-functioning social system. When people have unmet social needs, they desire social interaction.[13] When their belongingness tank is full, they curtail further interaction.[14] This process depends on having social energy. Because all social interactions are energy depleting, time alone is restorative. A study conducted among older adults in Switzerland found that periods of solitude and interaction shifted back and forth in predictable patterns.[15] Longer periods of time alone enabled longer subsequent social interactions, and longer social interactions were followed by rest and solitude. After too much conversation, people retreat into solitude (or at least want to) to recover and relax. Leisure is associated much more with being alone than with being around others.[16] If we believe social interaction has a certain amount of nutritional content, we can also accept that, as we can with food, it's possible to overdo it. On the interiority side, people have to work up an appetite to enjoy socializing.

Quality of conversation also plays a critical role. People are often contentedly alone after highly rewarding but high-energy social interaction.[17] People want some "me time" after intense interactions. But the quality of that time alone depends on how satisfying the conversation preceding it was.[18] Rewarding conversation consumes social energy as it meets the need to belong, which then turns into satisfied solitude later in the day. Restorative time alone refills depleted energy (thanks, mitochondria) while the need to belong slowly rises, eventually leading people to seek conversation and connection. Both "Satisfied Solitude" and "Connected while Conversing" are part of the uppermost, prosocial part of figure 1, which includes the states of sociability and interiority.

Connected and Disconnected Sociability

A theme of this book is that relationships are interdependent, brought into existence through communication. From mundane chitchat and gossip to expressing love and sharing intimate thoughts,

---

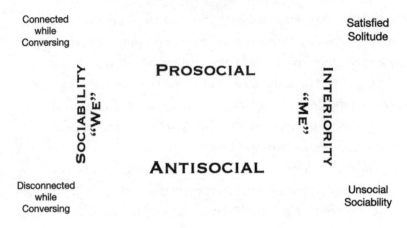

Figure 1. States of sociability and interiority.

relationships are forged, continued, and renewed through talk.[19] The sociability part of figure 1, on the left-hand side, represents the whole range of conversations we have in daily life, whether with close friends or with new acquaintances. Being social can be hard to get right. Sociability risks feeling uncertain, unwelcome, unknown, and misunderstood. Sociability, like time alone, includes prosocial and antisocial aspects. And we seek different people for different types of conversations. Some friends are great for having fun with, some are better for deep conversation, still others are good problem solvers and collaborators. Whom we choose to talk to depends on the emotions we want to experience, make sense of, or cope with.[20]

Let's consider why we do (or don't) talk to strangers. The need to belong exists to orient us toward the formation of enduring and close relationships. Yet as much as two-thirds of our daily social interactions are with people whom we aren't terribly close to — it's an even higher proportion for working adults.[21] We talk to strangers, acquaintances, classmates, coworkers, and on and on. On days when people feel happier, more upbeat, and more energetic, they tend to be more open to the world, friendlier, and warmer. They're more willing to smile and greet one another and listen and laugh together. And on days when people feel stressed or tired or in a foul mood, they're often reserved, terse, and inwardly focused. The researcher Jordi Quoidbach and his team conducted a mammoth study of interactions of nearly 31,000 French citizens. They discovered a fascinating pattern: when people feel bad, they're more likely to seek out close friends and family. When people are happier, they're more likely to talk to strangers – even though those interactions with strangers are generally less pleasant than talking with a friend or romantic partner. This suggests that, when it comes to talking to strangers, people borrow from their happiness reserve and make a little gift of it to someone else.[22]

So when are people most likely to give that gift? Quoidbach and his colleagues answer that question in terms of the *hedonic flexibility principle*. The idea of hedonic flexibility is that people talk to strangers when they have some happiness to spare. Once people take the risk of talking to strangers and find that they had more fun and liked the new person more than they had predicted, they're more likely to take that risk again.[23] Sharing our happiness in this way allows us individually and collectively to construct a healthier social world. It builds a bridge to another person whom we can learn from and talk to, and who may help meet our future need to belong. This bears a striking similarity to anthropological studies of friendship. Throughout the world, gift giving, particularly in the form of sharing broadly in times of abundance, is the bedrock of friendship.[24] We also give from what we can spare to people we don't know very well. This makes it possible to create new relationships and expand our support network.

By contrast, everyday conversations can also result in feeling stressed out, upset, disrespected, or rejected. Research demonstrates that these negative experiences weigh three times more heavily than accepting and inclusive conversations, but they're also, fortunately, relatively rare.[25] The most common way that people cope with rejection is to seek social support. In particularly hard times, such as life-threatening events, people rely on their closest family and friends to make it through.[26] We seek out connecting conversation to find reassurance and care. These acts of sociability help us grow and thrive despite adversity.[27] In this way, social disconnection can motivate connecting communication.

These tensions aren't resolvable. People associate the presence of others, compared to being alone, with both more positive emotions like closeness and more negative emotions like anxiety.[28] This is also true in close relationships. Sharing one's hardships and vulnerabilities is one of the core expectations of friendship, yet it can also be understood as burdening others with one's problems.[29] It's a long-standing finding in communication and psychology research that deeper disclosures help develop intimacy and closeness, but listening to more emotionally intense talk is draining.[30] What's troublesome about friendship and what's valuable about it are often one and the same. The quest to eradicate negativity or drains on emotional energy can reduce the likelihood of experiencing deep feelings of connection that come about from being a confidant and source of support.[31]

Extraversion-Introversion

During the pandemic, many people felt that Jim Gaffigan was right; the lockdown seemed like an introvert's paradise. Given the importance of this idea culturally and theoretically, it's worth considering. But let's first take up the popular claim that social interaction is unpleasant or even less beneficial for introverts. Is sociability relatively more rewarding for extraverts?

In the first chapter of the classic children's book *Anne of Green Gables,* Matthew Cuthbert and Anne (with an "e") are getting acquainted.[32] Reflecting on her talkative, imaginative nature, Anne worries she's talking too much: "Matthew, much to his own surprise, was enjoying himself. Like most quiet folks he liked talkative people when they were willing to do the talking themselves and did not expect him to keep up his end of it." Upon reflection, he replies, "Oh, you can talk as much as you like, I don't mind." This lovely story invites a question: Do introverts suffer when they must be social or are they more like Matthew Cuthbert, enjoying being social when in good company? There's an intuitive appeal to the idea that this is all about personality. People who are more extraverted spend more time socializing and express a stronger preference for doing so. It seems logical, then, that introverts wouldn't get nearly as much out of being social. While it may seem intuitive, evidence doesn't support this conclusion. The experimental design is a great simulation of making more-introverted people be social. In studies where participants are assigned to act extraverted, they report feeling more positive emotions, more connected, and more likely to have their need to belong satisfied.[33] People even feel better when they're just in an extraverted state of mind.[34] It doesn't matter whether people are more introverted or more extraverted to begin with — the benefit of acting extraverted appears to apply broadly.

There's another possibility. Maybe extraverted people get more out of their social experiences because of familiarity or preference. Again, this doesn't seem to be the case. Whether introverted or extraverted, people experience similar levels of happiness and positive emotions in social situations.[35] Several additional studies add weight

—

to these experimental claims. Taking tens of thousands of moments out of the days of over two thousand undergraduate students, researchers first tested whether more-introverted or more-extraverted students got more out of being social.[36] Personality didn't matter. Being social seems to feel better, especially when it's face-to-face (not online) and with close friends. The most-extraverted students didn't get a bigger bump to their well-being when they were social. The most-introverted students didn't get a bump to their well-being when they were alone.

An eleven-year study of the leisure time of twelve thousand adults from the Netherlands revealed similar results. Spending more nights per week on social activities was associated with greater happiness and life satisfaction.[37] Again, these benefits were seen across all personalities. In some studies, more-introverted people have been found to experience the greatest increase of well-being and life satisfaction when they socialized more, perhaps because it's comparatively rarer for them to do so.[38] This interpretation fits with a study conducted during the initial lockdown period of the pandemic.[39] The conventional wisdom was that sheltering in place was more enjoyable for people who didn't like to be social. Yet everyone who experienced a loss of connection during lockdown – whether more introverted or more extraverted – tended to feel lonelier and less happy. Extraverts' social opportunities dropped more dramatically (because they had more social experiences to lose), but the loss of social time was unpleasant across the board.[40]

What about friendship? It does seem to be the case that people who are more extraverted are more open to talking to strangers and tend to keep in touch with a larger circle of contacts both online and offline.[41] Further, both extraverted and introverted people tend to pick friends with similar personalities to their own.[42] But introversion tells us very little about the ability to have good friends.[43] By keeping their network of relationship partners tight and close, introverted people can more deeply invest in the people they like most, which enables deeper conversations.[44] This is a good strategy to avoid being spread thin by trying to keep in touch with too many people.[45] Whether more introverted or more extraverted, people can and do have high-quality friendships.

"Unsocial Sociability" and the Disconnection of Conversation

One of the challenges of social life is that to enjoy the benefits of being social, we must risk tedious and dull conversation as well as unfamiliarity, uncertainty, and disagreement. Being around others to some degree invites struggle and conflict. Connection and disconnection are unavoidable parts of what it means to rely on others, to be interdependent. On the interiority side of disconnection in figure 1 lies something insidious. Immanuel Kant, the German philosopher, in his essay "Idea for a Universal History from a Cosmopolitan Point of View," stated that a person isolates from others because of the "unsociable characteristic of wishing to have everything go according to his own wish." This characteristic is part of what Kant called *unsocial sociability,* which is humans' natural "propensity to enter into society, bound together with a mutual opposition which constantly threatens to break up the society."[46] What Kant meant is that when people are driven by unsocial sociability, they're antisocial by disposition, viewing the people around them as obstacles to their goals or wrong for not adopting their own point of view. One of the ingredients of unsocial sociability is feeling bitter about needing other people. It's a reluctant, grudging admission of interdependence. We resist the opinions of others because we favor our own point of view and consider ourselves superior to others.[47]

The thing is, there's some truth to the idea that being social can lead to withdrawal – or as Kant would say, to feelings of mutual opposition. When people are in a bad place (hurt, angry, or depressed), conversation with them can be exhausting.[48] When someone needs help, they can do all the talking while their companion does all the listening. Going through a rough time leaves people self-centered and even hard to be around, as countless Dear Abby and Ask Amy columns can testify. Ideally, friendships balance costs and benefits over time, so that neediness and support go both ways. Being a friend means being there for somebody when they're not at their best. This is what interdependence looks like on the sociability part of the continuum. The interiority component of antisociability is dangerous insofar as it seizes on the natural tendencies we all have toward self-interest. As Kant warned, this tendency, if unchecked, has the potential to break up society because it combines self-favoritism with isolation.

Unwanted Interiority

In her beautifully illustrated book *Seek You: A Journey through American Loneliness*, Kirsten Radtke shares the following story: "As a kid, there was some connection between a lack of independence and loneliness. I was prevented from finding people who would make me not lonely. It was a trap and I was aware of it but didn't know a way out."[49] Feeling trapped is indeed a potent emotion. Just as we can feel trapped in a dead-end job or a lease that restricts our freedom, we can feel trapped in a relationship or even a conversation. Loneliness is typically defined as the distance between the amount of companionship we desire and the amount we have. This means that a person can have little company but be perfectly content with their situation, perhaps even preferring more time alone.[50] Consider Beatriz Flamini, who in 2021–23 spent five hundred days alone in a cave in southern Spain—albeit with a research team remotely monitoring her health, preparing her food, and removing her waste every few days. Upon leaving the cave, Flamini said to reporters that her extended period of solitude was "excellent, unbeatable," and that she "didn't want to come out."[51] On the other hand, a person can have frequent social interactions but be lonely. This means that the ability to choose to interact when we want to is key to understanding this process. The very notion of choice is complicated given our constant mobile connectivity.[52] Solitude protects our privacy and integrity. Choice is a crucial component because it shapes our social experiences when we're alone and with others. Living alone is a good example of something that people don't always choose. It could happen because of migration, when leaving for college, when navigating divorce or separation, or, as in Kirsten Radtke's story, when prevented from finding friends to help exit the trap of loneliness.

Research indicates that all people at all stages of life are more likely to experience loneliness when they live alone.[53] That does not mean living alone is without benefits. But the balance of benefits and drawbacks can get out of whack when living alone is not by choice. Living alone or being alone when one would prefer not to is called involuntary solitude, a damaging state of being. Social deprivation, particularly in extreme cases, such as solitary confinement, is linked to a long list of negative outcomes.[54] Everyday manifestations of involuntary solitude, such as the feeling that there's nothing to do but to be alone—the very definition of lacking choice—are deeply unpleasant.[55] As unsatisfying as involuntary solitude is, it doesn't always motivate a desire to talk to strangers or to reach out to friends. Why not? Let's explore the vast research on loneliness for an answer.

Loneliness Can Become Self-Perpetuating

The late John Cacioppo's research on loneliness is unparalleled.[56] His work, which he conducted with numerous collaborators, advanced the world's understanding of loneliness in empirically rich and deeply empathetic ways. Beginning with the assumption that loneliness is a necessary feeling of longing that motivates social actions and choices, Cacioppo argued that this system can go off the rails. Rather than helping repair lost connection, loneliness can exacerbate the very isolation it's built to correct. Cacioppo, along with Louise Hawkley, defined loneliness as an "aversive condition that promotes inclusive fitness by signaling ruptures in social connections to motivate the repair or replacement of those connections."[57] When people experience loneliness as a temporary feeling in a day, they're motivated to interact socially.[58] When loneliness is chronic, however, it has harmful effects on physical and mental health. It also changes how people perceive the world. According to the evolutionary theory of loneliness, which Cacioppo articulated comprehensively in one of his final publications with his partner, the neuroscientist Stephanie Cacioppo, when people feel that they lack the desired amount of social connection, they become more hypervigilant toward "social threats." Chronic loneliness, in other words, can put us on high alert for signs of rejection from others.[59]

An overly inward focus becomes habitual for the chronically lonely, which leads to poorer partner attention skills, a lack of self-disclosure to friends, and less participation in organized groups.[60] People experiencing chronic loneliness can become less sensitive to the needs of others as they withdraw to prevent further rejection.[61] This means that the very actions that could reduce loneliness are avoided. People who are chronically lonely often unconsciously communicate to others, "Leave me alone." Unfortunately, people will often intuit this preference and try to respect an isolated person's wish to be isolated.[62] Acts of self-protection, which can be functional in the short term, can't reduce loneliness when they become habitual. Ultimately, the homeostatic system adapted to maintain relationships can become severely dysregulated under conditions of chronic loneliness.

Loneliness, it's critical to note, isn't the same thing as introversion or a preference for solitude.[63] Each has its own pattern of behavior. While more-introverted people prefer solitude and embrace it as an opportunity for restoration, reflection, and quietude, lonely people typically don't prefer solitude – they often find it unpleasant.[64] Compared to chronic loneliness, introversion is not a problem to be solved but a preference for lower levels and different types of sociability, such as intimate conversations with close friends. Certainly, more-introverted people can sometimes feel lonely, and lonely people might sometimes enjoy solitude. Because loneliness depends on what people want relative to what they have, a person can have very few friends or loved ones in their lives but be happy. There's no consensus about the "right" number of friends. The proper number depends on the quality of, and access to, loved ones. Having just one loving person at home can help stave off loneliness and boost longevity.[65] Embracing solitude or preferring fewer social events isn't a barrier to having good relationships or investing deeply in existing friends.[66] Indeed, people who prefer solitude may have deeper relationships than those who don't appreciate its value.[67]

An enormous study of Dutch citizens that included over 53,000 people revealed loneliness can be understood in part as a problem of structural disadvantage: individuals who were less well educated, were in financially precarious situations, or had mental health challenges were more likely to be lonely, no matter their age.[68] Permanent residents of the Netherlands from non-European backgrounds were also more likely to be lonely, as their older social networks were disrupted during emigration and their integration in society was stymied by discrimination. Loneliness is also exacerbated by stress, particularly work stress.[69] Work stress saps time and energy that is needed to bond with others, leaving people diminished and isolated. If people are busy working to make ends meet, while balancing constant demands of family life — especially the care needs of children and older family members — their time for connection is decreased. A great deal of loneliness is not of our own making.[70]

When Does Interiority Become Isolation?

Loneliness casts light on humans' amazing capacity to adapt. Almost anything can seem normal. Social life is no different. You get used to it. The pandemic demonstrated this the world over. Stay-at-home orders changed who we could safely interact with face to face. Life for many was less rushed, yet also much lonelier.[71] This led people to rely increasingly not only on video-calling through Zoom and FaceTime to connect with others, but also on old-fashioned phone calls. In the United States, for instance, during the first weeks of the pandemic in 2020, the rate of voice calls was double the peak day in 2019, which happened to be Mother's Day.[72] Over time, though, these efforts to reach out to loved ones and friends — and the connection resulting from these efforts — dropped off.[73] People grew more distant from their friends in the year following the outbreak of the pandemic. This trend toward less time with friends, unfortu-

---

74

nately, was well under way before COVID-19. Time spent with friends constituted 10.8 percent of free time in 2003 and only 5.4 percent of time in 2019. This time further declined during the pandemic.[74]

Loneliness also accompanies certain periods of life. Upon leaving college, for example, graduates face the reality of a diminished social life. This is also a period when expectations of mobility in pursuit of career goals increase. Without the easy access to friends and acquaintances provided by a college campus, many young people become accustomed to a less social life and consequently suffer loneliness. Studies indicate that young people, in general, are experiencing especially high rates of loneliness.[75] Researchers have also identified this same pattern of lost sociability among older adults after they retire, especially when the retirement is involuntary—that is, occurring earlier or later than they would have wanted.[76]

It doesn't take long for newfound social isolation to become normalized.[77] One study found that after ten hours of experimentally mandated social isolation, participants wanted badly to interact socially with someone.[78] The participants, however, desired *less* social interaction during their day of isolation than they had in a regular day of their life. This suggests that the more accustomed people get to being isolated, especially when they have no other choice, the more they become resigned to it. Another study found that as loneliness increased throughout the day, people were less likely to do something about it.[79] They instead reacted with passivity and sadness; this was especially true of people who were typically accustomed to friendly relationships with other people. A day of isolation was more fatiguing and vitality depleting compared to a normal day.[80] People wanted social contact but lacked the energy to do something about it.

The constant availability of mobile technology and social media probably plays a role as well. People turn to social media when they feel lonely, but social media aren't very good at making people feel socially satisfied. It's like a social snack—temporarily redirecting the feeling of disconnection but failing to satisfy needs fully.[81] Turning to social media as a primary source of belonging may instantiate a more worrying pattern: people who tend to rely on social media to address their need to belong appear to experience only a greater need to belong and greater social media use over time.[82] People often turn to social media when they're more distressed, but that doesn't necessarily alleviate their negative feelings. It does, however, seem to lead them to use social media more.

Humor and Nostalgia

Where does this leave those who wish to move out of the unsocial sociability corner of figure 1? It can be difficult. Social anxiety and loneliness aren't trivial concerns, nor are they easily overcome, but they can improve with treatment. Severe cases need professional care. What about more everyday feelings of unsocial sociability? What did Jeff tell his friend who felt so ambivalent about rejoining her social life?

Jeff has had a postcard hanging in his office for more than twenty years. It shows a woman looking tired and stressed, with the words "Other people ruin everything" arranged above her head. The rich irony of this postcard is that we're all villains in other people's heroic narrative, and yet we still favor ourselves in the story. Sometimes you've just got to laugh at the impossibility of it all. Humor can be a salve for the predicament we're all in. We need and love people, but people are also the source of a lot of misery and disconnection.

———

Jean-Paul Sartre is famous for writing, "Hell is other people," in the play *No Exit*. The play's premise — three people who are unknowingly stuck in hell together — is strikingly similar to the recent serial comedy *The Good Place*. Neither the classic play nor the recent show concludes with fatalistic pessimism. Later in life, Sartre suggested something entirely different: "Heaven, on the other hand, is very simple — and very hard: caring about your fellow beings."[83] Echoing similar sentiments, Sartre's contemporary and sometimes friend Albert Camus pleaded: "In a world whose absurdity appears to be so impenetrable, we simply must reach a greater degree of understanding among men, a greater sincerity. We must achieve this or perish."[84] Despite the absurdity of it all, perhaps with a bit of levity we can emerge with a renewed sense of comforted solitude. What's more, we may feel better equipped to handle being social again.

Another possibility is finding some peace in nostalgia, which research suggests can lessen the negative effects of feeling socially isolated.[85] Nostalgia reminds us that love and care aren't so far away, helping us overcome negative feelings caused by periods of isolation.[86] In a study combining survey and experimental designs conducted in the United States, the United Kingdom, and China during the lockdown period of the pandemic, Xinyu Zhou and her colleagues found that nostalgia helped combat loneliness and increase feelings of happiness.[87] Along these same lines, researchers have begun testing the effectiveness of reminiscence therapy among older adults, an approach that aids people in their recall of positive memories to reduce loneliness.[88] Researchers have also turned to virtual reality technology to help older adults, including those with mild to moderate dementia, lessen feelings of loneliness by reconnecting them with positive family memories in immersive digital environments.[89] Sharing memories and identifying pathways to becoming more socially connected can help people feel willing and able to connect. These connective experiences can kindle hope.

Perhaps the most important pathway to getting out of a mentality of unsocial sociability is to take the risk to be social again. Sociability can be an antidote to the antagonism and vanity that take hold when we're overly self-focused. Excessive emphasis on our own needs — however real and difficult they are — can crowd out the recognition that we're imperfect, but we deserve to have friends. And we have something to offer others. The unsocial sociability corner says, "All I need is myself; other people aren't worth it. My point of view is better than theirs anyway." In the later part of his career, Nick Cave, a legend of post-punk music and no stranger to seriously anti-social and antagonistic lyrics in his earlier years, lost his teenage son in a tragic accident. He released a series of raw and painful albums about his grief and loss. In response to an interviewer who asked about the importance of communication when people are at their worst, Cave responded, "It seems to be essential, even if just as a corrective for the bad, unexpressed ideas we hold in our heads."[90] This returns us again to the obligations that we must adopt to build hormetic stress. Cave's insights are reinforced by research that indicates people's need to be right, to be superior, to be antagonistic to the views of others melts away when in conversation with a responsive partner.[91] Such experiences pull people away from their defensive stance and out of interiority. Because responsiveness communicates to people that they have inherent value, it makes them better able to admit their own limits and mistakes. This suggests that we should try to communicate responsively with the people around us. It's perhaps the most straightforward way to foster less interiority among the people in our social worlds.

Chapter 5

SOCIAL INERTIA IN AN AGE OF INTERIORITY

We've discussed how building and maintaining relationships has inevitable challenges, while also being the bedrock of a fulfilling life. To build strong relationships, we must be committed to the cause. Yet for so many of us, this commitment seems to be on the wane. Consider the following:

- Teenagers' social time outside the house has been in free fall ever since Gen X grew up. In 1987 incoming college students spent 13.5 hours a week socializing with friends, but by 2016 that time had shrunk to 9.1 hours. Most of the decline occurred after 2010.[1]
- Laura Carstensen, director of Stanford University's Center on Longevity, has found that Americans ages fifty-five to sixty-four are far less socially engaged with their communities than were people of the same ages two decades ago.[2]
- Membership in places of worship has fallen from 70 percent of Americans in 2000 to less than 50 percent in 2022. Weekly attendance at churches, mosques, and synagogues shrank from 35 percent of Americans to less than 25 percent.[3]

· From 2003 to 2019, Americans' leisure time went up
(on average), but time spent in the company of others went
down. Many people have more time. They choose to spend it
alone.[4]

For at least thirty years, hours and hours of time each and every week that were once spent talking or hanging out for its own
sake have evaporated. It isn't only the pandemic that has caused
these changes, although it significantly exacerbated existing trends.
In 2020 stay-at-home orders gave many Americans, on average, another half hour a day in leisure time, but social distancing mandated
*un*sociability. Not surprisingly, the amount of time spent outside the
house shrank 42 percent from 2019 to 2020.[5] Yet for workers re-
lieved of certain responsibilities, such as their daily commutes,
working hours increased and time alone took up the rest of the newfound time.[6] Time alone has been increasing for at least three decades.[7] Most of the lost social time is in the category of going out
with friends or being invited over for dinner. The portion of free
time spent going out with other people or going to parties declined
from 22 percent in 2003 to 17 percent in 2019.[8] People are appor-
tioning fewer and fewer of their moments each day to opportunities
for connection.

Confronted with these trends, governments across the world
are increasingly concerned about loneliness — and for good reason.[9]
Loneliness and social isolation, as we noted in chapter 1, are better
predictors of mortality and morbidity than smoking and being over-
weight.[10] Government reports, experts, advice columnists, and news
agencies are all singing the same tune: we have to build better and
more supportive relationships, socialize more, and take control of
how and when we communicate. If it were only so simple. Although

well-intentioned, advice to prioritize connection often misses the fact that people aren't connecting with others for wide-ranging reasons. The barriers are a mix of powerful perceptual, dispositional, and structural forces. If we're advised to connect but don't have the resources to do so, we'll inevitably fall short in meeting our needs and our collective goal of a less lonely society. We seem to be living in an age of interiority in which it's increasingly difficult to find the time, energy, and companions with whom to form meaningful relationships.

This chapter focuses on the historical trends of interiority and why being overly stressed and socially taxed may be key reasons for a lack of connection. A desire to be alone is a feature, not a bug, in our design, yet — at this period of history — the amount of time spent alone has increased. We'll examine why interiority is joined by a greater focus on the self and how this is complemented and hastened by new technologies. We'll also discuss how interiority is both a trend and a reaction, created in a time when barriers to connect feel very real.

Social Time Is Short and in Decline

In the United States, vast losses of social time over at least the last three decades have plunged the social climate into a much colder place. To understand why, we will begin by exploring how Americans generally use their time. Each year since 2003, the U.S. Department of Labor has conducted the American Time Use Survey, which collects a day in the life of over ten thousand people. Each minute of a twenty-four-hour day is accounted for. When did you wake up? What did you do then? And then? And so forth. To get a picture of how people use their time, we analyzed the data from 2003 through 2019.[11] There are as many weekend days recorded as weekdays, so we present these two patterns of time separately in figures 2 and 3. Because we're interested in people's waking hours, the roughly one-third of life spent asleep is not shown.

Work dominates most people's weekdays, when averaged across full-time or part-time employees, students or retirees. The data indicate that, on average, over six hours a day, five days a week, are spent working, with another hour being tacked on each day of the weekend. Add in a twenty-minute commute, and 45 percent of our weekdays are spent in service of work. Working has also become more solitary. The percentage of Americans working remotely quadrupled during the pandemic and was still twice as high in 2023 as it was in 2019. The second-most time-consuming activity is watching TV (which includes streaming media on any device). Although this activity is negatively related to life satisfaction both within a day and over a lifetime, people prefer to watch TV rather than participate in most other activities. It occupies two and a half hours per weekday and three and a half hours per weekend day (figs. 2 and 3).[12]

There are many demands that constrain time further—cooking, housework, laundry, child care, and shopping. Americans are busy people. Where do social routines fit in? People, on average, report reserving less than forty minutes a day during the week and seventy minutes a day on weekends for socializing. The ten minutes a day spent making phone and video calls or writing letters and personal emails adds a little more social time.[13] Of course, people enjoy one another's company without talking. It's nice to have someone around to sit or relax with or to accompany us on errands. Even there, time is scarce and shrinking. Examining time diary data from the United States and countries across Europe, the economist Daniel Hamermesh found that romantic partners who share a home spend only about an hour each day awake, at home, doing the same thing.

—

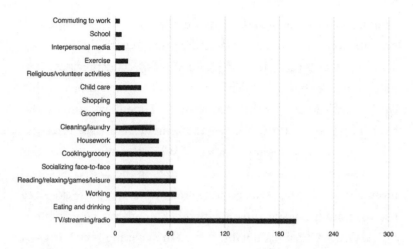

Figure 2. Average time spent on activities during weekends (in minutes), 2003–19. Figure does not include time sleeping. *Source:* U.S. Bureau of Labor Statistics, "American Time Use Survey."

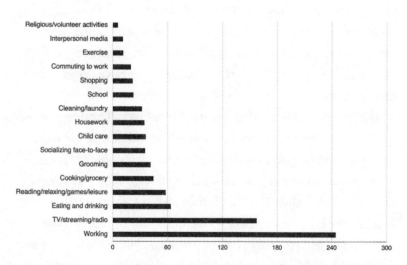

Figure 3. Average time spent on activities during weekdays (in minutes), 2003–19. Figure does not include time sleeping. *Source:* U.S. Bureau of Labor Statistics, "American Time Use Survey."

Couples are home doing different things for an additional hour (for example, one person eating while the other gets ready for work). Time together for couples with children is especially precious: couples who have children under five years old see their time together cut in half.[14] Even this time has shrunk. Time diary studies that stretch back to the 1960s suggest that Americans are spending less leisure time in the company of others.[15] While they have, on average, nearly twice as much leisure time now than in the past, they spend most of it alone. If we're not even spending time with those closest to us, we're surely not spending it with other members of our communities. One of the most notable trends in declining sociability is a reduction across forty years in time spent hosting or attending parties or get-togethers, visiting one another, and entertaining guests.[16]

Why is social time such a small part of the tapestry of our days? Where does that time go? We might be tempted to think we're spending our surplus time focused on home and family. Research based on time-use data indicates that there are clear benefits from these activities, particularly when they're shared, but a rise in "family time" doesn't seem to explain where leisure time is going.[17] One clue is what people do when they get their time back. The onset of the pandemic drastically reduced time spent outside the house and increased leisure time at home.[18] Although many people had fewer obstacles to socializing at home, they chose not to. When we compare data from December 2019 with those from December 2020, we find that the hour and a half of social time spent with people outside the house turned into only a half hour with people in the home. That last hour? People often chose to spend it alone. What do people do when alone? They sleep, watch TV, and play video games. Despite the exaggerated rhetoric about the harms of social media, it isn't the killer of face-to-face time it's portrayed to be.[19] Rather, decade-over-decade comparisons of free time suggests that video games and TV are increasingly dominant forms of entertainment while people are alone.[20] In general, and during the pandemic particularly, very little free time is used to reach out and connect with people outside the house (in person). Despite the uptick in phone calls and video chats during the shelter-in-place period, mediated communication did not make up for the time once used to hang out in person.[21] Clay Shirky, a New York University professor and author, coined the term *cognitive surplus* to describe the free time Americans devote to media consumption (often alone) instead of creative endeavors (often collaboratively).[22] It seems clear that we have a "connective surplus" as well, one that leaves hours upon hours on the table when we could be cashing them in on social interaction.

Time in Life

Americans use their time differently at different stages of their lives and at different times of day, yet the lack of prioritization of social time cuts across all groups. We examined what teens and young adults (fifteen to twenty-four years old), middle-aged adults (forty to forty-nine years old), and older adults (sixty-plus years old) did with their time in 2019 (before the disruptions of the pandemic) during the week. Teens and young adults mainly go to school, and middle-aged adults mainly go to work. As any working parent knows, middle-aged adults work longer hours than their children go to school. This frees up quite a bit of time for young people to do as they please, particularly for college students. For adults over sixty, work time decreases to about an hour a day and school time is nearly zero. At this stage of life, TV often takes center stage — four and a half hours a day during the week.

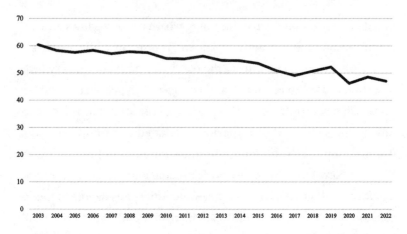

Figure 4. Average time spent socializing (in minutes per day), 2003–22. Includes socializing and communicating with others, attending or hosting parties, and personal media time (including voice calls). *Source:* U.S. Bureau of Labor Statistics, "American Time Use Survey."

No matter people's age, social time doesn't appear to be a priority. All age groups, on average, reported about the same amount of time socializing: teens and young adults (thirty-two minutes per day), middle-aged adults (twenty-eight minutes per day), and older adults (thirty-five minutes per day). Whether full-time employees or full-time students, young people averaged about the same amount of time socializing. For older adults, time gained by retirement didn't tend to increase social time.[23] Given the clear evidence that time spent socializing is on the decline, we're shaving off time from an already small piece of the pie. In both the United Kingdom and the United States (the countries with the best available data), the total amount of time spent socializing has declined by at least 25 percent in the last three decades.[24] This downward trend can be clearly seen in the United States data between 2003 and 2022 (fig. 4).

Barriers to Connection — Why Is Interiority on the Rise?

If being social is so beneficial, then why is interiority on the rise? What's going on? Here we'll explore two trends — work and technology. The need to belong doesn't exist in a vacuum. There are many obstacles to spending time with others. Few people have the freedom, control, and resources to optimize their social health. People need food, shelter, clean water, and a sense of safety before the need to belong can bring about its full benefits.[25] The pursuit of basic needs, accomplished in many societies mainly through paid labor, supersedes the quest for social needs.[26] Work constrains people's ability to interact with nonwork friends and family simply as a matter of time. While work may increase contact with others in the workplace, time for the relationships we choose is reduced. Work becomes a steeper obstacle when it's the number one priority in life.

Cross-national data reveal that, more than any other cause, time spent working takes away from the time people spend together.[27] Education, work, career — these prized goals are often pursued relentlessly. Many of the rewards offered by work can offer a great deal of in-the-moment pleasure, and industrialized countries throughout the world prioritize work as a source of value and virtue for their citizens. The impact of work even cuts across socioeconomic lines: people in the top 5 percent of income-earning households work the most hours per day.[28] This shift from spending time socially to spending time working is notable because it suggests that having the means is no excuse or reason to live a life of leisure — making more money is treated as a good reason to keep working.

Mobility, Intentionality, and Technology

In Jeff's book *Relating through Technology,* he expressed his fear that the celebration of technology's potential has obscured the ways that it has restructured the routines of our days.[29] Technological advances have done much good for human relationships—we need to be clear about that. More than ever before, relationships can endure across geographic divides. This is important when people need to move around for work and educational opportunities. Geographically separated grandparents and grandchildren, for instance, can develop relationships with one another through technologies like FaceTime in ways that were previously impossible.

But the fact that technology facilitates long-distance relating comes with trade-offs, one of which is that distance renders relational connection a more *intentional* process. Communicating with distant loved ones—friends, grandparents, or romantic partners— often requires careful planning. We have to schedule the right times to chat, sometimes across disparate time zones. We have to text one another and remember to reply in a timely fashion. When we no longer share a community defined by physical space, connections atrophy unless considerable effort is made, and this effort only grows as our day-to-day work and child-care demands mount. To have occasional face-to-face meetings with distant friends and family, flights and trains must be booked and boarded. The benefits we draw from our long-distance friend and family relationships, in short, often require a good deal of effort from us.

Further, technological connection appears less capable than routine face-to-face contact of keeping relationships intact.[30] In the year following the outbreak of COVID-19, 50 percent of Americans reported having lost touch with at least a few friends, and the declines were particularly steep for young people.[31] As social distancing rules were lifted, 39 percent of people reported having friends that they interact with only through media. The embrace of technology for relational maintenance — including relationships between people who live relatively close to another — makes relationship building and maintenance more effortful and harder to make routine. Paradoxically, then, increased technological change, which presumably frees us up to connect when and how we want with others, can leave us feeling ever more stuck — struggling to build new relationships and keep old ones alive.[32]

Consider the present moment in contrast to historical patterns of sociability. For most of human history, communication was implicit or structured into daily life through geographically situated places: the workplace, the community, and the home.[33] In fact, some of the desire to seek solitude was in response to the obligations of sociability inherent in cramped domestic spaces.[34] In such a world, social interactions, including interactions with friends and family, required less intentional action to occur. In this way, mobility and technology free us up to be *less* social. These trends are exacerbated by other developments, such as frictionless technology. Friction occurs when human-to-human contact accompanies arranging, planning, or purchasing services or goods.[35] Frictionless technologies remove social obligations to leave home, talk to others, and engage in our community. Food delivery apps, self-checkout lines, and online shopping can increase convenience while decreasing human contact and opportunities to interact. This is reflected in time-use trends showing that people spend less time than they used to shopping outside the house.[36] Frictionless technology embodies the zeitgeist of interiority.

In the past, one category of friend was the trusted and valued commercial trading partner. Such friends extended credit, engaged in honest dealings, shared local gossip, and could be relied on to keep their promises. Such friendships (although we don't call them that) still exist. It's an exaggeration to extend this definition to our favorite cashier or barista, but not by much. If these social interactions and relationships are deleted in the name of reducing friction, this is one less group of people to talk to and trust. Research suggests that conversations with such folks matter for our well-being, especially on days when we have less access to close others.[37] Not only does mobile technology give us an excuse not to interact with the people we meet when we're out and about, but the elevation of frictionless technology atomizes the social potential of community life through commerce.

On top of all this, we live in an unprecedented era of media choice, as we have at our fingertips nearly infinite media content to be consumed anywhere, on demand, with few restrictions of time or place. Although there are financial barriers to accessing content, these barriers are small compared to those that existed thirty years ago, when a person had to be near a TV at a certain time to watch one episode, shown once (until reruns), from a limited set of options. The embrace of media on demand reflects our values. We all crave the satisfaction of accomplishing things. When spending time hanging out with others, however, there's typically nothing tangible to be accomplished.[38] Finishing a series on Netflix or watching the football game — these are things to be checked off a list, often alone.[39] The idea of families gathering around the TV to watch together has been in decline for at least thirty years and, as devices and platforms have continually proliferated, it's now a thoroughly outdated image.[40] Media content is self-selected and increasingly personalized — to levels that will only increase with the continued integration of AI into our lives. Algorithms already pick shows, content, stories, and news bits just for you. Soon, with minimal effort, AI will generate entire immersive worlds finely tuned to our tastes. Media content is there for us, whether we tend to it or not, at any hour of the day. Unlike friends, media are never inconvenienced by our schedule.

Spending time with other people puts you at risk of feeling unsettled, unloved, and annoyed. You can't swipe left mid-sentence to find someone better to talk to. Social interaction is hard work; it takes energy.[41] Think about how much effort it can take just to exit gracefully from a face-to-face conversation.[42] People demand things from us in ways that media use doesn't. Expectations of geographic mobility in careers, the work involved in long-distance relationship maintenance, frictionless technology, and endless media choice all encourage the societal shift toward interiority. These trends reflect our cultural values back to us. They all suggest that we can, and should want to, reduce our social obligations. Ironically, this increases the burden on the individual. As boundaries of space are removed and prioritization of convenient solutions increases, we're forced to prioritize our own social health in a broader climate of interiority. No one else can do it for us.

Normalization and Sense Making

Each of the barriers to socialization—work, technology, and media choice—is accompanied by cultural rationalizations that favor interiority. The way we make sense of things is both constant and collective. Relationships, conversations, and experiences are influenced by the structures people inhabit. These factors have long been with us, but the current climate of interiority seems to give us no incentive to expend the social energy required to be in relationship with one another. It limits our moments to connect and constrains our ability to get our need to belong met — as can be seen in rising rates of loneliness among younger adults. Social time is somehow both less valued collectively and more precious individually.

Rather than push against these trends, it's easier to embrace them. When problems feel uncontrollable, interiority feels like a safe solution. Faced with the difficult reality of finding enough time to spend with others and recognizing the inherent difficulties of starting from scratch with new acquaintances, it's utterly reasonable that people would embrace an interior life. Compared to making new friends or repairing existing relationships, media are much more controllable and manageable. The rationalization of a less social life at both an individual and cultural level seizes on existing arguments about the importance of being alone and then reapplies them to present-day challenges. This process casts interiority as a manageable and even healthy way to deal with lost sociability. Unlike high school, a task at work, or even binge-watching a streaming series, relationships aren't achieved — they're never finished.[43] In an existential sense, this is to our benefit. The endless renewal necessitated by our relationships requires us to show our value and appreciation to others. For the purpose of building a social routine in competition with other more immediately satisfying activities, the lack of achievement is a problem. Aversion to the social energy investments required to make and keep relationships is a barrier to meeting our need to belong and to have a satisfying life through sociability.

Human relationships take time and effort. Most people would like to have a social life in which rewarding social interaction is plentiful and readily accessible. But this is impossible if we make ourselves available only when we want to. To have friends, we have to make and keep friends. If we want to have people in our lives, we must be accessible to them. If our jobs or other obligations have crowded out maintaining relationships in the past, others may simply not be available when we need them in the future. Even the surgeon general, Vivek Murthy, who recently wrote an excellent book on rising loneliness, admitted that he found himself lonely because he allowed his own relationships to deteriorate because of his commitment to work.[44]

The need to belong is fast becoming the only need in many developed nations that still requires other people. It's quite possible to feel independent, in control, and competent in a nearly hermit-like state in many developed countries. Needs like food, water, and shelter can be attained through mobile connectivity and the frictionless, deliverable economy. Relationships depend on available and responsive friends and loved ones. This is true whether we reach out to people through media or seek them out in person. Phone calls and texts are particularly valuable when we need someone the most, but someone must accept the call or respond to the text, or even come over to find us. We're ultimately reliant on other people's choices to make time for us. This is where the wholehearted embrace of interiority is so dangerous. It doesn't affect just one person. Removing the obligations of social life drains precious social resources – human presence, shared time, conversational practice, and relational effort – from all of us.[45]

What does this mean practically? Let's begin by admitting that it can be incredibly hard to prioritize relationships right now. Although many people have more leisure time than previous generations did, they also have less company.[46] Lost social time and fewer interactions are losses for everyone. They're multiplicative, not just cumulative. Second, it's increasingly normal not to go out, not to prioritize relationships, not to keep in touch, and to make excuses rather than accept social invitations. This normalization of interiority makes it harder for everyone to make friends and keep in touch. Intentionality has never been more consequential for our social health.

You may be thinking, "I am doing just fine. I have friends and I spend time with them." This may be true. The loss of social time and the prioritization of relationships are unevenly distributed. Some people are thriving in their relational lives and others are really suffering. Critically, individual thriving is not the same thing as societal thriving. As scholars of belonging specifically acknowledge, we might feel as if *our* social needs are met without recognizing that our belonging can be a source of exclusion for others.[47] A good way to think about the age of interiority is to consider other public health challenges. Just as the Western food diet has harmed nutrition, the Western communication diet seems to be doing the same for social interaction.[48] The broader trends and inherent interdependence of social life mean this shift toward interiority is consequential—physically and socially—for everyone.

Many solutions that are out there are, at best, incomplete. Whether the advice is "talk to strangers" or "make friends," it assumes people completely control their social world. Such guidance also assumes people have resources to make connections, even though we know such resources are not uniformly available. To spend more time with friends, one must have friends and geographic access to them. Friends must also be responsive to our invitations. Many people, as we will discuss in the next chapter, are marginalized and forced to keep connections limited for their own safety. This is why a one-size-fits-all solution to isolation and loneliness may be well intentioned but is often wrong.

So what choices do we have? Whether we're introverted or extraverted, everyday conversations have a calorie-like quality that renders sociability a potential source of well-being for many. Although there's clear evidence that face-to-face interactions carry the most weight in promoting connection, a phone call is a close second place, especially for friends and family far away. Making time to talk — really talk — appears to be the key.[49] A social regime nourishes our social health in the short term and improves life satisfaction, well-being, and longevity in the long term. We need one another. Yet we must accept that the process of connection is hard work, and that there are limits to what we can handle.

Hormesis Revisited

The gerontologist Elissa Epel, of the Weill Institute for Neurosciences and the Center for Health and Community at the University of California, San Francisco, proposed a way to integrate the social conditions of stress with existing biological models.[50] This work included the concept of hormesis that we discussed previously. Such work is important given that many of the best predictors of longevity and healthy aging are social. When it comes to human thriving, lacking quality relationships hurts and having quality relationships helps. Vitality — our global sense of renewed energy — is a by-product of getting one's social needs met. Problems arise when the conditions of stress are chronic and uncontrollable. Poverty, a lack of consistent caregiving in childhood, and abusive relationships all impair healthy aging.[51] The GUTS model of stress that we described in chapter 1 also shows how such conditions lead to feelings of chronic unsafety that keep people in a constant state of destructive stress.[52] Faced with ongoing and uncontrollable stress, we become stuck in a state of hypervigilance.[53] Such circumstances are not only exhausting, but also damaging to internal organs. This is among the many reasons why structural racism and chronic poverty have biological effects on health and longevity. Internal organs wear out when stress and its consequence, inflammation, are unrelenting and everywhere.

These stressors force energy trade-offs. Managing stress consumes a substantial amount of cognitive, affective, and physiological resources, taking away from the energy that individuals can devote to each other.[54] The stress may be contagious. People providing excessive support for others experience increased depressive symptoms.[55] Zero stress, however, means the body lacks opportunities to develop resilience and for cellular "housecleaning" activities that slow cognitive and physical aging.[56] An example of this hormetic process is the biological benefit of exercise and strength training (and maybe the occasional polar plunge). Physical stress in the form of exercise can lead to muscle growth and cell rejuvenation. Similarly, social stress can develop coping skills and emotional regulation, creating a bank of resources that a family can draw from in tough times.[57] In fact, close relationships can be understood as interdependent and dynamic stress-management systems. This is where the space between a person's social health and physical health is bridged. Consider the older adults in the Experience Corps who reported increased stress but also greater feelings of purpose in life (while also showing improved cognitive health).[58] Social stress, though sometimes unpleasant, can contribute to vitality. In a study of older adults in Chicago, participants were asked to identify people in three categories — those they found very supportive, those they discussed important matters with, and those they found demanding and who were sources of stress and anxiety. Loneliness was found to be lower for participants who reported more people in all three categories — even the demanding category.[59] These findings underscore the point that connecting with others enriches us and demands things from us.

———

A word of caution: this is not a more-is-better solution. Voluntarily increasing one's exposure to social stress by caring for another person who needs support is healthy only if this stressor pushes a person to the optimal zone of social stress (typically, from too little social stress to a moderate amount). Once pushed too far, social stress wears down the energy reserves, eventually stealing from other processes, from sleep to cell restoration.[60] This leads to the following conclusion: it's good for us to be occasionally, intentionally, and meaningfully stressed out by other people.

Protecting Relationships from the Flaws of the People in Them

There are times when we all think, "Ugh, I don't want to deal with other people." Or, in frustration, we ask, "Why do I have to go through all this? It's so much work." The reason, it seems, that our evolution favored a hormetic system is *because* relationships are difficult and inconstant. Consider what would happen if people didn't have motivational processes that encouraged more effort when they're stressed by other people. We all make mistakes. We all can be petty, selfish, unkind, and unresponsive to other people's needs. But people are also necessary to have families, to love and laugh, and to thrive. If we write off everyone in their moment of need or when they aren't perfect in our eyes, then we lose a lot. Relationships are, ultimately, fragile.

Fortunately, the resilience we build when we have a belongingness system that favors hormesis keeps us going back when people cause us stress. To grow, we must keep trying, keep forgiving, and keep loving people, especially when they need us most. When this functions optimally, it prevents a minor disaster, which is the loss of a necessary relationship owing to a moment of selfishness or obnox-iousness. Given that we're all selfish and obnoxious sometimes, hor-mesis explains why these mechanisms promoting relational repair can also be ruinous. When social stressors (or environmental stress-ors) are chronic, unrelenting, or downright cruel, our stress levels are uncontrollable and unstoppable.[61] Those are the exact condi-tions that Elissa Epel describes as being harmful to our survival and growth.[62]

To be clear, we're not advocating enduring abusive and danger-ous relationships for the sake of growth. People in such circum-stances are well beyond a healthy zone of hormesis. Neither overly exhausting nor understimulating social routines are ideal. The mod-erate, in-between space of hormesis is a place of growth and re-newal. Maybe you're thinking, "Who has time for all this?" That's a totally fair question. Relationships, like all things that take time, don't exist outside our other daily commitments. Work and TV/streaming have long been major obstacles to social time, and our social routines were severely disrupted by the pandemic. We're at a place of societal deficit.

In a climate of interiority, the problem stems from a lack of energy. Chronic work stress contributes to loneliness.[63] Many jobs require social interaction, and some, like customer service, sales, teaching, and child care, especially so. An entire day of socializing with strangers, coworkers, and clients for pay is exhausting, and it leaves little time or energy for pleasant social interaction and being a responsive listener. Workplace stress is a major source of exhaus-tion; it makes it harder to recover after work and replenish energy by the next morning.[64] The very real demands on time and energy di-minish our social time. When people say, "Who has time to date?" or "Making friends as an adult is impossible!" they're speaking to the reality that careers and other obligations leave little to be spent on relationships of choice. We have no more bandwidth. The hormesis model suggests that there's little benefit to adding social stress if you're already chronically stressed. Working harder when your social energy and free time are already badly taxed will do little to promote growth and resilience, which means that the benefits of hormesis are most applicable to people who are socially understimulated. When people have free time to give, the stress of new relationship building is most likely to be revitalizing.

Balancing Energy Costs through Social Routines

Habits are powerful things. Patterns have a way of reinforcing themselves. For good or ill, what we do day-in and day-out builds habits that are hard to break. Today's habits enable and preclude future choices. All choices are embedded in patterns, and choice is the essence of changing the pattern. It's less energy to go with known, familiar, and safe routines than to choose to do something different. Relational energy is like a catalytic process. Catalysts are agents that lower the total energy costs. Chemical reactions require a lot of start-up energy — often in the form of heat. Once the reaction has begun, however, the energy costs plummet. Social routines are catalysts for relationships. Whether a new routine is habitual (calling your sister once a month) or due to a life change (a new job or new roommate), it can be a catalyst to relational development and lower future energy costs. If you find yourself having social energy to spend or recognize in yourself an unmet need to belong, one crucial path to renewal is breaking social inertia through small, simple acts of connection. Choosing to take on social obligations, such as making an effort to show kindness to strangers or volunteering for organizations like the Experience Corps, could be the first step toward realizing the benefits of hormetic stress.

Everyday conversations are a combination of choice and routine. There are conversations that we choose to have and that are familiar to us (joking around with friends) and conversations that we don't choose to have but that are routine (work or school talk). Then there are unfamiliar conversations that we want to have (meaningful heart-to-hearts) and those that we'd prefer not to have and that are not part of our normal routine (fights or arguments). In our research, the people who felt their relationships were the easiest to maintain were the people who chose their routines.[65] Greater choice when it comes to everyday interaction is also linked to having better days and greater overall life satisfaction.[66] Choosing a routine of connection can take a good deal of effort at first, but if it strengthens our relationships, it can conserve energy over time. After all, the least effortful interactions are familiar conversations that we want to have with people we know well, which, again, is why spending time with good friends can sometimes feel so effortless.

Feeling understood in a relationship is life sustaining and vitality building partly because it's energy efficient. When people have a lot of energy to give, they have the most to gain from taking on more social stress. In other words, having low-energy connections conserves energy now and renews energy in future — both through energy conservation when we get comfortable and familiar and through the vitality gained by getting our need to belong met. People are often reluctant to invest their energy in others when they're relationally *under*stressed. You can see this reluctance in social inertia (a lack of prior routine) and when people discount the benefits of interactions. To get started, small investments of energy could pay off. This can start with making plans to see people you already know well. This could even be taking opportunities to chat with the people in your routine spaces, such as those at work or school. Don't worry about having a deep conversation; mere acknowledgment of your shared space and experience is valuable. Each act we take to socialize with other people has the potential to benefit us personally, while also enhancing our well-being by cultivating future interactions. Small investments into building a routine are worthwhile.

In the long term, giving our social resources to other people through communication is an energy investment. In the future, those relationships might buffer us from stress or help us recover when new hardships arise. People who believe they have support tend to respond to stress in less reactive ways. They have the hopeful pathways and agency to keep going, thinking, "I've got this," rather than, "I'm doomed."[67] This is quite practical. If you have help, such as a large and supportive social network, then you can probably roll with changes or problems. If you don't have help, then every single problem is bigger and more taxing — and your body reacts commensurately. Romantic couples experience renewal and vitality when they work through a conflict. Succeeding in the face of struggle builds a couple's capacity and ability to do so again in the future. Energy expended in relationships can convert into a stress-buffering investment. The total sum of energy we have invested in another person — quite literally hundreds of hours of social energy — becomes an invaluable resource that would be unrecoverable if we lost that relationship. The motivation to keep trying in relationships not only builds resilience to future stressors, but also makes it easier to manage stress when it comes.

The implications here are clear. We must budget our social energy to save it for meaningful interactions and meaningful relationships. There's an important place, too, for low-energy, small-stakes interactions with people in our communities. There are several pathways, as we discuss in chapter 7, toward building a healthier social life. Whatever pathway is best suited to us, we should obligate ourselves to being social, not despite — but because of — the stress it causes. It's for our own good. It lights the fires — generates the heat — we need to catalyze connection.

Chapter 6

WHEN SOCIETY ANTAGONIZES CONNECTION

In her captivating memoir, *Corrections in Ink,* Keri Blakinger recounts her harrowing experiences in a county jail (and later, state prisons) in the state of New York following an arrest for drug possession. Blakinger vividly describes the tenuousness of relational life for people in prison. Relationships between inmates are often forced, as they share unnervingly close quarters—usually devoid of walls or stalls—where "simply going to the bathroom can turn into a shamefest."[1] In prison, Blakinger writes, "up is down, everything is gray, and the supposed rules make no sense."[2] The life of an incarcerated person, she says, is "bound by a new and secret set of rules and mores" where privacy is impossible, indignity normative, and powerlessness assumed.[3]

Jails and prisons, as Blakinger depicts them, reflect what the sociologist Erving Goffman termed "total institutions," which fundamentally alter the assumed rules and expectations that typically govern everyday social interaction.[4] People in prison indeed have little control over how, when, and with whom they interact. And even though, as Blakinger writes, small moments of connection for incarcerated people do occur in between unannounced transfers and reassignments, that connection is always antagonized. Total institutions, by design, change — if not completely mortify, as Goffman put it — a person's sense of self and their relationships with others.[5]

Total institutions are the starkest, most dramatic examples of how structural pressures influence moments of communication. Structural pressures are the forces, seen and unseen, that push people toward and pull them away from one another and shape the rules and expectations of interaction in any given moment. Structural pressures exist at a higher-order level of analysis than the individual — they're the settings and contexts in which day-to-day social interaction transpires. In total institutions, these forces control all facets of the who, why, how, and when of day-to-day interaction. This is part of the reason that total institutions can be so harmful — they take away people's autonomy to intentionally seek out the types of interactions that meet their needs, especially those related to belonging.[6]

Even if we aren't living under the control of total institutions, structural pressures from various sources still affect our everyday experiences of social interaction.[7] In the words of the Columbia University sociologist Mario Small, social interactions are often, at least to some extent, "institutionally mediated," which has consequences for how we communicate and for our potential to connect with others.[8] The people available to us to interact with each day (to spend energy on), as well as the norms and expectations operating in those interactions, are influenced by the organizations and environments that we spend a lot of time in. Recognizing this fact opens our eyes to the opportunities and limits of our day-to-day social interaction. Throughout this chapter, we provide examples of some of the prominent structural constraints on our day-to-day interaction, with particular emphasis on the places we live — our neighborhoods, towns, and cities. We consider the consequences of these pressures for the diversity of our interactions, our worldviews, and our belongingness across groups.

Although the structural pressures on our interaction stem from larger forces beyond our control, often with deep historical roots, our choices still matter. Social theorists describe this as a fundamental tension between agency and structure, whereby our social interactions simultaneously create the society we live in and are shaped by the society we live in.[9] The communication scholar Malcolm Parks's concept of a *social-contextual perspective* nicely frames the inseparability of social structures and social interaction. As Parks stated, "Interpersonal relationships and broader social structures are communication patterns . . . [and] have no existence apart from the communication practices in which they are enacted."[10] In other words, communication between people, over time, builds the institutions, rules, expectations, and cultural codes that guide our lives. At the same time, the institutions, rules, expectations, and cultural codes that are already in place — created through the totality of past interactions — exert force on the types of communication experiences people are likely to go through. This basic assumption, that micro-level social interactions are intertwined with macro-level social forces, has varying implications. On the positive side, it suggests that we can live in a better world if we attend to how we interact with others within our day-to-day moments. On the negative side, it suggests that if we aren't attuned to them, existing structural forces rooted in distrust, fear, and hate can continually guide our patterns or interaction in ways that deepen division.

Space, Place, and Social Interaction

Some people, if given the chance, jump at the opportunity to spend a day in nature, hiking in the woods or lounging at the beach. Others prefer a busy city, neon lights, and endless options for food and entertainment. Intuitively, we know that physical environments shape what we do and how we feel.[11] Environments also affect how we communicate with others and therefore can also shape our well-being.[12] If we think critically about our environments, we see how they facilitate and restrict our interactions. Environments, for instance, influence our interaction potential, or whom we might come in contact with, particularly in terms of face-to-face interactions.[13] But even our online interactions, such as email and video meetings, especially those concerning work, are implicated. The shift to remote work that many people experienced in recent years, for instance, drastically changed opportunities to develop workplace relationships. And for younger workers in their first job, remote work restricts their chance to develop workplace friendships and mentor relationships.[14] Lacking workplace relationships is consequential because research indicates that positive workplace relationships can increase subjective well-being and serve important instrumental functions, such as guidance on navigating workplace norms.[15]

Environmental factors at a much larger scale, such as the population density of a city, influence the sheer likelihood of encountering other people on a day-to-day basis. If you're in a major metropolitan area and walking downtown, you simply have a higher probability of meeting someone than if you were in a rural environment.[16] Population density, then, is a structural force larger than any single person or group that influences the nature of our moments of day-to-day interaction. Such pressures are influential, but not completely determinative, which is consistent with the notion of the aforementioned agency-structure tension. Consider that while population density affords greater opportunity for interaction, the degree to which people capitalize on these opportunities is subject to choices they make. We're unlikely, for instance, to interact with people around us, even in crowded spaces, if we're all looking down at our phones.

Beyond the potential to interact with people in general, environments shape the specific characteristics of people we might interact with, especially with regard to race and ethnicity, age, and socioeconomic status. The authors of this book spend a large part of their days on college campuses, which makes interactions with people in their late teens and twenties more likely than if they worked in, say, a skilled-care facility. This obvious example about how space can shape interaction potentials can lead to deeper — and, in some cases, troubling — insights about how physical environments restrict interaction — and therefore connection — along racial, economic, and political lines.

Consider that many Americans continue to live in segregated spaces; this continually shapes social interaction patterns. The history of racist government practices, such as redlining — a New Deal-era government policy whereby neighborhoods with Black residents were systematically blocked from government-backed home loans — has played an outsize role in determining the demographic composition of cities and neighborhoods (while also limiting Black Americans' access to home ownership, a primary source of wealth generation). Various reports indicate that many U.S. communities and larger regional areas are as racially and economically segregated as ever, despite the fact that diversity is increasing in the country as a whole. The vast majority of U.S. communities that were redlined in the 1930s continue to be populated mainly by people of color, and for all the strides the United States has made with regard to civil rights in housing following the Fair Housing Act of 1968, racial segregation of U.S. cities has persisted. According to researchers at the University of California, Berkeley — Stephen Menendian, Samir Gambhir, and Arthur Gailes — over 80 percent of major U.S. metropolitan areas are more segregated today than they were in 1990. Government policies, argue Menendian and his colleagues, have multifaceted "lingering effects."[17]

One such lingering effect is that discriminatory policies have reduced the probability of people communicating and developing relationships across racial and economic lines. These effects span generations because when communities are segregated, their schools can be, too. As a 2022 report by the U.S. Government Accountability Office indicated, although school segregation was slightly down from 2014–15 to 2020–21 (from 47 percent to 43 percent of schools), it remained pervasive.[18] The thorniness of community and neighborhood segregation is apparent when we consider research showing that segregation can persist even when people's stated preferences favor diversity.[19]

Communities aren't segregated just by race and ethnicity, but also on the basis of political ideology.[20] In a pattern that began at least four decades ago, many Americans, without necessarily knowing it, seem to be prioritizing politics when signing a lease or mortgage, creating identifiable "red" or "blue" communities. The journalist Bill Bishop termed this phenomenon "the big sort." Using demographic data and voting behavior, Bishop argued that zip codes and neighborhoods have become "isolated islands" of ideology where residents "cluster in communities of like-mindedness."[21] "Americans," says Bishop, "have used wealth and technology to invent secure places of minimal conflict" where they "spend more time with people like themselves."[22] The structural forces fueling ideological sorting can, like school segregation, be exacerbated by unconscious preferences.[23] Liberals and conservatives, for instance, sometimes move to different parts of a city (or to different cities altogether) because they're seeking amenities that happen to map onto their respective political views. Liberals, for example, tend to value living close to art museums, whereas conservatives tend to value proximity to places of worship.[24]

Casting additional light on the ways in which physical entities can serve as ideological proxies, David Wasserman of the *New York Times* found correlations between voting in the 2016 presidential election and voters' proximity to specific retails chains. Democrats? More likely to live near Whole Foods, Lululemon, Urban Outfitters, and Apple stores. Republicans? Cracker Barrel, Tractor Supply Company, Hobby Lobby, and Bass Pro Shops.[25] Citing Wasserman's analysis in his book, *Why We're Polarized*, Ezra Klein commented on the growing link between ideology and locality, arguing that "as the parties become more racially, religiously, ideologically, and geographically different, the signals that tell us if a place is our kind of place, if a community is our kind of community, heighten our political divisions."[26]

Drip by Drip

Many of the costs associated with segregation and sorting are well documented, stark, and devastating.[27] Race-based residential segregation, for example, is tied to health disparities for communities of color.[28] Communities with higher concentrations of people of color not only receive fewer government resources, which undermines quality of life and schools, but typically live in spaces with higher environmental and health risks.[29] Segregated neighborhoods can also limit economic mobility. Social interaction—specifically, reduced diversity of social interaction—plays a role in this. Consider the remarkable research of the Harvard University economist Raj Chetty and his colleagues on the consequences of diversity of interaction and people's economic gains over time. Specifically, Chetty and his team analyzed links between "cross-class interaction" within communities and people's salaries over time.[30] The researchers measured cross-class interaction as the extent to which people with low socioeconomic status (below the median level) are friends with people with high socioeconomic status (above the median level). Their analysis revealed that cross-class interaction was related to greater economic outcomes for children from families with low socioeconomic status, which suggests that when kids from poorer families interact more often with kids from richer families, the kids from poorer families have an increased likelihood of earning more money over time. Given the nature of the data, the researchers can't identify the specific reasons that cross-class interactions facilitate upward economic mobility. They speculate, though, that interacting with diverse people, including people of higher socioeconomic status, provides advantageous networking possibilities (for example, job opportunities through weak ties) and models for pursing educational and career aspirations. If children aren't given the chance to develop relationships with different types of people, there are numerous social and economic costs.

Some of the many costs of failing to connect with a diverse range of people become apparent over time, as Chetty's research shows. In this way, although any given moment of interaction—including what that moment of interaction is about, who is involved, and where it occurs — can seem of little importance, these moments add up over time and across people, much like the drops of water in a cave that form stalactites and stalagmites. Each drop seems insignificant, but over the years, the small bits of calcium from each drop contribute to something larger.[31] Thinking about social interaction in this way reveals other costs associated with the structural constraints that limit the diversity of interaction and connection with others. Moments of interaction in our seemingly mundane encounters can function as a "training ground" where we practice the necessary communication skills to manage the most difficult moments of our lives effectively. Think about neighbor interactions. When you move to a new place, introducing yourself and waving hello to a neighbor when you see them might not seem like a big deal. Over time, though, regular greetings can turn into occasional conversations, giving you the chance to learn a little bit about them — what they're like, how long they've lived in the neighborhood, why they moved there in the first place. These moments are the building blocks of trust and are vital for people's ability to forge relationships across demographic differences.[32]

The consequence of such moments lies not only in the fact that they make streets, buildings, and blocks more pleasant spaces to be in or that they can spark new friendships. Such moments can save lives in times of crisis. According to research by Daniel Aldrich of Northeastern University, good relationships with your neighbors are a matter of life and death when disaster strikes. In his book *Building Resilience: Social Capital in Post-Disaster Recovery,* Aldrich points out that it's typically neighbors, not police, firefighters, or paramedics, who are first responders in disaster situations. Building bonds in the good times can ensure that people look out for one another in the bad times. Aldrich has also found that communities with stronger interpersonal connection between members also recover more quickly from disaster events and are more likely to rebuild in their existing neighborhoods than they are to relocate.[33]

Structural factors directly affect the likelihood that this type of neighborhood connection will occur. Cities with better social infrastructure, for example, have been found to fare better in disasters. Social infrastructure includes libraries, playgrounds, parks, ball fields, public pools, walking paths, community centers, and social establishments like coffee shops and pubs.[34] Aldrich notes that when it comes to natural disasters, there are four "determinants of mortality": geographic conditions (for example, sea level), the intensity of the hazard itself (for example, size of a storm), economic conditions (for example, income level of people affected), and social conditions (for example, strength of social ties and social infrastructure). Of the four factors, Aldrich contends that social conditions are often the most overlooked and underappreciated, despite their lifesaving potential.[35]

Social infrastructure is beneficial to community connection because it brings people together—face-to-face—in ways that would otherwise never occur. As Eric Klinenberg wrote in his book *Palaces for the People: How Social Infrastructure Can Help Fight Inequality, Polarization, and the Decline of Civic Life,* "Countless close friendships between mothers, and then entire families, begin because two toddlers visit the same swing set."[36] In urban, suburban, and rural communities, libraries are especially important physical spaces for human connection.[37] Beyond providing important access to books, libraries are key meeting spaces for older adults who live alone and people seeking support, such as first-time parents. Klinenberg argues that investments in public institutions such as libraries increase community members' social health and their resilience to natural disasters simultaneously. We need such investment more than ever in an age of interiority. Or, as Klinenberg put it, "In a world where we spend ever more of our time staring at screens, blocking out even our most intimate and proximate human contacts, public institutions with open-door policies compel us to pay close attention to the people nearby."[38]

But do Americans even talk to their neighbors anymore? They do — some of them, anyway. A Pew survey, for instance, revealed that 26 percent of Americans say they know most of their neighbors and an additional 57 percent know some of their neighbors.[39] It stands to reason that if a combined 83 percent of Americans know at least some of their neighbors, they probably interact with them from time to time. The survey results supported this conclusion, as roughly 70 percent of people who said they know at least some of their neighbors reported that they talk to them at least once a month. Cities and towns need to capitalize on and promote these small moments of social interaction by investing in shared community spaces.[40] In short, it's not just individuals who need to spend social energy on connection. It's governments, too.

The Dividends

The personal and social costs of failing to connect with people in our communities are numerous, and these costs can be deepened if we live in demographically homogeneous spaces.[41] Regularly interacting with people different from ourselves, even in small talk — at times, specifically in small talk — can contribute to our becoming better communicators. A professor at the University of California, Santa Barbara, Tania Israel, writes and conducts workshops to help people talk more openly and productively about controversial issues.

Talking about challenging topics requires the kinds of responsive communication skills that take time and practice to develop. These skills include patiently allowing people to make their points before speaking, refraining from signaling judgment through nonverbal cues, and asking clarifying questions. "We are not born with the skills that contribute to successful dialogue," writes Israel in the book *Beyond Your Bubble: How to Connect across the Political Divide.*[42] Being responsive to others takes effort, energy, and practice. Israel reminds us that to productively engage in challenging conversations, such as those involving value-based disagreements, we need to exercise our skills. Everyday conversations with the people around us, especially people who are different from us, are the training grounds. We can practice responsive communication when we're chitchatting with our neighbors or even when we strike up a conversation with someone at the DMV. By exercising these skills in low-stakes, mundane moments of talk, our skills are honed for when we need them most—in those emotion-ladened, physically and mentally taxing conversations about divisive social issues.

The best way for people from different ideologies to improve relations with one another is first to learn how to talk about their interests outside value-based issues. Two experiments conducted by Erik Santoro and David Broockman showed that, when Democrats and Republicans were asked to talk to each other about their "perfect day," their feelings of warmth and perceptions of cross-party respect drastically increased.[43] These gains, however, were short-lived, which suggests that regular conversation—in all its glorious mundanity—might be an initial waypoint on the long road toward less bitter views of political rivals. And as we go further down that road, we need what the psychologists Stephen Antonoplis and Oliver John call O2.[44] O2 is openness, curiosity, and open-

---

114

mindedness about diverse people and experiences. Although O2 is a personality trait, it can also be developed through practice. In fact, it has to be practiced for it to make a difference. Unless we put these kinds of pro-dialogue communication skills to use, they atrophy.

Failures to connect with others in our communities — especially people who are different from us in terms of race, age, and economic resources — are missed opportunities for what Heather McGhee, in her book *The Sum of Us: What Racism Costs Us and How We Can Prosper Together*, calls solidarity dividends. Solidarity dividends are the societal-level gains that all people can experience if they intentionally pivot away from distrust of one another and toward connection and care. This can take time, as distrust is often rooted in powerful structural forces, including race-based prejudice that has been transmitted from generation to generation. People from highly resourced and privileged groups bear the burden of this shift toward openness to diverse experiences, given the structural advantages they have been afforded throughout our nation's history. McGhee convincingly argues that solidarity dividends, cultivated in part through greater openness and connection with diverse others, can spark better policy decisions at all levels of government and for all people.[45]

There are real structural and psychological barriers to these important conversations. When neighborhoods become more ethnically, economically, and racially diverse, and when people interact with different types of people, biases often are exposed that might otherwise stay hidden.[46] As we enter diverse spaces, moreover, we can operate from a default sense of mistrust that stifles relationship development.[47] One study, for example, found that when you heighten perceptions of inequality between communicators, such as by highlighting their economic differences, their desire to develop a relationship with one another is reduced.[48] Clearly, there are initial barriers to relationship building across differences that we can't overcome unless we're committed to the cause.

Positive intergroup interaction — that is, interaction between people from different demographic and cultural groups — is essential to building a more inclusive, trusting, and caring society.[49] Research demonstrates that positive intergroup contact can be beneficial in numerous ways, such as by increasing trust perceptions and reducing prejudice.[50] Changing hearts and minds in an enduring sense, though, necessitates more than just pleasant chats. A massive study of intergroup contact that surveyed nearly thirteen thousand people across sixty-nine countries found that when people from societally advantaged groups have more frequent pleasant social interaction with people from societally marginalized groups, support grew among the advantaged individuals for social change and toward greater equality for all.[51] Still, this and other research paints a complex picture when it comes to the benefits of intergroup interaction for social change across people from different groups, including people from historically disadvantaged groups.[52] The research also indicates that pleasant talk is best conceived as an entry point to the kind of deeper conversation that's foundational to larger-scale social change. People, especially those from advantaged groups, must be willing to have deeper, potentially face-threatening talk about structural inequality and ways they can help in reducing it.

We also need to remember that intergroup interaction can sometimes be unsafe, depending on people's circumstances. Some people might not have the requisite safety — psychological or physical — to reach out to strangers. Stigmatized identities of various types, such as undocumented status, transgender identity, or identification with a disability can make it risky, even life threatening, to seek connections with people outside an inner circle of trust. Marginalized people are often excluded from social networks and lack legal protections in ways that directly threaten their health and well-being, which further highlights why the burden is on people with the greatest resources and privileges to make their communities more welcoming and inclusive.[53] A takeaway message of this chapter, then, is that not everyone has the luxury of seeking out connection with the people around them, no matter how much they value or desire it.

When We Talk, We Argue (Necessarily So)

In the field of communication, there's an important tradition that emphasizes the importance of everyday talk. Everyday talk includes the full range of interactions we have with people — from mundane chitchat and gossip to expression of affection and serious conversations.[54] Although scholarship on everyday talk is wide-ranging, one of its key influences was the work of early twentieth-century sociologists within the symbolic interactionist tradition, such as Charles Horton Cooley and George Herbert Mead. These scholars argued that our sense of self (that is, who we understand ourselves to be within the larger society) is constructed, sustained, and altered through the social interactions we have each day. Through our accumulated moments of interaction over our lifetimes — more precisely, our *interpretations* of those moments — we come to understand our place in the world.[55]

Extending these ideas, Steve Duck has long argued that everyday moments of talk do far more than we realize.[56] Duck contends that any time we talk to someone, we offer them a *rhetorical vision*.[57] We present a set of arguments — *lines,* to use Erving Goffman's term — about how we view ourselves and the world around us.[58] In

---

any moment of talk, often without our realizing it, our rhetorical vision is on display, telling others (a) who we believe we are (individually and in relation to others) and (b) how we believe the world operates. It's through talk, Duck says, that we test the validity of our rhetorical visions in both subtle and obvious ways.[59] People's responses to how we talk tell us whether they support or reject our understanding of ourselves and the world. In this way, everyday moments of communication, whether they're composed of small talk, political discussion, romantic banter, or brainstorming at work, are always consequential.[60] In sum, our interaction presents arguments and claims — often beyond our awareness — about what we think is true, valuable, moral, and just. And our partners in conversation, whether they know it or not, are constantly confirming or rejecting our arguments and claims.

If we take the rhetorical vision perspective seriously, we can't help seeing how important small moments of interaction are. It shows, for instance, how psychological factors such as trust play out in talk. If we have low trust for the people in our communities, that low trust manifests itself, if only subtly, in our words and actions.[61] We might keep our heads down, focused on our mail, to avoid interacting with neighbors when we see them. These are lost moments, crystalizing a vision of the self as separate from others.[62] Turning away from others in our communities can be part of a vicious cycle, reinforcing a vision of the world as cold and unwelcoming. The rhetorical vision concept also reinforces how influential structural pressures can be, especially those that severely limit the types of people we interact with. If we find ourselves in patterns — because of structural constraints and personal choices — where we interact only with people who know us well, are similar to us, and operate from the same worldviews, we lose opportunities to have our rhetorical visions challenged and amended in ways that make us more open to others (heightening our O2). In other words, we miss vital time on the communication training ground. Interacting with a diverse range of people, some of whom are going to be open to connecting and listening to us despite potential areas of disagreement, offers us the opportunity to reconsider and improve our views of others, be more accepting, and ultimately build meaningful connections over time.

Communities Rebuilding for Connection

There's only so much any one person can do to push back against societal forces that antagonize connection and reinforce *homophily,* or people's tendency to interact and form relationships with people similar to themselves.[63] Communities can nevertheless band together to build connections across people. Often this involves community members and leaders rethinking their policies and systems and creatively finding ways to bring people together. We can look, for instance, to a place named Frome (pronounced Froom), a town of thirty thousand in Somerset County, England, where civic leaders, doctors, nonprofit organizations, and community members joined forces to adopt structural changes in the interest of fostering connection across a diverse range of people. Together, they developed the Compassionate Frome project, whose primary mission is the fight against loneliness, especially among the most vulnerable community members, such as those struggling with chronic disease management, exhausting family caregiving roles, and unexpected life transitions that restrict their time and energy for social contact. Helen Kingston, a physician, saw the need for such a program when she realized that many of her patients were suffering from chronic loneliness that was exacerbating their health problems.[64]

Kingston and her collaborator, Jenny Hartnoll, a community development specialist, created Compassionate Frome to ensure all people in the community have opportunities for companionship and are aware of free resources that might offer them tangible assistance with food, clothing, or shelter. They created easily accessible service directories that doctors and local community members could quickly recommend to others. They also recruited a volunteer army of community connectors. With only a few hours of training, anyone can become a community connector, and over a thousand people have done so. These include taxi drivers, hairdressers, police officers, and store clerks. Dr. Julian Able and Lindsay Clarke, in their book *The Compassion Project: A Case for Hope & Humankindness from the Town That Beat Loneliness,* estimate that twenty thousand conversations a year between community connectors and community members have been created through this project.[65] These conversations involve everything from discussions of housing resources to digital media lessons to friendly conversations about everyday experiences.[66]

Compassionate Frome has also created talking cafés, talking benches, and workshops for crafts and woodworking. All are welcome, free of charge; the goal is to build friendships among people who would otherwise never meet. Need-specific groups sometimes emerge from the talking cafés, such as diabetes or heart disease support groups.[67] For some folks — such as a ninety-two-year-old retired grocer named Joe, who's the primary caregiver for his wife (who has severe disabilities) — the talking café is their only chance to connect with people.[68] Compassionate Frome has been a success by any metric. Many people in town say that it has changed their lives by building friendships and support that previously had no space in which to emerge. The project has also improved the quality of care, reducing emergency admissions in Frome's hospitals by 14 percent over a four-year period, even as the rate of emergency admissions trended upward in nearby communities.[69]

Over four thousand miles from Frome, in a coffee shop in the tiny downtown of Rocky Ford, Colorado, community members – mainly farmers in eastern Colorado – created the Coffee Break Project. Its motto: "Do you look after your neighbors as close as your crop or herd?" Much like Frome's talking café, the Coffee Break Project aims to build connections among community members, many of whom are struggling. In rural farming communities, like those throughout eastern Colorado, social disconnection and the persistent stresses of farming are serious but sometimes hidden threats to people's lives. In these communities, rates of depression, anxiety, and suicide have sky-rocketed in recent years.[70]

The Coffee Break Project is just one component of the COMET model, which was developed through a collaboration between concerned community members and the local health system. COMET stands for Changing Our Mental and Emotional Trajectory. Like Compassionate Frome, COMET aims to increase awareness of mental health challenges and access to appropriate resources. It does this in large part through encouraging community members to reach out and support one another. Cassady Rosenblum, who wrote about COMET in the *New York Times,* described the program's objectives: "While people in places like Yuma [Colorado], population 3,500, may balk at the mention of a therapist, they probably already treat their local bartender like one. What if that bartender was trained, even a little, to recognize symptoms of emotional distress and intervene? What if everyone in town was?"[71]

Still, as Rosenblum writes, COMET is, at best, a partial solution. Building friendships and connecting people with mental health services are important, but the challenges farming families face are monumental. When your fortunes rise and fall because of unpredictable and insufficient seasonal rainfall, when unexpected frosts can destroy months of work overnight, and when geopolitical events in faraway countries can quickly put you in the red, high stress and anxiety are inevitable.[72]

The same challenges of connection, albeit due to very different causes, exist in places where diversity of interaction is lacking owing to segregation and sorting. Still, efforts to build social connections through structural change, even changes as small as those developed by the Coffee Break Project, can make a difference. They can help keep people from feeling totally isolated in their worst moments — the very thing that leads people to contemplate self-harm. These types of efforts don't fix the roots of disconnection or reverse decades of powerful structural constraints that counteract connection, but the chance to chat over coffee and a donut lets a little light in, offering companionship and a sympathetic ear, perhaps even some helpful tips on farming through ongoing drought conditions. It orients people toward, rather than away from, their neighbors. It's a nudge toward social interaction that, over time, can support people's visions of themselves as interdependent, relevant, and obligated to one another.

Chapter 7

LIFE IN A SOCIAL BIOME

Mustering enough energy to leave a state of inertia—to fight through personal and structural barriers—is a difficult part of any change. In this chapter, we propose seven small, achievable strategies that you can use to start your reinvestment in your social energy, each backed by solid empirical evidence. Before discussing those strategies, we believe it's helpful to think about our life as lived out in a series of small everyday moments. Each moment, as we bounce from social interaction to time alone, is seemingly insignificant, but it holds tremendous potential for building better personal social health and ultimately a healthier society. One of our motivations for writing this book was to offer readers a research-based way to understand and talk about the individual and aggregate moments of communication and connection that transpire in daily life. With that goal in mind, this chapter will propose a new way to conceptualize communication and social health. We call it the *social biome*.

A biome is a biological and ecological concept. In its most basic sense, a biome is the plants, animals, and climate of a given region. Desert, grasslands, and tropical forests are all biomes with distinct characteristics. A biome defines life in a place. Biomes, however, aren't just about physical and biological factors external to humans. Every single human, in fact, constitutes a biome. As you probably know, each of us has a *microbiome* composed of trillions of bacteria, fungi, and viruses living in and on our body, especially in our stomach.[1] We each have more microbes in our gut than cells in our entire body.[2] These microbes influence all aspects of our life, and, in fascinating ways, shape who we are. It can even be argued that the bacteria *are* us, given that they eat what we eat and grow and change with us from our birth to our death.[3]

Scientists are accumulating voluminous research on the human microbiome. With astounding accuracy, they can now catalogue our gut microbes. As we change, such as when our eating habits change, so too does our microbiome. Poor dietary choices, and perhaps even a cross-country flight, can wreak havoc on our microbiomes.[4] Promising research in animals paints an exciting picture of a future in which alterations to gut bacteria might decrease seizures caused by epilepsy, alleviate depressive symptoms, or lessen the effects of autoimmune diseases, but such promises are tenuous.[5] Will eventual treatments benefit everyone equally? It's impossible to know. The microbiome is staggeringly complex. Moreover, each one of us—and our trillions of microbial companions—is embedded within larger biomes. In other words, we all live in unique nutritional and hygienic environments that influence the nature of our microbiome. A true wonder of the microbiome is its remarkable capacity for both reanimation and resilience.[6] It's the culmination of the choices we make, such as the foods that we eat, as well as the environments we just happen to be born into. Although strategic dietary and lifestyle changes or medical interventions can alter our microbiome—and potentially the nature of the "gut-brain axis"—

these alterations are conditioned by many factors that exist beyond our understanding and, probably, our control.[7]

If we zoom back out from the guts of individual humans to the interrelations among people, we move from the human microbiome to the human social biome. Rather than microbes in your gut, your social biome is composed of the people in your social ecosystem and the moments of interaction you have with them. Your social biome, like your microbiome, is both created by you and furnished to you. It's highly tenuous and highly durable. And, perhaps most important of all, your social biome, like your microbiome, has much to say about the quality of your life. Your social biome, for instance, depends on good social nutrition to function at its best. Social scientists studying human sociability confront the same complexity as natural scientists studying the microbiome. Just as the microbiome is composed of trillions of microbes from hundreds of species with complex and interconnected effects, one person's social life is composed of millions of moments of varying forms of social interaction embedded within relational, cultural, and historical layers. There are innumerable factors — verbal, nonverbal, environmental, technological, institutional — involved in studying just one social interaction. And when we think about social interaction across multiple people's lives at the same time, the complexity is daunting.[8] All this variability explains why relational life is challenging and why people differ in their basic understandings of the purpose of communication.

To work through this complexity, let's start with some basic questions. These questions can also guide your own process of discovering where to get started. With whom do you interact every day and where? What do you tend to talk about? Did you choose to have these interactions or are they required of you? How much variation is there in the types of people with whom you talk and the types of interaction you have? How do you usually feel when you're alone? Do you get a say in how much time alone you have and how you spend it? How much do you rely on digital technology to facilitate your interaction? Your answers to these questions are entry points to understanding your own individual social biome. By thinking carefully about your patterns of interaction and the conditions under which your social interactions transpire, you get glimpses of the totality of your social world, including what's there or absent, what's said or left unspoken. When we start to frame our lives as a series of moments of communication, we see the building blocks of our identities, worldviews, and relationships. If it's true that we are our gut bugs, it's also true that we are our social interactions.

In a Moment

The social biome as a concept grew from our discussions with one another as we were conducting research on people's everyday experiences of social interaction and time alone.[9] Our research built on the interaction diary approach we reviewed in chapter 1, and we asked people to track their social interaction experiences over time, often through brief surveys we sent to their smartphones throughout the day. We sought to identify patterns and routines of relating that provide insight into people's social health and well-being. We propose that people's unique social biomes are composed of all their moments of day-to-day interaction. Each moment of interaction, moreover, is characterized by five key parts: *emotion, routine, people, episodes,* and *structure.*

- Emotion entails the feeling of the moment, including social emotions such as connection, loneliness, hope, and happiness. Even the most complex emotions can be understood as occurring in individual moments.[10]

- Routine refers to the ways that the moments in our days are organized – the patterns of our social life. Every moment has potential to build routines. If you look back on your day, week, or month and can recount what you typically did, this is your routine. The routines we construct include the typical people, emotions, and forms of talk we have. They're important because they represent what is usual, while creating the backdrop against which change can occur.

- People in the biome include your entire network of actual and potential interaction partners, from close friends to acquaintances and strangers. These are the people deeply embedded in our daily routines as well as the people we just happen to meet because of the social environments we frequent. Children, romantic partners, and roommates are present in many of our moments. On workdays, any number of colleagues or customers share our moments. There are also the easily overlooked people, such as those you might briefly chat with in your neighborhood or while shopping at a grocery store.

- Episodes are the content and format of conversations and messages occurring within moments. Communication episodes are essentially what you're doing in your conversations, such as catching up, making plans, fighting, or engaging in small talk. This aspect includes the different media you use to communicate, such as voice calls, video chats, texts, and social media.

- Structure refers to the social, cultural, and historical forces that enable and constrain the types of emotions, episodes, people, and routines in our moments. Structure represents wide-ranging proximal and distal factors that shape the construction of our social biomes. These factors can be material, such as social infrastructure, as well as temporal, such as time pressures placed on us by long work hours and commutes. The concept of structure also captures the idea that these moments become patterned over time. Emergent patterns of talk construct and constrict our rhetorical vision of the world. Recall from the last chapter that rhetorical vision is the set of implicit arguments we make, based on the nature of our communication, about how to view ourselves and the world around us.[11]

By thinking about our days as a series of moments in this way, it becomes apparent that our days are often patterned on the basis of whom we talk to, what we talk about, and how we accomplish that talk through various modes of communication — all embedded in larger social and cultural structures. These moments create the links among different people and reflect why we view our lives as we do. This process includes our global evaluations of our lives. In our research, for instance, we found that people's life satisfaction — assessed by their agreement level with statements such as "If I could live my life over, I would change almost nothing" — is linked to their perceptions of randomly sampled moments of social interaction in their daily life.[12] A growing body of social scientific research suggests that simple evaluations of moments of interaction and time alone are robust predictors of big-picture questions about life. Our lives are very much the aggregation of our momentary social experiences. It's from this vantage point that we recommend the following approach to creating a healthier social biome.

The Seven Elements

Although there are some general patterns found across groups of people, patterns can also be highly idiosyncratic because our routines are shaped by our unique needs and the constraints placed on us. There are no "perfect" patterns that everyone should follow. Although relationship science has established some consistent and clear characteristics of good social health, it's far from being able to offer precise estimates of how many friends or how many conversations a person needs to maximize social well-being. There's enormous variability between people: our social health depends on what we need at a specific stage in life, on a particular day, or within a given conversation. In other words, many roads can lead you there.[13]

There can also be too much of a good thing, which economists call *declining marginal utility:* after a certain point, the more you do something, the less you get from it. Enjoyable things — like food, exercise, or sex — fit this formula.[14] Some is good, healthy, enjoyable, but too much is . . . well . . . too much. Optimal social health functions similarly. There's strong evidence that the positive effects of social interactions on such outcomes as happiness, longevity, and mortality flatten out the more interactions someone has.[15] The gain from going from zero to some social interactions is big. The gain from going from frequent interaction to interacting all the time is zilch. A social gathering with friends, family, and acquaintances that occurs between once a week and once a month is probably just about right.[16] More time with friends, family, and acquaintances after that is extra work and doesn't necessarily add much to happiness. Even the benefits of having more friends drop off after a point.[17] We can't possibly keep in touch with everyone. Across too large a network, we can't develop the depth of friendship and solidarity we need for meaningful conversation or social support. And we can become overwhelmed, to the point of being stressed out, by caring for too many people.[18] The seven strategies we offer in this chapter should be held in balance with one another to add variety to your social life. None of these strategies should be carried out endlessly or to the point of

---

crowding out other good things, and they're subject to numerous caveats. We acknowledge change is easier said than done. Habits toward greater connection are difficult to establish, and research-based practical guidance must honor that complexity. Informing people to simply "prioritize interaction" or "choose connection," as if rewarding social interaction can be turned on like a light switch, is unlikely to be helpful.

Element One: Communication with Strangers

When Jeff was growing up, driving on the highways of northeast Kansas required stopping to pay the tolls. Tollbooth operators exchanged tickets for payment, back then in cash. Jeff has a clear memory of his father's typical conversation with tollbooth operators. As his dad pulled out his wallet, he would boom out, "Howdy! How is your day going?" As is Kansan custom, he liked to comment on the weather — good or bad. Its unpredictability was particularly worthy of comment. In a moment of teen insecurity, Jeff asked why he did that. His dad said he challenged himself to make that conversation the most pleasant exchange that person had that day.

This idea is true to the nature of a healthy social biome. Yet by focusing primarily on close relationships, researchers have often overlooked the importance of talking to strangers. Only about 40 percent of our social interactions are with close relationship partners, which leaves 60 percent or more with strangers and weak ties.[19] If we count every "I would like a black coffee with a little cream," "No thank you, I don't want a receipt," and "Thank you so much" as a social interaction, then it's likely the portion of interactions with strangers and acquaintances would be even higher. Just as our food and drink choices shape our gut microbiome, each point of contact with people out in the world shapes our social biome.

In our evolutionary past, humans had more tightly knit social networks and interacted with very few strangers.[20] In industrialized countries, particularly in urban centers, this ratio has flipped; there's an endless sea of strangers. The entire service sector is built on interactions among strangers. It makes perfect sense that there are benefits to spending quality time with people you see repeatedly and depend on for safety and comfort. Yet we can also benefit from being social with people we barely know. Several studies have found that talking to strangers in everyday places can be a resource for improving our days. One study had participants interact in a friendly manner with their barista at Starbucks in Vancouver and found that these little prosocial acts boosted happiness.[21] Another study asked participants to interact with fellow commuters on trains and buses in Chicago and found they had a better ride to work.[22] Interestingly, this study's findings were exactly the opposite of what study participants thought would happen. A third study, on the London Underground, recruited a group of people known to be notoriously taciturn. Again, little moments of interaction with strangers made the Tube ride more pleasant and made people happier.[23] Londoners who had these conversations said they felt encouraged to do it again in the future.[24] Merely noticing the small benefits of interaction may increase our sense of connection and belonging in our communities.[25]

Frequent interactions with acquaintances and strangers are associated with less loneliness and higher life satisfaction. Matthias Mehl and his colleagues reported, for example, that "compared with the unhappiest participants . . . the happiest participants . . . spent about 25 percent less time alone (58.6 percent vs. 76.8 percent) and about 70 percent more time talking (39.7 percent vs. 23.2 percent)."[26]

The benefits of being social appear across a range of personalities and life situations, including people in treatment for serious illness.[27] In France, the happiest people spent twice the amount of time in the company of people (70 percent) than the least happy did (37 percent).[28] These interactions may take only a few seconds. A study conducted in Turkey discovered that simply saying "Thank you" or "Have a nice day" while talking to a cab driver can give people a boost in happiness.[29] Having a task-focused conversation, such as one about traffic or a location to be dropped off, offered no such benefit to riders.

Our advice here is not to go around aimlessly greeting everyone you see or interrupting conversations. Clearly, this would not only violate norms and produce negative outcomes, but also run counter to the values of respect and care that we're aiming to uphold. We also must recognize that people might not respond to us as we want them to. Our warm greeting to a service provider, for example, might be net positive for us, but it's just one interaction among the dozens required of them that day. Some people are also more comfortable than others talking to people for various reasons related to personality, culture, and neurodiversity (among many other factors).[30] We also noted earlier that not everyone feels comfortable interacting with strangers because of stigmatization, discrimination, and real risks of violence. They have to prioritize their safety and, in some cases, avoid people who aren't trusted insiders. In fact, recognizing how beneficial stranger interactions can be to our health and well-being further underscores how harmful laws and practices of exclusion are in our society. Ultimately, what we're suggesting is that when opportunities present themselves for small talk with someone new, we should try to make the most of those moments. They're chances to send small signals of acknowledgment, dignity, and responsiveness to others within a routine of sociability. The goal is not to strike up a long conversation or develop a new relationship with everyone we meet. Rather, it's to cultivate a habit of responsiveness, recognizing that even small moments can be consequential to individual- and community-level well-being.

Element Two: The Quality of Interactions

As we've discussed, wide-ranging research suggests that time spent socializing with close friends and family can contribute to greater life satisfaction, less loneliness, and a longer life. The quantity of communication, including small talk, can be important—a topic we return to a bit later. The quality of communication, however, despite being more influential on outcomes, has received considerably less research attention than quantity. Part of this is because good communication can be hard to measure. In our research, we have identified four types of conversations that we think matter: meaningful talk, catching up, expressing affection, and joking around.[31] Having just one of these conversations can increase connection, decrease stress and loneliness, and improve the quality of our days.[32] Such conversations can be shared with anyone. We have found that the who and the what of conversation both matter—separately.[33] We asked 116 people about their recent social interactions at five random times a day for five consecutive days. Across the 2,722 interactions that the participants reported on, high-quality interactions boosted connection and happiness no matter whom it was with.[34] Taking time to catch up, joke around, or have a meaningful conversation with someone feels good and lowers stress and loneliness.[35] One clear directive emerges from these findings: when possible, steer conversations toward something meaningful to you. This can combat loneliness and enhance well-being.[36] Meaningful talk can involve talking about something you like, day-to-day problems you face, or more emotionally challenging experiences. Even people who aren't as comfortable or excited about engaging in more in-depth ways can benefit from doing so.

Even more important is to direct conversations toward things important to your conversation partner. In our own research and scores of other studies, experiencing perceived responsiveness from others appears to improve the quality of people's days and their well-being.[37] A healthy social biome is both cause and consequence of these little acts of kindness and sociability. Happy people are probably social attractors who facilitate deep social encounters and friendly greetings and encourage strangers to approach them for questions and conversation. Yet deeper conversation and friendly gratitude can also cause us to feel more connected. Just as catching up and joking around can build intimacy, deep conversations instill a sense of meaning in our lives. Practice how to have such interaction in ways that feel authentic to you (without putting too much pressure on yourself to gets things exactly "right").

Element Three: The Diversity of Moments

Making strong social connections across diverse types of people is one of the most difficult challenges we face in our everyday lives. Just as some meals make us feel good but might not be all that healthy for us in the long run, a diet of *only* familiar and comfortable social time doesn't necessarily make those moments completely good for us — or society. Diversity of interaction within our social biomes, including interactions that challenge our rhetorical visions, might be fundamental not just to a well-lived life, but also to a just and thriving society. We can think about this the same way microbiologists think about the benefits of increased biodiversity in gut bacteria for warding off disease. Having moments of interaction with a diverse range of people can lead to a host of beneficial health and social outcomes.

Thus, the third element of a healthy social biome is *social interaction diversity*. Different communication episodes across different types of people, even if they're challenging or uncomfortable, can ultimately promote well-being for ourselves and society. Individuals (and the societies they live in) are unlikely to thrive if they interact only with a limited range of people and have only a limited range of conversations. We learn about ourselves by interacting with others; it's through interaction that our worldviews are set forth, evaluated, and potentially confirmed. (This is the good social stress we discussed in chapter 3.) How we view others is tightly linked to how we talk to others. Stated in the simplest terms, interacting with few people, about similar topics, day in and day out, results in a worldview that lacks nuance and diminishes our appreciation for people with different life experiences. A lack of diversity in our daily conversations can fuel what we described earlier as the unsocial sociability part of our nature. It can be healthy to have our views challenged, to think beyond our own point of view, and to better understand the experiences of others, as these factors can enhance empathy and compassion.

Researchers point to several reasons that interaction diversity may be so valuable. One is that social network diversity—that is, how many different types of people we interact with—increases the flow of valuable and unique information to people.[38] Research also indicates that interacting with a wide range of people can even support positive mindsets, such as optimistic thinking.[39] But there are barriers to seeking out such interactions, one being our own expectations. Studies indicate that people often learn more from talking to strangers than they initially thought possible.[40] Because talking to people we don't know is inherently uncertain, we might be tempted to discount what they have to offer. At a more macro level, structural constraints can limit who's available to us to interact with each day. Research suggests these perceptual and structural impediments are detrimental to our well-being. Indeed, large studies of healthful social habits suggest that interacting with a variety of different people each day is beneficial.[41] Friends, family, colleagues, teammates, neighbors, spouses, and children all have something different to offer us (and we to offer them). The need to belong, then, can be satisfied through a variety of pathways, from deep conversation with trusted friends and family to small talk with someone completely new and different from us.[42] Interaction diversity is beneficial because it opens us up to new perspectives and ways to feel cared for and belong (as well as ways to communicate care and belonging to others).

Element Four: Choosing Sociability

Have you ever thought how weird it is that you don't completely choose your friends? Friends at work? HR did that. School friends? Zoning boards did that. We often don't even choose our family members. The angry teen shouting, "I didn't choose to be born!" isn't exactly wrong. There's considerably less choice in our social circumstances than we might imagine. By comparison, day-to-day social choices are more controllable. Some days, and at some times of day, we can choose to be alone or in the company of others. Although we are often obliged to interact, such as when we're at work, some conversations are more freely chosen, and those are the conversations that research has found we enjoy the most. Specifically, studies reveal that social volition, or the degree to which a social situation is freely chosen, as opposed to being forced on us, is positively associated with well-being.[43]

The ability to seek and connect with people when we want to – such as when our need to belong is heightened – is necessary for a healthy social biome. Want is typically measured by estimating how willing people are to work for something. Wanting interaction with someone is powerful; it expresses commitment and value to another person, thus shaping the meaning of an interaction. Wanting to be there is probably quite apparent to others, even if it's never said out loud. When we want to be there, we're likely to communicate nonverbally: You matter to me, what you say is important, and I am giving you my attention and energy here and now. By contrast, feeling that someone doesn't want to talk to us, or would rather be talking to someone else, can feel as hurtful and unsettling as choosing to interact feels energizing and affirming.

In our research, we found choosing to have conversations is part of living the good life. We drew from over ten thousand moments embedded in five hundred people's days and found that people who reported having more choice about how to spend their social time were less lonely and happier. By contrast, people who felt more constrained in their choices tended to report less satisfaction and fewer positive emotions.[44] Other research has found that college students who have more choice in whom they interact with feel more positive and fewer negative emotions and have a greater sense of meaning and life satisfaction.[45] Research also shows that older adults are more energetic, happier, and connected during interactions they choose to have compared to interactions required of them.[46] In many situations our choices are limited. Environments and social conditions of various types can rob us of chances to reach out to others. But these constraints also highlight why taking advantage of the opportunities we do have to reach out to others is so valuable. They also underscore why making ourselves available to people who need connection can foster positive moments across our social biomes. Those with the most to give – the greatest connective surplus – have the most capacity to support others with their time and attention. Choosing to socialize when we can, and making ourselves available to others, can change the trajectory of a day and a lifetime.[47] Small changes in how we respond to others, and the extent to which we look out for one another, can set us (and the people in our social biomes) on a path toward greater social well-being.

This process certainly depends on where you start. It's likely that people who have few opportunities for friendship and socialization at work, for instance, benefit the most from more socializing in their free time. When it comes to social life, it's also best, if possible, not to put all your eggs in one basket. Here, too, though, we must acknowledge that with variety and choice comes risk, and that risk is greater for some than for others. Yet whenever it's possible and sufficiently safe, accepting the risks and socializing might be the best choice. Social stress is necessary to gain the benefits of growth through social hormesis. Even if we risk rejection when we reach out to others, there are potential gains to be had from developing a new friend or a stronger relationship with a neighbor. It's important not to get too complacent, even when we're comfortable with the routine moments of social interaction in our social biome.

Element Five: Digital to Analogue

Many people in the Global North have access to digital technologies that offer opportunities to connect over distances that were conceivable only in science fiction just forty years ago.[48] These tools of connection have limitless potential to bridge geographic divides. They're crucial for families who are kept apart by forces outside their control, like families of migrant laborers, families of people who are incarcerated, and romantic couples in long-distance relationships.[49] As Jeff discussed in his book *Relating through Technology*, even though technology can help maintain relationships, that doesn't mean that people always use it in that way. On average, people devote twenty to thirty times more minutes to nonsocial entertainment media than to phone calls, video chats, and texting each day. This translates to three to four hours versus ten minutes daily.[50] Choosing not to keep in touch when the opportunities are there has consequences. Although young adults reported that geographic distance is the single greatest barrier to keeping friends, 40 percent also acknowledged that they simply had not made time for their friendships.[51] Mobile and social media have made it easier than ever to keep in touch, but many of us just don't do a very good job of making it a priority. Changing our habits in terms of keeping in touch can start with something pretty basic. Consider the importance of a simple text message to someone who needs it. Communicating through text is better than not communicating at all.[52] People get the most benefit from mediated interactions when they are at their loneliest—whether for a day, for a week or for over a year.[53] That is why we recommend climbing the *ladder of communication* at your own pace. The lowest rung might be looking at what friends and family have posted on social media (along with likes and comments). Online people watching, especially during your downtime, can be a good way to keep involved with the people you care about.

The next rung on the ladder is messaging with small groups or one-on-one. Group chats offer opportunities to joke around, send memes, and keep in touch. This is a low-effort and convenient tool for connection for families and friends alike. The next rung up is direct messaging or texting. People often underestimate the value the recipient places on receiving a friendly text.[54] Texting is probably most valuable when two people engage in a back-and-forth exchange that approximates conversation, but even just a one-way message can work. Here's some advice: if you think of a friend, send them a text (or an email if that's your preference) without expecting a response. This is especially important when your friends or family are struggling; send them a message just letting them know you're thinking of them.

After that rung on the ladder comes video chat and phone calls. Phone calls are probably the only modality of communication that's substitutable for lost face-to-face contact.[55] The research on video chat is still in the works, but it does hold promise. Unfortunately, much of the video-call research is conflated with the necessity and stress of Zoom calls during the pandemic and in the context of workplace communication. We would guess, however, that for people who enjoy and are familiar with video calls, they're probably just as good as (and perhaps better than) old-fashioned phone calls.

Face-to-face conversations are at the very top. Spending time with friends and loved ones face-to-face is a very good use of time when it comes to belonging, but, as we've discussed, there can be benefits to well-being from being social with *anyone*. Climb the ladder, knowing that each rung is better than the one below, but also knowing that some communication is often better than none.

Element Six: The Social Energy Ratio

The sixth factor is what we call the *social energy ratio*. This combines the rewarding feelings of connection and the desire to put less energy into interactions. We believe that high-ratio interactions are high in good social calories. Meaningful conversations are an example of a high-ratio interaction — such conversations are emotionally intense and expend a lot of energy while also producing numerous long-term benefits. Intriguingly, small talk is also a high-ratio episode. This might seem counterintuitive given that small talk is often perceived as lacking in substance and many people say they hate it. Yet such conversations can be connection enhancing even if they're neither deep nor energy intensive.[56] Consider office small talk. Rather than being dreadful and loathed, research has found that office chitchat often enhances people's self-reported sense of positivity and their sense of community at work.[57] These are some of the benefits that many (though certainly not all) remote workers have reported missing when they aren't at work physically. Given the potential benefits of such small talk, the onus is also on employers to create opportunities and spaces — in-person and virtual — for employees to comfortably engage in small talk.

Part of the value of small talk is its efficiency. People lacking available social energy can maintain a relationship by engaging in a low-energy yet connecting conversation (for example, stopping by just to say hi). The degree to which a conversation is pleasant, not how long it takes, is a good indicator of its value.[58] We've found that the ratio of energy to belongingness in daily conversations is associated with having more-positive and less-negative feelings in people's lives and greater choice regarding the people they converse with.[59] Engaging in high-ratio interactions may help us manage our mood and homeostatic needs. It gets us out of our own heads for a little while and makes us more aware of the others around us and the events and goings-on in our surroundings. In other words, the benefits of high-ratio interactions could be attributable to simply having some company.[60]

As a final point, our research has found that interactions with a low connection-to-energy ratio can be miserable. Conversations that people must have for their jobs, such as interacting with demanding customers, are typically rated as high in energy but low on connection. They don't really help people get their need to belong met and they drain the limited resources of social energy. Conflicts are perhaps the most draining in this regard—very low connection and very energy intensive. People tend to really dislike spending energy on conversations that don't make them feel connected to the people around them.[61] The ratio idea is a handy way to realize that not all conversations have to be "heavy-duty" or deeply personal to keep our social biome healthy. And considering that low-ratio interactions are often demanded of us in our jobs—that is, they fulfill functional needs—we must find moments of high-ratio talk whenever we can. Keep in mind, too, that small talk need not enhance momentary well-being to be beneficial, given that it can set the stage for future relational development.

Element Seven: Restorative Solitude

Road trip! The adventure, the open road, the promise of an exciting destination with your BFF riding shotgun. The two of you will spend dozens of hours cruising along with boundless opportunities to talk. But retreating into silence is important, too. We all know the trip can become quite uncomfortable if one person fails to respect the other's desire to have some space to themselves. Even if the trip is a wonderful balance of time together and time apart, friends rarely conclude the trip by diving into deep conversation. Even with both time and capacity for talk, we feel that we need some time alone.

Solitude and time to recover are absolutely necessary for a healthy social biome. We were rather surprised to find in our research that the best predictor of whether people felt satisfied with their lives or were generally lonely was how they answered the question "Would you like to be alone or with other people?" in the moments they were by themselves.[62] In short, wanting the solitude we have appears to be associated with greater well-being. That said, as we've discussed, people's answers about alone time are linked to their larger patterns of relating to others. Further, although time alone matters, what you do with that time matters even more. Solitude is best spent restoring, relaxing, and making the most of it. One of the best ways to enjoy that time is to take things down a notch, reduce stress, and be quiet.[63] Relaxation and energy recovery are even more important after challenging days at work.[64]

Restorative solitude is interiority that isn't in opposition to others. As we discussed in chapter 4, being social and being alone are two parts of the same whole. As David Vincent wrote in *A History of Solitude*, it's "the cultivation of interior solitude, among crowded lives, that makes society endurable."[65] In fact, solitude is most restorative when it occurs after positive social interaction experiences. The calm and peacefulness of well-spent solitude appears to pique people's feeling of wanting to reconnect, once restored.[66] Solitude appears to be most potent when combined with the concept of choice. Being alone because you're choosing to be alone is associated with in-the-moment good feelings (and the absence of bad feelings) as well as overall life satisfaction.[67] In this mobile era, it may be necessary to make yourself digitally unavailable to fully realize the benefits of social withdrawal.[68]

A final note about solitude: research suggests that living alone, especially for older adults, can reduce the likelihood of experiencing

---

143

restorative solitude. Such solitude can instead be unwanted and marked by loneliness. Yet research also demonstrates that such loneliness can be attenuated by factors such as social support and positive neighbor relationships.[69] Currently, about a quarter of U.S. households consist of people living by themselves.[70] Thus, to foster moments of restorative solitude across members of our social biomes, we have to look out for one another, especially people who don't have strong social networks in place. Their likelihood of experiencing restorative solitude is partly dependent on our choices to reach out to them to facilitate high-ratio, enjoyable, and responsive moments of interaction.

Let's also be clear about what we're *not* saying.

- We're not saying that this process is free from discomfort, disappointment, and mistakes. Communication is inherently messy, interdependent, and uncertain, and, short of coercion, you can't make other people do what you want. This is a process. It's not a recipe for guaranteed success.
- We're not saying that this process is free from risks or vulnerability. We should push ourselves, within reason and ethics, to be vulnerable, not only in established relationships but in new relationships, including those with people different from us. We grow and learn in moments when we encounter other ways of seeing the world.
- We're not saying that social health is free of loneliness. Loneliness is part of being human and is a crucial internal sign of an unmet need to belong. It's not possible or desirable to avoid all moments of disconnection, disapproval, and misunderstanding. Spending time alone, moreover, is necessary to recharge and regroup.
- We're not saying this is a one-size-fits-all solution. Your social biome is always changing. It changes when exciting new

things happen, such as moving to a new city, getting a new job, having children, and falling in love. And it changes in times of loss and turmoil, too. All social change will alter the makeup of your social biome and require revisions to the way you communicate in your day-to-day life to foster well-being for yourself and the people around you.

It's tempting to comb through patterns of interaction and come up with a magic number: X hangouts + Y phone calls + Z friends = happiness. Despite headlines with "five simple tricks" that will grant you "magic powers," the science is nowhere close to being able to offer such recommendations. The human social biome is far from mapped. What people need to do depends on their social routines. It starts with how people allocate their time each day. If you live with a roommate or have a partner and children, you probably don't need to schedule as many outside-the-house social events to facilitate extra social interaction (and you might not have much time or energy to do so). For people firmly embedded in active social networks, a valuable social interaction could be one long phone call, one happy hour, one catch-up lunch, or one game of pickup basketball with a friend every other week. Likewise, those with jobs in the service or retail industries might require more time alone to recharge and relax. People whose jobs offer fulfilling social obligations — that is, they have good friends at work or enjoy the social part of the job — probably have lower social needs. Making time for friends outside of work and the home is important, but not everyone needs the same frequency of interaction beyond their normal social routine. All routines are built from a mix of volition and chance. Prioritizing connection takes energy. Over time, the energy expended becomes less and less as connection becomes a habit. It's never too late to build a social routine, through some trial and error, that will contribute to living a better life in the long run.

As researchers and teachers, we're often asked: What should we do to increase connection, make friends, and live a more social life? In the spirit of these honest and important questions, we wrote this chapter to offer clear, direct answers. Yet we do so with humility. Our seven elements seem to make people personally responsible for problems that are bigger than they are. The same is true of physical health. We live in a world where many of us move around less than people did in the past. This makes it seem like it's all up to the individual to adopt solutions — get a standing desk, get in your steps, hire a personal trainer. That's unfair. Sustained solutions *can't be at only the individual level*. We need community-level and governmental support to give people the capacity to connect and have restorative solitude.[71] Affordable and available child care, access to high-quality and timely health care for young and older adults, and sufficient wages to keep people from having to work multiple jobs just to make ends meet — these are also essential if we're to find the time, space, and energy to follow the recommendations we've made in this chapter.

We've argued that we live in a world that often doesn't seem to prioritize our time together — an age of interiority. Changes in technology and work only exacerbate our challenges. Yet for those who have the choice and the available energy, the evidence is clear. We must increase our social obligations, daily and continually, to avoid a prolonged state of social inertia. Caring for people takes social energy. Taking on the burdens of others is tiring. Loving people involves sacrifice. Yet these experiences represent the most important work we'll do in our lives. If you still struggle with taking steps toward greater sociability, think of your future self. Think about the present you in relation to who you were and want to be. Start with an attitude of beneficence – be nice to your future self. Your future self deserves something good! When we follow through with our social plans or make efforts toward sociability, we should thank our past self for setting it up: "Thank you, past self, for doing the things necessary to make today more social." When there's an opportunity to meet new people, think of your future self. It's true that the work of self-presentation and relating can be a little uncomfortable. But it's probably better than you think.[72] We should take the risk of spending that extra energy for our own good. The choices of today can shape tomorrow.

Chapter 8

HOPE IN OTHERS

It was a startling realization in March 2020 that talking to people was the main risk factor for viral infection. More conversation meant more risk. On top of that, the absence of places to safely gather with people and the fear of casual conversation cruelly shoved us all further down the path of interiority that started decades ago. As we look around, and certainly as we read in the news, the world seems to be constantly on fire—metaphorically and literally—which perhaps only intensifies our desire to retreat. Therein lies one of our grandest struggles. To foster a healthier social biome for ourselves and those around us, we need social routines that encourage us to engage in activities we enjoy, repeatedly, with other people.[1] Everyday conversations, especially with responsive others, make us more accepting of others, reduce our need to be right, and help us become less self-focused.[2] There appears to be value in just trying to be more social in pursuit of hormetic stress, whereby we grow through relational struggles and obligations.

Yet we've also argued that human connection, while a fundamental need, can be hard to come by for individuals and societies.

Just being more social is not always easy. The communication that builds connection in our everyday moments is often taxing, laden with trade-offs, and restricted by the systems we live in. Loneliness and disappointment will always be fundamental (and necessary) challenges for all of us. And, paradoxically, the harder we try to connect with others, the more frustrated we can become when we don't feel our efforts are recognized or reciprocated. But to the extent that we try to push through the discomfort and disappointment, we can improve our relationships and find meaning in our lives. Connecting with others can be a pathway to a more hopeful future—for ourselves, our relationships, and our larger communities. Hope can echo throughout our social biomes in small moments of connection between people. And that's why we end this book reflecting on the construction of hope through communication.

There's plenty of evidence that hope is on the wane. People report despair about their children's future, low trust in governments, and existential dread caused by climate change.[3] Many people feel quite literally under attack because of marginalized racial, ethnic, and gender identities.[4] Just in case that wasn't enough, we've been warned that AI might one day turn against us. If we're living in an age of interiority, we could just as easily contend that we're in an age of hopelessness. But what does it mean to be hopeful or hopeless? In day-to-day conversation, we say things like we're "holding out hope" or "trying not to get our hopes up." Such comments suggest that hope is, at best, an intentional suspension of disbelief or, at worst, willful ignorance of the cold, hard reality of life.

This latter view of hope—as a foolish illusion or dangerous obliviousness to the way things really are—was held by some of history's most famous thinkers.[5] As far back as 750 BCE, Hesiod wrote about hope being among the evils inside Pandora's box.[6] Over the last seventy years, however, social psychologists have offered us a radically different view of hope. Although they also conceptualize hope as residing in the mind, they don't view it as detached from reality. It's not the blind faith, folly, or escapism that philosophers such as Plato, Nietzsche, and Schopenhauer bemoaned.[7] Hope is instead firmly grounded in people's goals for their lives and the lives of those around them.[8]

The late psychologist C. R. Snyder, along with his collaborators, has been especially instrumental in revolutionizing the social scientific study of hope through his prolific research of hope theory. According to hope theory, hope is all about goals, where goals are defined as "mental targets" — things we want to make happen or keep from happening.[9] "Hope, in its simplest form," said Diane McDermott and C. R. Snyder, "is the inner knowledge that one has the ability to set and pursue goals, as well as to solve problems all along the way."[10] We have goals related to all spheres of our lives, such as school, work, health, and relationships.[11] Goals can be short-term (I want to make sure my son has a fun birthday party this weekend; I want to finish this project tonight) or long-term (I want to learn a new language; I want to be a supportive friend or trusted partner).

By situating hope in goals, Snyder differentiated people with high and low hope based on the ways in which they think about their goals. There are two important components of the hopeful mindset, which Snyder termed *pathways* and *agency* thinking. Pathways thinking concerns the ways or "routes" through which we can achieve our goals. It's the *waypower* of hope. We also need *willpower* (or agency thinking) to persevere when the going gets tough and our routes get blocked. Agency thinking is our sense of self-belief through which we can successfully pursue the routes we envision through pathways thinking.[12] The more challenging the goal, the higher the likelihood that we're going to face numerous obstacles in our pursuit of it. Agency thinking keeps us going, rerouting if necessary.[13] Hope theory contends that it's the combination of pathways and agency that determines our levels of hope.[14]

For people of all ages, pathways and agency thinking supports positive outcomes in numerous life domains, including school, athletics, work performance, and recovery from health challenges and natural disasters. A study of Division I track - and - field athletes found that pathways- and agency-thinking levels predicted their season-long performance, even after accounting for coaches' ratings of the athletes' natural physical ability.[15] Following Hurricane Katrina, a study found that pathways and agency thinking was linked to family coping.[16] A study of retail, mortgage banking, and telecommunication professionals found that pathways and agency thinking predicted objective indicators of achievement, such as sales figures over a year's time, even after accounting for workers' cognitive ability and sense of self-efficacy.[17]

Hope focused on identifiable goals, as opposed to some ambiguous sense of optimism about the future, helps us see hope in moments of everyday life that we might otherwise miss. Every time we see children working diligently on a drawing or a puzzle, coworkers doing their best to help a customer, or friends giving their full attention to one another over coffee, we see hope in action. Within these moments, people are devising goals, pursuing pathways, and employing agency to accomplish what they view as important and meaningful. Often, these goals are directly linked to belonging.

Responsive Hope and Human Dignity

We've discussed how responsiveness, which is communication that expresses care, support, respect, and validation, is foundational to meeting our need to belong. It's also foundational to hope. Building on hope theory, Andy's research shows that hope in the form of pathways and agency thinking is rooted in moments of connection with others during day-to-day social interaction. Having responsive communication partners not only satisfies our need to belong, but also fuels our belief that we can achieve meaningful goals in our lives. Across multiple studies, Andy has found that people who report higher levels of hope also report greater feelings of connection to others throughout the day, which suggests that emotional connection supports pathways and agency thinking.[18] In one of those studies, Andy, along with Andreas Neubauer and Christopher Otmar, tracked undergraduate students' social interactions over a ten-day period using a smartphone app; they found that greater levels of day-to-day connection with others led to increases in the students' levels of hope over the study period.[19] Connection with others, moreover, was positively predicted by the amount of perceived partner responsiveness the students reported across their moments of interaction—with loved ones, acquaintances, and strangers. Because responsiveness makes us feel accepted and valued for who we are, it fosters our self-confidence and belief in our ability to go after meaningful goals, even when the goals seem hard to reach. Without such moments of affirmation, our self-esteem withers, and so too does our capacity for envisioning, and ultimately achieving, the goals we find meaningful. Without responsive communication, hope can't be built or sustained.

The idea that hope is fostered in small moments of connection within our social biomes is consistent with what the philosopher

Victoria McGeer calls *responsive hope*. Writing about her vision of responsive hope in the article "The Art of Good Hope," McGeer proposed that "an individual's capacity for hoping well depends on that individual's being responsive to the hope of others and, beyond that, participating in or even building a community of others who are likewise responsive to hopeful lives beyond their own. . . . Our success as hopers has an irreducibly communal dimension."[20] If we live in social biomes where people do their best to be responsive to one another in small moments of day-to-day communication, hope can flourish across the biome — even if only drip by drip. Our individual senses of pathways and agency are linked to our treatment of others, or, as McGeer so perfectly put it, other people are the "keepers of our hope."[21] This includes people we hardly know. This was evident in Frome, where "health connectors" were trained how to listen carefully to people, often strangers, to help them identify and achieve their goals. As Julian Able and Lindsay Clarke described, "A health connector will ask questions that bring to the surface what really matters most to the patient and then they can set goals together and formulate a plan. This process of goal setting differs from that of care planning, which is a medical process. . . . By contrast, goal setting is about improving well-being and a positive way of engaging with matters important to the patient's life — such as overcoming the emotional difficulties of loneliness or the grief of bereavement, or the problems raised by practical issues such as those of housing and employment."[22]

When we accept the idea that hope is communal and not just personal, we better appreciate how much is riding on our treatment of one another in everyday moments of talk.[23] We can further simplify this: hope can emerge only in social biomes where people treat one another with basic human dignity. Even if we adopt the prevailing psychological definition of hope as being composed of pathways and agency thinking, we must recognize that these forms of thought flourish only when our need to belong is met. And this can happen only when people uphold one another's dignity in moments of everyday social interaction.[24]

For health researchers such as Nora Jacobson, dignity is, at its core, about tensions between inclusion and exclusion in our everyday life. Jacobson defines dignity as the "abstract, universal quality of value that belongs to every human being simply by virtue of being human."[25] Just like hope, dignity can be something perceived by the self, but it's primarily constructed through communication between people. Dignity is at stake in each interaction we have with other people, whether those people are our closest relational partners or complete strangers. Highlighting this fact, Jacobson reconceptualizes social interactions as *dignity encounters*. Within everyday dignity encounters, our conscious and unconscious communicative behaviors have the power to reinforce or harm people's dignity. Moments of social interaction marked by high partner responsiveness allow hope to grow and dignity to be honored, whereas communication that vilifies, exploits, taunts, and discriminates robs people of their hope and rejects their dignity.[26]

Social biomes in which interactions repeatedly violate people's dignity are inherently corrosive to individual and societal well-being. As Donna Hicks, an international conflict mediator and author, argues, "Our emotional radar is set at a very low threshold for indignities."[27] Hicks's writing and mediation work demonstrate that trust can't emerge or be sustained in spaces where violations are normative. Moments of indignity, moreover, are self-reinforcing: when people anticipate dignity violations in their everyday interactions, those expectations become incorporated into their vision of the social world. And when this vision leads them to anticipate a cold and unwelcoming social climate, possibilities for human connection are necessarily restricted. Their default approach to everyday communication becomes rooted in feelings of exclusion, fear, and unsafety. They therefore adopt a protective stance that interferes with their ability to enact and perceive responsiveness. Indignities, in sum, reverberate insidiously throughout social biomes, calcifying into an enduring sense of hopelessness and disconnection.

(In)Dignity as Contagion

In his book *Ultra-Solutions, or, How to Fail Most Successfully,* the communication theorist Paul Watzlawick cast light on the vicious cycles of indignity and hopelessness that are perpetuated when people habitually approach social interaction from a defensive posture. We see this most clearly reflected in the tale of Watzlawick's fictional character Amadeo Cacciavillani, who enters every social interaction with deep mistrust of others and a win-at-all-costs philosophy. Watzlawick describes Cacciavillani as a "zero-sum player" whose "constant aggressive and defensive posture" is the embodiment of hopelessness and mistrust.[28] But Cacciavillani's vision of the world began to crumble one morning when, while walking away from his parked car, he heard rapid footsteps behind him. Assuming the worst, Cacciavillani was perplexed when he heard a voice shout to him that he had left his headlights on. What could possibly have made the stranger do this? Cacciavillani slowly realized the stranger was trying to be kind. How novel, thought Cacciavillani!

The stranger was clearly operating from a vision of the world foreign to Cacciavillani – one guided by dignity and obligation to others. This moment was consequential. We later learn that

Cacciavillani, upon finding a lost wallet stuffed with money, recalled this stranger's kindness and, unlike old Cacciavillani, who would have stuffed the newfound bills in his pocket and tossed the wallet aside, new Cacciavillani drove to the wallet owner's address and returned it, bills intact. And, "as luck would have it," wrote Watzlawick, "the owner of the wallet was himself an inveterate zero-sum player," and it was Cacciavillani's act of kindness that would eventually lead the wallet owner to rethink his own mistrustful vision of the world.[29]

There's a little bit of Cacciavillani and little bit of the stranger in all of us. The positive and negative parts of sociability are two parts of a whole. Our tendencies toward fostering hope and honoring dignity aren't completely of our own making, a result of the fundamental tension between structure and agency. We're products of our environments. Yet we also reshape our world as we live in it. If moments of everyday social interaction throughout our life have regularly violated our dignity, the world quickly feels to us like an unsafe place. And once we adopt a vision of the world around us as being unsafe, our ability to connect with others is reduced and our capacity for hope is dashed. We're left in a state of chronically high stress that wreaks havoc on our minds and bodies.

Hope-extinguishing indignities spread like infections in social biomes, breeding zero-sum players, some of whom are motivated less by malice than by an entrenched sense of unsafety. For many people, the world *is* unsafe. In addition to fears of interpersonal violence, unsafety is perpetuated by social conditions. Long work hours, economic precariousness, insufficient access to health care, and a general lack of a social safety net rob people of moments of calm and security. These factors put people in a state of chronic hypervigilance for threats in the social environment and make it impossible for them to give as much attention as they would like to their friends and loved ones.[30] And if they don't even have the requisite emotional bandwidth to be responsive to those closest to them, how could they ever muster the energy to be responsive to acquaintances, coworkers, customers, or strangers? In such conditions, individuals are well past the Goldilocks zone of hormetic stress. As the demands of modern life pose increasing threats to their attention, sense of safety, and social connection with others, these conditions necessarily undermine their capacity for responsive hope.

Hope for a Better Relational and Economic Future

Relationships aren't the only thing that matters when it comes to well-being and connection. Economics matter too. One of the primary pathways toward a better future for individuals and their families is higher education. But gaping inequities exist in higher education access and attainment in the United States. This is especially true, for instance, for children with undocumented status, who face numerous barriers ranging from ineligibility for federal financial aid to persistent fears of deportation for themselves and the people they love. These conditions can diminish children's hopes of bettering their (and their family's) future. Media messages that frame immigrants as outsiders further marginalize them and perpetuate destructive feelings of exclusion.[31]

Yet even in the face of these large-scale structural forces that can continually undermine children's sense of hope for their future, hope can still be kindled in small moments each day within people's social biomes. Parents, teachers, and friends can foster children's sense of hope by communicating messages that support the children's capacity for pathways and agency thinking.[32] Research conducted by Andy and Jennifer Kam, which surveyed over four hundred immigrant high school students (many of whom had undocumented status) over the course of an academic year, demonstrated just how important such communication can be.[33] The study asked students about their intentions to attend vocational schools and two- and four-year colleges, and students' day-to-day communication with important people in their lives, including parents, teachers, and friends. Of particular interest were forms of communication that enhanced students' pathways and agency thinking, termed *hope communication*. Hope communication includes conversations that help children think about and name their goals, develop routes toward their goals, and reinforce the children's sense of self-worth. The results of the study showed that students who reported regularly receiving hope communication (from parents, teachers, and friends) over the course of the academic year tended to have higher intentions to attend college. Yet results also suggested that such communication with children needs to be consistent over time or the positive effects go away, if not reverse.[34]

In chapter 6 we discussed how diverse social experiences, including interaction with people of higher socioeconomic status, are linked to economic mobility for people of lower socioeconomic status.[35] That research, however, could only speculate about why this is the case and suggest possibilities such as networking benefits or modeling. Another explanation, even if only a small one, is the communication of hope, which, when used by important people in children's lives like teachers and peers, builds up the children's sense of self-worth and helps them envision goals and routes toward those goals. Such messages might help fortify children's belief that they can create a better future for themselves and their families. We can help other people envision better futures in small moments of talk each day. Putting in extra effort in our conversations with young

---

people in ways that nonjudgmentally help them envision routes toward achieving their dreams can positively affect their lives. Such conversations are clearly not a panacea for society's ills. They can't eradicate racism and the many other structural barriers immigrant children face. They can't fix the financial precariousness associated with so many of society's inequities. Saying so would be naive, if not "cruelly optimistic."[36] But each moment of talk we have in our lives accumulates, as the social biome view suggests. And if enough people in children's lives reinforce their sense of value and potential, a supportive local communication climate (in an otherwise harsh national one) can be created that gives them their best chance to achieve the goals they find meaningful, thus pushing back against the forces of marginalization.

These small moments of hope communication with children can also help them create better personal relationships now and in the future. In another study Andy collaborated on with Jennifer Kam, this time surveying more than four hundred sixth- to eighth-grade students over the course of an academic year, they examined how hope communication from parents resulted in more positive family communication over time. Specifically, they looked at constructive conflict management between parents and children, which involves respectfully talking through disagreements and refraining from personal attacks. Parental hope communication and constructive conflict management were mutually reinforcing over time. That is, parental hope communication led to more constructive communication (when any conflicts arose), and this fed into more parental hope communication over time.[37] These results are consistent with what the psychologist Barbara Fredrickson and her colleagues term *upward spirals of positivity.* Summarizing their research of upward spirals, Fredrickson and her collaborator Thomas Joiner noted,

"Everyday positive emotions, as fleeting as they may be, can initiate a cascade of psychological processes that carry enduring impact on people's subsequent emotional well-being."[38]

Moments Echo

Moments of social interaction matter, we have argued, because they accumulate within social biomes, shaping our visions of ourselves and the world around us. Accumulation, in this sense, happens across the *new* moments of social interaction we have each day. Yet accumulation also happens when the same moments of social interaction repeatedly influence us over time. Humans are mental and conversational time travelers, frequently thinking and talking about our past experiences in everyday life.[39] We spontaneously replay past moments from our lives upwards of twenty times a day.[40] Our memorable moments of interaction include those marked by responsiveness and dignity as well as — sadly — unresponsiveness and indignity. In general, we don't remember much from our social interactions. Research on conversational memory indicates that, not long after a conversation takes place, we're lucky to remember 10 percent of what was said.[41] But research shows that certain moments of interaction stick with us throughout our entire lives, shaping our expectations, how we make decisions, how we evaluate stressful experiences, and how we judge the quality of our lives.[42]

Moments of criticism, rejection, and experiences of trauma in childhood — what Donna Hicks refers to as the "early imprints of indignity" — can haunt our memories and hijack our attention in everyday life.[43] This is an unfortunate byproduct of the brain's attempt to help us ward off future harm, reproducing painful memories as "warning signals" of the types of social encounters to avoid in the future.[44] Experiences of rejection and exclusion get integrated into our self-concepts in the form of negative self-talk, where we become the voice of our own harshest critics. We repeatedly tell ourselves that we're not good enough and no one can be trusted.

But what does this have to do with hope? Hope is, in part, about the stories we carry around with us — stories about the world and our place within it.[45] These stories are stored moments of social interaction that have occurred throughout our lives. Whereas moments of love and achievement support our sense of hope, moments of rejection and trauma undermine it.[46] Messages of indignity and unresponsiveness don't diminish our capacity to hope only once. They do so repeatedly, often in the form of self-talk. When children grow up being constantly criticized or belittled by adults, those voices of hurt become integrated into how the children learn to *intra*-personally communicate with themselves.[47]

Fortunately, memorable messages can also enhance our sense of hope and motivate us, such as when we think back to something inspirational a family member, teacher, or coach told us about how to navigate struggles.[48] Our hope, and the hope of others, then, is shaped by many factors — past and present. But at its core, hope is about our emotional connection with others — connection that makes us feel safe and emboldened to go after the goals we find most meaningful. We're the keepers of one another's hope. We're the keepers, too, of one another's sense of belonging. The momentary choices we make in everyday interaction can foster connection for ourselves and others over a lifetime. We must choose, to whatever extent we can, to build social routines and obligations to others, and to take small steps to break through social inertia, fostering hope and belonging in a world so hungry for them.

—

NOTES

CHAPTER 1. COMMUNICATING TO BELONG

1. The landmark study, "Social Relationships and Mortality Risk," was a meta-analysis — a study that combines results of previous studies — published by Julianne Holt-Lunstad, Timothy B. Smith, and J. Bradley Layton in 2010 in the journal *PLOS Medicine.* Several other sources also support the criticality of social relationships to positive health outcomes. Holt-Lunstad, Robles, and Sbarra, "Advancing Social Connection"; Holt-Lunstad, "Major Health Implications"; House, Landis, and Umberson, "Social Relationships"; Shor and Roelfs, "Social Contact Frequency"; F. Wang et al., "Systematic Review."

2. Holt-Lunstad, Robles, and Sbarra, "Advancing Social Connection"; Barzeva et al., "Quality over Quantity"; Feeney and Collins, "New Look"; H. Liu, Xie, and Lou, "Everyday Social Interactions"; Pinquart and Sorensen, "Risk Factor for Loneliness"; Sun, Harris, and Vazire, "Is Well-Being Associated"; Tonković, Cepić, and Puzek, "Loneliness and Social Networks"; Friedman and Martin, *Longevity Project,* 168; Vaillant, *Triumphs of Experience,* 342; Kroencke et al., "Well-Being"; Sandstrom and Boothby, "Why Do People Avoid Talking to Strangers?"

3. Hall et al., "Quality Conversation"; Kroencke et al., "Well-Being."

4. Throughout this book, we aimed to root our arguments and ideas in peer-reviewed research, mainly from the social sciences. Often we attempt to generalize from available findings and translate them as best we can to make them accessible. Even though the ideas we discuss are based on published research and theory, it's important to note that the available published research and theory are biased in that they mostly (though not completely) involve participants from North America and Europe and are published in English. We attempt to take into consideration the limits of our knowledge and the certainty of our conclusions, but such caveats can't always account for the vast array of differences that might exist in people's experiences with everyday communication and connection based on their unique situations and life experiences.

5. Ainsworth, "Attachments beyond Infancy"; Berkman et al., "From Social Integration"; Carter and Keverne, "Neurobiology of Social Affiliation."

6. Fredrickson, *Love 2.0*, 32–35, provides an overview of some of the research in this area.

7. Lieberman, *Social*, 20.

8. Campa, "Developmental Trends"; Mikulincer and Shaver, "Attachment Perspective."

9. Snyder, "Hypothesis," 264.

10. Barge, "Hope, Communication"; C. Davis, *Communicating Hope*, 104–13, 228; Merolla and Kam, "Parental Hope Communication."

11. Snyder and Feldman, "Handbook of Hope"; Snyder, Cheavens, and Sympson, "Hope."

12. Hippel and Smith, "Evolutionary Origins," 29.

13. Alberts et al., "Mapping the Topography"; Methot et al., "Office Chitchat."

14. Matthias Mehl and his colleagues' research revealed just how much talking many of us do in our day-to-day lives. Their work is also the source for the 16,000-words-spoken-per-day estimate we cited in the preface. Specifically, Mehl and his colleagues reported a mean of 15,958 words; Mehl et al., "Are Women Really."

15. Murray, "Needs, Viscerogenic," 369.

16. Craig Hill is one such researcher who contributed to the development of the needs perspective, in "Affiliation Motivation."

17. Denworth, *Friendship*, 121–24. As Lydia Denworth describes in that book, Baumeister and Leary began developing the need-to-belong concept in the summer of 1993. They then published "Need to Belong," a highly influential 1995 article explicating the need to belong. See also Allen et al., "Need to Belong," for a brief historical overview of the concept's development.

18. Leary and Downs, "Interpersonal Functions."

19. John Cacioppo proposed a concept called the social thermostat that serves a similar purpose and has a similar name. This concept is mentioned in J. Cacioppo and Patrick, *Loneliness*, 71.

20. Bryson, *Short History*, 450.

21. Allen et al., "Need to Belong"; Lieberman, *Social*, 19.

22. Gouldner, "Norm of Reciprocity."

23. Clark, Mills, and Powell, "Keeping Track"; Hall, "Friendship Standards."

24. Allen et al., "Need to Belong," 1142.

25. Hirsch and Clark, "Multiple Paths."

26. Hall, "Energy, Episode"; Quoidbach et al., "Happiness and Social Behavior"; Sandstrom and Dunn, "Social Interactions"; Granovetter, "Strength of Weak Ties."

27. Grammer et al., "Patterns."

28. Ruesch and Bateson, *Communication*, 23, 209; Wilmot, "Metacommunication."

29. Duck, "Diaries and Logs"; Wheeler and Nezlek, "Sex Differences"; Wheeler, Reis, and Nezlek, "Loneliness."

30. O'Connor and Rosenblood, "Affiliation Motivation," 514. Shawn O'Connor confirmed through email that they coined the term *social calories*. No authors they cited used that exact phrase.

31. Prentice, Halusic, and Sheldon, "Integrating Theories," 81.

32. Cheryl Carmichael, Harry Reis, and Paul Duberstein tracked the same group of college students for thirty years. At age twenty, the students kept a diary of their social interactions for one week. For young adults, the researchers found the quantity of social interactions mattered the most. The quantity of their social interactions at twenty years old predicted the quality of social interactions ten years later, when the researchers asked the same students to track their social interactions again. Looking up the same students one more time twenty years later, at age fifty, they found that those whose social patterns shifted from quantity to quality were happier, less lonely, more fulfilled. Carmichael, Reis, and Duberstein, "In Your 20s." See also Victor and Yang, "Prevalence of Loneliness," and Zhaoyang et al., "Social Interactions," for nuanced findings on the quality-versus-quantity issue.

33. Malinowski, "Problem of Meaning"; Coupland, Coupland, and Robinson, "How Are You?"

34. Coupland, Coupland, and Robinson, "How Are You?"

35. This meta-analysis, conducted by Eran Shor and David J. Roefls and published as "Social Contact Frequency," analyzed approximately 400,000 participants across ninety-one studies, and it found that risk of death was about 13 percent higher for people with low, compared to high, social contact. Social contact pertains primarily to quantity (not quality) of interactions, which is important to keep in mind. Interestingly, additional analysis suggested that contact might be especially beneficial when it is with weak ties. Further, in one of the tests the researchers conducted, the link between contact and mortality was significantly stronger for women than men.

36. Barzeva et al., "Quality over Quantity"; H. Liu, Xie, and Lou, "Everyday Social Interactions"; Pinquart and Sorensen, "Risk Factor for Loneliness"; Sun, Harris, and Vazire, "Is Well-Being Associated"; Shor, Roelfs, and Yogev, "Strength of Family Ties"; Tonković, Cepić, and Puzek, "Loneliness and Social Networks."

37. Milek et al., " 'Eavesdropping on Happiness.' "

—

38. Baumeister and Leary, "Need to Belong"; Feeney and Collins, "New Look." In Allen et al., "Need to Belong," 1138, Baumeister put it this way: "Desired social bonds have two aspects: frequent positive or neutral (just not negative) interactions, and an ongoing framework for mutual caring."

39. Hall, "Energy, Episode"; Hall et al., "Quality Conversation"; Kroencke et al., "Well-Being"; Sandstrom and Boothby, "Why Do People Avoid Talking to Strangers?"

40. Prentice, Halusic, and Sheldon, "Integrating Theories"; Sheldon and Gunz, "Psychological Needs"; Sheldon and Schüler, "Wanting, Having, and Needing."

41. Tomova et al., "Acute Social Isolation."

42. Hofmann, Vohs, and Baumeister, "What People Desire."

43. Allen et al., "Need to Belong."

44. Achterhof et al., "Adolescents' Real-Time"; Burnholt et al., "Technologically-Mediated Communication"; Kroencke et al., "Well-Being"; Macdonald, Luo, and Hülür, "Daily Social Interactions."

45. Dissing et al., "Smartphone Interactions"; Hall, Dominguez, and Mihailova, "Interpersonal Media"; Kroencke et al., "Well-Being."

46. Hall, *Relating through Technology*, 159.

47. Hall, Pennington, and Merolla, "Which Mediated Social Interactions."

48. Sheldon and Lyubomirsky, "Revisiting the Sustainable Happiness Model."

49. Hawkley et al., "From Social Structural Factors"; Hutten et al., "Risk Factors."

50. Kroencke et al., "Well-Being."

51. Ibid.; Quoidbach et al., "Happiness and Social Behavior."

52. Dunn and Lok, "Can Sociability"; Regan and Lyubomirsky, "Inducing Sociability."

53. Joshanloo, Sirgy, and Park, "Directionality."

54. Friedman and Martin, *Longevity Project*, 164; Vaillant, *Triumphs of Experience*, 342.

55. Tay and Diener, "Needs and Subjective Well-Being."

56. It's important to consider different types of human needs together. Once people's basic survival needs for shelter, food, and clean water are met, meeting the need to belong is critical. Another way to think about it is that meeting basic survival needs is vital and necessary to reap the benefits of belonging. Segal and his colleagues, for instance, found that individuals who were temporarily unhoused and experiencing at least one mental health disorder benefited from social support from friends and family only when their basic financial and safety needs were met. Segal, Silverman, and Temkin, "Social Networks."

57. Fredrickson, *Love 2.0*, 85.

58. Vangelisti and Brody, "Physiology of Social Pain."

59. Berkman et al., "From Social Integration"; Floyd et al., "Physiology of Affectionate Communication"; Holt-Lunstad, "Major Health Implications."

60. Brosschot, Verkuil, and Thayer, "Generalized Unsafety Theory," §1.2.
61. Berkman et al., "From Social Integration."
62. Afifi, Callejas, and Harrison, "Resilience through Stress."
63. Feeney and Collins, "New Look"; Stadler et al., "Close Relationships."
64. Gable and Bedrov, "Social Isolation."
65. Fardghassemi and Joffe, "Causes of Loneliness."
66. Reinhardt, Boerner, and Horowitz, "Good to Have."

CHAPTER 2. COMMUNICATION IS HARD
AND ALWAYS HAS BEEN

1. Goo, "Skills Americans Say." Ask employers who they're looking to hire and they'll also quickly point to communication skills. Refresh Leadership, "83% of Companies." The so-called soft skills revolution in hiring preferences has been growing for decades the world over and in all spheres of life. The World Health Organization has also long cited effective communication as one of the pillars of healthy individuals and societies. World Health Organization, "Skills for Health."
2. Baumeister and Robson, "Belongingness and the Modern Schoolchild," 106.
3. Bowker, "Predicting Friendship."
4. Hank and Steinbach, "Sibling Estrangement"; Scharp and Dorrance Hall, "Family Marginalization."
5. Freres, "Financial Costs"; Morrison, "Negative Relationships"; Sonnentag, Unger, and Nägel, "Workplace Conflict."
6. Cummins, "We're All Bad Neighbors."
7. Duck, *Meaningful Relationships*, 59–66.
8. Jacoby and Ochs, "Co-Construction"; Stewart and Koenig Kellas, "Co-Constructing Uniqueness."
9. Gottman, Driver, and Tabares, "Repair during Marital Conflict." That's not to say there isn't a remarkable amount of coordination happening during most conversations we have. Even conversations in which misunderstanding is occurring can be coordinated in basic ways. People, for instance, are usually able to accomplish basic turn taking in conversations or recognize utterances as statements or questions. Thus, coordination and misunderstanding can occur simultaneously and at different levels. Sillars and Vangelisti, "Communication."
10. One of the world's leading scholars of competent communication, Brian Spitzberg, once put it this way: "There are as yet no unproblematic criteria for good communication." Spitzberg, "What Is Good Communication?" 114. Even in the study of conflict management in romantic relationships, where decades' worth of research has been conducted, the psychologists Nickola Overall and James McNulty

note in "What Type of Communication" that studies aren't always able to delineate inherently constructive versus destructive behavior. In other words, a great deal of nuance exists.

11. Douglas, "Expectations about Initial Interaction"; Frisby, Sidelinger, and Booth-Butterfield, "No Harm, No Foul"; Gallois, Watson, and Giles, "Intergroup Communication"; K. Tracy, *Everyday Talk*, 17–20.

12. Baxter, "Interpersonal Communication as Dialogue"; Duck, *Meaningful Relationships*, 57.

13. Philipsen, "Theory of Speech Codes." Another key factor regarding meaning construction in these types of situations is the extent to which friends perceive one another's goals as positive in nature. As Ildo Kim and Nicholas Palomares note in "Role of a Bystander," this is what differentiates playful teasing from hurtful bullying.

14. Du, Derks, and Bakker, "Daily Spillover"; Ferguson, "You Cannot Leave."

15. Cegala, "Affective and Cognitive Manifestations"; Merolla, Hall, and Bernhold, "Perseverative Cognition"; Pasupathi and Rich, "Inattentive Listening."

16. Bavelas, Coates, and Johnson, "Listeners as Co-Narrators"; Enfield, *How We Talk*, 109–19.

17. There's a long line of research on the benefits of person-centered support. High and Dillard, "Review and Meta-Analysis." Yet there's also important research showing that person-centered support isn't necessarily the best form of support in all situations and moments. Shardé M. Davis's research on Black women friends' discussions of their experiences receiving racial microaggressions, for instance, suggests that communication indicative of low person-centeredness, such as redirecting a conversation toward the self as opposed to the support seeker, can play valuable roles in the support process. This is further evidence of the complex nature of communication effectiveness and its dependence on context and people's identities. S. Davis, "When Sistahs Support."

18. Gottman, *Science of Trust*, 201.

19. Lists of active-listening tactics often appear in popular press articles focused on achieving success in business. Popularization of the term *active listening* in business contexts had led some scholars to shun the term altogether. Part of this has to do with the fact that typologies of tactics can oversimplify the listening process, which is a mix of behavioral and perceptual elements attributable to all people involved in an interaction. Kluger and Itzchakov, "Power of Listening," 124.

20. Hall, *Relating through Technology*, 186; S. Tracy, "Let's Talk."

21. Manusov, "Interpersonal Communication," 104.

22. Lipetz, Kluger, and Bodie, "Listening Is Listening."

23. Bodie et al., "Listening Competence."

24. Korobov, "Discursive Approach."

25. Weger et al., "Relative Effectiveness." There's wide-ranging research on advice in various contexts and sophisticated theoretical models to explain when advice is and isn't received well on the basis of factors such as message features, timing, and communicator characteristics. We direct readers to Erina McGeorge, Bo Feng, and Lisa Guntzviller's "Advice," an in-depth review of this literature.

26. Spitzberg, "What Is Good Communication?"
27. Baxter, "Interpersonal Communication as Dialogue."
28. H. Clark and Fox Tree, "Using *Uh*."
29. Knapp, Hall, and Horgan, *Nonverbal Communication*, 351; Enfield, *How We Talk*, 2.
30. Lipetz, Kluger, and Bodie, "Listening Is Listening," 87.
31. Gottman, *Science of Trust*, 74.
32. Gottman and Silver, *Seven Principles*, 11. See also Gottman, *The Marriage Clinic*, 8–11, for more comprehensive discussion of what he sees as the limits, as well as the benefits, of active listening and other forms of communication within his larger research and therapeutic paradigms. Importantly, he notes that behaviors indicative of active listening are most important when people in close relationships are talking about challenges involving other people, as opposed to sharing frustrations involving each other's behavior. In *The Marriage Clinic*, Gottman also describes the origins of the active-listening concept.
33. Solomon et al., "Dynamic Dyadic Systems."
34. Gottman, *Science of Trust*, 23.
35. Itzchakov et al., "Communicating for Workplace Connection."
36. Cohn and Fredrickson, "Beyond the Moment."
37. Lipetz, Kluger, and Bodie, "Listening Is Listening."
38. Carl and Duck, "How to Do Things"; Watzlawick, Beavin, and Jackson, *Pragmatics*, 226–27.
39. Afifi, Merrill, and Davis, "Theory of Resilience."
40. Stulberg, "For People to Really Know."
41. Stafford, "Communication and Relationship Maintenance"; Stamps, Mandell, and Lucas, "Relational Maintenance, Collectivism"; Madlock and Booth-Butterfield, "Influence of Relational Maintenance." We defined maintenance as keeping relationships "healthy." Healthy, when it comes to relationships, can mean many different things. For some relationships, it might mean sustaining high levels of emotional closeness. Other times, especially in nonintimate relational contexts, it might mean keeping a given relationship in a state that you want the relationship to be in, and this might not involve high levels of emotional closeness.
42. Johnson, Galambos, and Anderson, "Skip the Dishes"; Madlock and Booth-Butterfield, "Influence of Relational Maintenance"; Ogolsky and Bowers, "Meta-Analytic Review."
43. O'Keefe, "Logic of Message Design," 89. Interestingly, as O'Keefe's work indicates, message design logics are most apparent in complex communication situations, where many goals are probably salient for communicators. A good example is when a

manager needs to fire an employee. The manager wants to be clear about what's happening and why. They want to inform the employee of the organization's policies for termination. At the same time, they also probably want to be respectful of the other person and cognizant of the short- and long-term difficulty they might experience following this news. When firing someone, it's likely that the expressive message designer will be as straightforward as possible about what's occurring and how they feel about the situation. If they feel sad that this is happening, they will say it. If they don't, they won't, even if expressing empathy is the polite thing to do. The conventional message designer, however, will be highly attuned to terminating someone "by the book," while also politely offering their situationally appropriate regret about the situation. The rhetorically minded message designer is likely to go above and beyond conventional professionalism, endeavoring to construct a persuasive narrative for how the fired employee should understand the situation. The termination, they might say, while certainly a setback, is but a temporary one; in fact, looked at from just the right angle, this is an opportunity for growth, paving the way to new and fulfilling opportunities in the long run. Finally, it's important to note that we've applied the message design logic concept here to individuals as if people default to only one logic in all their communication. People can adopt different logics at different times and in different contexts. Design logics are therefore often conceptualized at the message level, rather than the person level.

44. Dainton and Zelley, *Applying Communication Theory*, 62–65; O'Keefe, Lambert, and Lambert, "Conflict and Communication."

45. Edwards and Shepherd, "Theories of Communication."

46. Vangelisti, Knapp, and Daly, "Conversational Narcissism." One intriguing caveat is in order about conversational narcissism. Although it appears to be universally despised and detrimental to relationships, there's one place where it can sometimes (and sadly) yield benefits: the workplace. As Vangelisti, Knapp, and Daly explained, persistently tooting one's horn can get one's work noticed in organizational settings lacking robust ethical standards of accountability.

47. Lipetz, Kluger, and Bodie, "Listening Is Listening."

48. Marzoratti and Evans, "Measurement of Interpersonal Physiological Synchrony"; Wells et al., "Positivity Resonance."

49. Lin et al., "Friends in Sync."

50. Lipetz, Kluger, and Bodie, "Listening Is Listening."

51. Reis, Regan, and Lyubomirsky, "Interpersonal Chemistry."

52. Weger et al., "Relative Effectiveness," 24.

53. Reis, Clark, and Holmes, "Perceived Partner Responsiveness," 204. To understand the interplay of generalized social perceptions and micromomentary features of communication relevant to positive emotions during social interaction, see Reis, Regan, and Lyubomirsky, "Interpersonal Chemistry."

54. We adopted the note-melody metaphor with regard to gestalt psychology from the writing of Susan Fiske and Shelley Taylor in *Social Cognition*.

55. Although perceived partner responsiveness and listening are considered related constructs, researchers maintain that they're not the same. Kluger and Itzchakov, "Power of Listening."

56. Stafford, "Communication and Relationship Maintenance"; Scott, "Longitudinal Examination."

57. Winkielman and Nowak, "Beyond the Features."

58. Lemay and Clark, "How the Head."

59. Crasta et al., "Toward an Optimized Measure," 339.

60. Manusov, "Interpersonal Communication," 115.

61. Baxter and Montgomery, *Relating*.

62. Wilmot, "Communication Spirals," 329.

63. Hochschild, *Managed Heart,* 197; Garrosa et al., "Energy Loss"; S. Tracy, "Locking Up Emotion."

64. J. Cacioppo and S. Cacioppo, "Loneliness in the Modern Age."

65. Kashdan and Roberts, "Social Anxiety"; Honeycutt, "Imagined Interactions."

66. This idea is also nicely captured by Brené Brown's notion of the "vulnerability hangover" that people can experience following self-disclosure. See Burns, "How to Nurse an Oversharing Hangover." Brown spoke about the vulnerability hangover and the importance of constructively managing shame in her TED Talk "Listening to Shame."

67. Neff and Davidson, "Self-Compassion."

68. Duck, *Meaningful Relationships,* 161.

69. Fortunately, we know from the communication researcher and theorist Howard Giles and his colleagues' extensive research on communication accommodation theory that this type of tailoring often happens without our consciously realizing it. There's a natural tendency for us to adapt to the communication needs of relationship partners. See, for instance, Gasiorek, "Theoretical Perspectives," and Soliz, Giles, and Gasiorek, "Communication Accommodation Theory," for overviews of this work. This is important to keep in mind because it reinforces the idea that we shouldn't give up too early on the prospect of developing a relationship, say a friendship, with someone with whom our initial interactions are stilted or awkward. Intentionality in our communication nevertheless remains critical to continually ensure we're communicating in ways that are most likely to honor people's unique understandings of good communication.

70. Sasaki and Overall, "Constructive Conflict Resolution." The importance of shared-meaning construction features in other models of relational communication, such as John Gottman's sound relationship house theory, which is especially applicable to long-term romantic relationships; Gottman, *The Marriage Clinic,* 105–7; Gottman, *The Science of Trust,* 1, 37.

71. Hawn, "Civility Cudgel"; McCullough, *Beyond Revenge,* 49–61.

72. Caughlin, "Multiple Goals Theory"; Sillars and Vangelisti, "Communication."

73. Gilligan, Suitor, and Pillemer, "Estrangement."

74. Dailey, "Confirmation in Personal Relationships"; Donovan et al., "Labor of Talking."

75. Itzchakov and Reis, "Perceived Responsiveness Increases Tolerance."

76. McCullough, *Beyond Revenge*, 14; Merolla, "Forgiveness Following Conflict," 234–46.

77. Boothby et al., "Liking Gap"; Sandstrom and Boothby, "Why Do People Avoid Talking to Strangers?"; Wolf, Nafe, and Tomasello, "Development."

78. Surveying some of the liking gap research in her book *Social Chemistry: Decoding the Patterns of Human Connection*, Yale University School of Management professor Marissa King similarly concluded that we too often hold a "self-deprecating and defeatist attitude about [our] social life" (23).

79. Wolf, Nafe, and Tomasello, "Development."

80. Riggio and Crawley, "Nonverbal Skills." And the diminishing returns of perfectionism go beyond communication, applying to well-being more generally, and some research shows that people who strive the hardest to be happy are the least likely to be happy. Zerwas and Ford, "Paradox."

CHAPTER 3. TOWARD OPTIMAL SOCIAL STRESS

1. Carlson et al., "Impact of the Baltimore Experience Corps."

2. Varma et al., "Experience Corps Baltimore."

3. Ibid., 1043.

4. Epel, "Geroscience Agenda."

5. Hans Selye's concept of eustress also captures the idea that stress can be positive. Selye, *Stress without Distress*.

6. Bobba-Alves, Juster, and Picard, "Energetic Cost"; Raichle and Gusnard, "Appraising the Brain's Energy Budget."

7. Raichle and Gusnard, "Appraising the Brain's Energy Budget."

8. Harvard Health Publishing, "Calories Burned."

9. Ibid.

10. Bobba-Alves, Juster, and Picard, "Energetic Cost."

11. Ibid.

12. Lieberman, *Social*, 19.

13. This research on anxiety and energy expenditure was cited by Bobba-Albes and her colleagues in "Energetic Cost." For the original study, see Schmidt et al., "Resting Metabolic Rate." It's important to note that a study conducted by a different team of researchers on men and women of varying ages, but using a different measure of anxiety from the one used by Schmidt et al., did not find the same link between anxiety and resting metabolic rate. Wilson et al., "Life Stress." Caution is

therefore needed when interpreting results regarding an association between anxiety and resting metabolic rate.

14. Dominguez et al., "Working Hard"; Hall, "Energy, Episode"; Hall and Davis, "Proposing the Communicate Bond Belong Theory"; Hall, "How Many Hours"; Hall and Merolla, "Connecting Everyday Talk"; Hall, Mihailova, and Merolla, "Typicality and Volition"; Hall et al., "Social Bandwidth."

15. D. Davis, "Development and Initial Tests," 13.

16. Lavrusheva, "Concept of Vitality."

17. Uziel, "Individual Differences."

18. Stijovic et al., "Homeostatic Regulation."

19. R. Collins, "Emotional Energy."

20. Martela and Sheldon, "Clarifying the Concept."

21. Bobba-Alves, Juster, and Picard, "Energetic Cost"; Matthews and Tye, "Neural Mechanisms."

22. Ryan and Frederick, "On Energy."

23. Hall and Merolla, "Connecting Everyday Talk"; Luo et al., "Alternating Time Spent."

24. Luo et al., "Alternating Time Spent."

25. Matthews and Tye, "Neural Mechanisms"; Stijovic et al., "Homeostatic Regulation."

26. R. Collins, "Emotional Energy"; Hall et al., "Social Bandwidth"; Luo et al., "Alternating Time Spent."

27. D. Davis, "Development and Initial Tests"; Dominguez et al., "Working Hard"; Hall et al., "Social Bandwidth"; Hall and Davis, "Proposing the Communicate Bond Belong Theory"; Hall and Merolla, "Connecting Everyday Talk."

28. Hall et al., "Social Bandwidth."

29. Ibid.

30. Cameron et al., "Empathy Is Hard"; Hall, "Energy, Episode"; Hall et al., "Social Bandwidth."

31. Fernández et al., "Why We Socially Interact."

32. Hall, "Energy, Episode"; Hall et al., "Social Bandwidth."

33. Miller, Considine, and Garner, " 'Let Me Tell You.' "

34. Hall et al., "Social Bandwidth."

35. Merolla, Otmar, and Salehuddin, "Past Relational Experiences."

36. Leikas and Ilmarinen, "Happy Now"; Luo et al., "Alternating Time Spent"; Hall, "Energy, Episode."

37. Hall, Mihailova, and Merolla, "Typicality and Volition."

38. Uziel, "Individual Differences."

39. These quotes came from the data set analyzed in study 1 in Hall et al., "Social Bandwidth."

40. Hall, *Relating through Technology*, 67.

41. Boland et al., "Zoom Disrupts."
42. Ramstead, Badcock, and Friston, "Answering Schrödinger's Question."
43. Communicate Bond Belong (CBB) theory, which Jeff proposed with Daniel Cochece Davis, includes a principle of energy conservation. Ramstead and his colleagues identified this as the free-energy principle, which is a neuroscientific theory of brain and behavior that states that organisms seek to minimize internal entropy by avoiding the expenditure of energy on unexpected outcomes. This principle suggests that energy conservation counteracts the forces of entropy in all organisms' physical environment. Humans, thus, seek out and shape their local environments to minimize energy expenditure, while seeking to meet fundamental needs, such as nutrition, safety, and inclusion. The free-energy principle suggests that organisms seek to optimize the use of time and energy, which steers them away from high-energy states, both in terms of arousal and in terms of energy expenditure in social interaction. This is consistent with the human energy management principles that CBB theory is based on (D. Davis, "Development and Initial Tests"). Excess energy spent on interaction reduces the available energy to accomplish other goals, which would be maladaptive from an evolutionary point of view. Hall and Davis, "Proposing the Communicate Bond Belong Theory"; Ramstead, Badcock, and Friston, "Answering Schrödinger's Question."
44. Hall, "Energy, Episode"; Hall, "How Many Hours."
45. Cameron et al., "Empathy Is Hard"; Hall et al., "Quality Conversation."
46. Kam and Merolla, "Hope Communication."
47. Epel, "Geroscience Agenda."
48. Hall and Davis, "Proposing the Communicate Bond Belong Theory."
49. Hruschka, *Friendship*, 56.
50. Whillans and Dunn, "Valuing Time over Money."
51. Kahneman, "Cutting through the Noise."
52. Dunbar, *Friends,* 44; Hall, "How Many Hours."
53. Snap, "Friendship Report 2020."
54. Liming, *Hanging Out,* xix.

CHAPTER 4. BALANCING CONNECTION AND SOLITUDE

1. Finkel, *Stranger,* 19, 23–24, 152–53; Finkel, "Strange Tale"; Kottke, "The Last True Hermit." It was Kottke's blog post that introduced us to Knight's story and Finkel's accounts of it. Fittingly, Knight's two social interactions during his time in North Pond were brief and defensive. In Finkel's book *Stranger in the Woods,* Knight recalls that his first interaction amounted to a mere "Hi," which he muttered head-down as he quickly walked past a hiker. The second interaction, taking place about twenty years later, was with three men who were returning home after ice fishing. Knight, Finkel wrote, doesn't remember saying a single word to the men.

One of the men, however, told Finkel that he recalls Knight saying a few things, mainly concerning Knight's wish to be left alone.

2. Hall and Merolla, "Connecting Everyday Talk."

3. Some of the ideas in this chapter first appeared in Jeff's writing for the *Wall Street Journal*: Hall, "Price We Pay."

4. Vincent, *History of Solitude*, 1–25.

5. Hall, "Price We Pay"; Kumar and Epley, "Undersociality Is Unwise."

6. Vincent, *History of Solitude*, 15–16.

7. Gaffigan's interview aired on CBS on July 2, 2021. Video of the interview is available at https://www.youtube.com/watch?v=efiYHtlxjuE.

8. Campa, "Developmental Trends"; Mikulincer and Shaver, "Attachment Perspective."

9. Vincent, *History of Solitude*, 15–16.

10. All relationships involve partners managing unresolvable tensions between autonomy and connection. As Leslie Baxter, a communication researcher and theorist, stated in "Dialectical Contradictions," "No relationship can exist unless the parties forsake individual autonomy. However, too much connection paradoxically destroys the relationship because the individual entities become lost" (70).

11. Hall and Davis, "Proposing the Communicate Bond Belong Theory"; Hall and Merolla, "Connecting Everyday Talk."

12. O'Connor and Rosenblood, "Affiliation Motivation"; Hall, "Regulation of Social Interaction"; Reissmann et al., "Role of State Feelings."

13. Hall, "Regulation of Social Interaction"; Hall et al., "Social Bandwidth"; Reissmann et al., "Role of State Feelings."

14. Hall, "Energy, Episode."

15. Luo et al., "Alternating Time Spent."

16. Uziel, "Individual Differences."

17. Hall, "Energy, Episode."

18. Hall et al., "Social Bandwidth."

19. Duck, *Meaningful Relationships*, 9–15.

20. Cheung, Gardner, and Anderson, "Emotionships."

21. Hall, "Energy, Episode"; Quoidbach et al., "Happiness and Social Behavior"; Sandstrom and Dunn, "Social Interactions."

22. Quoidbach et al., "Happiness and Social Behavior."

23. Algoe, "Find, Remind, and Bind"; Sandstrom and Boothby, "Why Do People Avoid Talking to Strangers?"

24. Hruschka, *Friendship*, 69.

25. Bernstein et al., "Within-Person Effects."

26. Hruschka, *Friendship*, 97.

27. Afifi, Callejas, and Harrison, "Resilience through Stress"; Feeney and Collins, "New Look."

28. Uziel, "Language of Being Alone."

29. Eramian, Mallory, and Herbert, "Friendship, Intimacy"; Hall, "Friendship Standards."

30. N. Collins and Miller, "Self-Disclosure."

31. Eramian, Mallory, and Herbert, "Friendship, Intimacy."

32. Montgomery, *Anne of Green Gables.*

33. Jacques-Hamilton, Sun, and Smillie, "Costs and Benefits"; Regan and Lyubomirsky, "Inducing Sociability"; Zelenski, Santoro, and Whelan, "Would Introverts Be Better Off."

34. Wilt and Revelle, "Extraversion."

35. Jacques-Hamilton, Sun, and Smillie, "Costs and Benefits"; Milek et al., " 'Eavesdropping on Happiness' "; Mueller et al., "Happy Like a Fish in Water"; Wilt and Revelle, "Extraversion"; Wilt and Revelle, "Big Five."

36. Kroencke et al., "Well-Being."

37. Kuper et al., "Who Benefits."

38. Sun, Harris, and Vazire, "Is Well-Being Associated."

39. Folk et al., "Did Social Connection."

40. Entringer and Gosling, "Loneliness"; Folk et al., "Did Social Connection."

41. Hall, Pennington, and Lueders, "Impression Management"; Harris and Vazire, "On Friendship."

42. Bahns et al., "Similarity in Relationships."

43. Harris and Vazire, "On Friendship."

44. Sun, Harris, and Vazire, "Is Well-Being Associated."

45. Miritello et al., "Time as a Limited Resource."

46. Kant, "Civilization and Enlightenment," 41; We credit Radmila Prislin and William Crano's essay "Sociability," 39–40, for bringing Kant's ideas regarding unsocial sociability to our attention.

47. It's astonishing (and often comic) how far this is said to go. As Mark Leary discussed in his book *The Curse of the Self: Self-Awareness, Egotism, and the Quality of Human Life,* we tend to favor people who share our birthday, our name, and first and last initials over those who don't. Nearly everyone, moreover, rates themselves above average, rarely believes that other people are as exceptional as they are, and evaluates their own virtues to be more objectively valuable than the virtues they don't possess (e.g., "I may be unathletic, but I am smart and being smart is better"). Leary notes that even our self-serving biases have biases: people routinely underestimate how much they're biased. In other words, we think, "People are generally biased, but I am less biased and self-serving than the average person."

48. Cameron et al., "Empathy Is Hard"; Strazdins and Broom, "Mental Health Costs."

49. Radtke, *Seek You*, 93.

50. Burger, "Individual Differences."

51. Treisman, "Spanish Athlete Spent 500 Days Alone."

52. Campbell and Ross, "Re-Conceptualizing Solitude."

53. Hall, Dominguez, and Mihailova, "Interpersonal Media"; Hawkley et al., "Are U.S. Older Adults"; Holt-Lunstad et al., "Loneliness and Social Isolation"; Tonković, Cepić, and Puzek, "Loneliness and Social Networks"; Victor and Yang, "Prevalence of Loneliness."

54. Arrigo and Bullock, "Psychological Effects."

55. Tse, Lay, and Nakamura, "Autonomy Matters."

56. J. Cacioppo and Hawkley, "Loneliness"; J. Cacioppo et al., "Loneliness across Phylogeny"; Hawkley and Cacioppo, "Social Connectedness and Health."

57. J. Cacioppo and Hawkley, "Loneliness," 228.

58. Reissmann et al., "Role of State Feelings."

59. J. Cacioppo and S. Cacioppo, "Loneliness in the Modern Age."

60. J. Cacioppo and Hawkley, "Loneliness."

61. J. Cacioppo et al., "Loneliness across Phylogeny."

62. D. Ren and Evans, "Leaving the Loners."

63. J. Cacioppo et al., "Loneliness across Phylogeny."

64. Burger, "Individual Differences"; Cacioppo et al., "Loneliness across Phylogeny."

65. Holt-Lunstad et al., "Loneliness and Social Isolation"; X. Ren, "Marital Status."

66. Harris and Vazire, "On Friendship."

67. Burger, "Preference for Solitude."

68. Hutten et al., "Risk Factors of Loneliness." See also Victor and Yang, "Prevalence of Loneliness."

69. J. Cacioppo and Hawkley, "Loneliness." See also S. Cacioppo et al., "Loneliness and Implicit Attention to Social Threat."

70. Loneliness might also have a heritable component, meaning some people are born with a greater likelihood of being lonely because, for instance, of their heightened sensitivity to social environments. Social conditions, however, greatly influence loneliness and necessarily interact with whatever portion of loneliness is based on genetics. J. Cacioppo and Hawkley, "Loneliness"; J. Cacioppo et al., "Loneliness across Phylogeny"; Spithoven et al., "Genetic Contributions."

71. Entringer and Gosling, "Loneliness."

72. Kang, "Humble Phone Call."

73. Hall, Dominguez, and Mihailova, "Interpersonal Media"; Hall, Pennington, and Merolla, "Which Mediated Social Interactions." Lapowsky and Benita, "Where Did All Your Zoom Friends Go?"

74. Atalay, "Twenty-First Century of Solitude."

75. Luhmann and Hawkley, "Age Differences"; Victor and Yang, "Prevalence of Loneliness."

———

76. Shin et al., "Nature of Retirement and Loneliness."

77. The homeostatic processes regulating social contact and solitude operate from an individual's typical social set point. In other words, the drive to increase or decrease social activity is in relation to what people are typically accustomed to. It's adaptive for a homeostatic system to be responsive to changing circumstances. Major life events or environmental changes can change individuals' set points. If a person's social set point becomes much lower than before, then a "high" level of social contact in an isolated period might be lower than a "low" level of social contact during a social period. The neurologists Gillian Matthews and Kay Tye's review of animal models, "Neural Mechanisms," suggests that animals that are forced to experience conditions with very low social contact behave much like humans with high trait loneliness. This is consistent with Reissmann and his colleagues' study of social interactions, "Role of State Feelings," which found that individuals' trait levels of loneliness affected how social they were in general—which reflects a low social set point. Yet everyone's daily social behavior was influenced by their previous desire to interact at earlier times in that day, which suggests a similar homeostatic system for everyone. This raises the question: How much isolation leads to a change in the set point? Matthews and Tye in their animal studies suggest that changes lasting several days—but maybe much longer—could shift a set point. To find an answer for humans, the degree of social deprivation that would have to be experimentally induced would be unethical. Thus, although the time it takes to shift a set point is unknown, it appears that (a) social contact is regulated in a homeostatic fashion, and (b) individuals at the lowest set point are those most likely to experience high trait loneliness. This suggests they are the least likely to be able to get their need to belong met. In fact, this chronic state of social deprivation leads to a higher allostatic load over time and to pernicious health outcomes (Epel, "Geroscience Agenda").

78. Stijovic et al., "Homeostatic Regulation."

79. Arpin, Mohr, and Brannan, "Having Friends."

80. Stijovic et al., "Homeostatic Regulation."

81. Hall, *Relating through Technology*, 65; Z. Wang, Tchernev, and Solloway, "Dynamic Longitudinal Examination." J. Cacioppo and Patrick, *Loneliness*, 260.

82. Jarman et al., "Examination of the Temporal Sequence"; Z. Wang, Tchernev, and Solloway, "Dynamic Longitudinal Examination."

83. Gerassi, *Talking with Sartre*, 130.

84. Camus, *Lyrical and Critical Essays*, 346.

85. Routledge et al., "Nostalgia as a Resource."

86. Zhou et al., "Counteracting Loneliness."

87. Zhou et al., "Restorative Power of Nostalgia."

88. Hoang et al., "Interventions."

89. Afifi et al., "Using Virtual Reality."

90. Petrusich, "Fragility of Life."

91. Reis, Regan, and Lyubomirsky, "Interpersonal Chemistry." Responsiveness can ease the generalized lack of safety people feel in their day-to-day lives, which is consistent with the GUTS model discussed in chapter 1. A renewed sense of safety is critical in light of scholars' contention that psychological safety is a precondition for experiencing positive affect (intra- and interpersonally) throughout the day. C. Brown and Fredrickson, "Characteristics and Consequences."

CHAPTER 5. SOCIAL INERTIA IN AN AGE OF INTERIORITY

1. Twenge, Spitzberg, and Campbell, "Less In-Person."

2. Tergesen, "Your 401(k) Isn't Enough."

3. *Economist,* "America's New Exceptionalism."

4. Atalay, "Twenty-First Century of Solitude."

5. Ibid.

6. Kun et al., "Where Did the Commute Time Go."

7. Rinderknecht et al., "Understanding the Growth."

8. Atalay, "Twenty-First Century of Solitude."

9. National Academies of Sciences, Engineering, and Medicine, *Social Isolation.*

10. Holt-Lunstad, "Major Health Implications."

11. The U.S. Department of Labor surveys between 9,000 and 14,000 Americans every year, spread out over the year, yielding a total of 210,586 days of data from 2003 to 2019, approximately evenly split between weekend days and weekdays. Sampling a similar number of days during the week and on weekends is a surveying choice by the U.S. Department of Labor. The number of days surveyed is based on the number of participants, not days. In other words, the technique doesn't attempt to capture every day over seventeen years equally. We elected to include only prepandemic measures because the pandemic disrupted both data collection and Americans' typical routines. When they're available, we supplement these analyses with pre-, during, and post-pandemic comparison studies. The categories for figures 2 and 3 were created using the following ATUS data categories: Shopping includes travel to shop; Exercise includes walking, golf, weightlifting, working out, health-related self-care, and travel to exercise; School includes homework, studying, and travel to school; Religious/volunteer activities includes services, practices, volunteering, and travel to religious or volunteer activity; Interpersonal media includes telephone calls, emails, and letters; Socializing face-to-face includes attending or hosting parties, talking or reading to household children; Child care includes playing, traveling, homework, pickups, and attending events for children; Cooking/grocery includes cleanup after cooking, travel to the grocery store, and buying food;

Housework includes lawn and garden care, household organization and planning, caring for pets, interior decoration, interior maintenance, financial management, sewing, vehicle repair, exterior cleaning, storage; Cleaning/laundry includes two codes; Grooming includes bathing and dressing and hygiene; Eating and drinking is one code; Commuting to work is one code; Working includes both primary and secondary jobs; Reading/relaxing/games/leisure includes thinking, playing games through computers and in person; TV/streaming/radio includes going to the movies.

12. Atalay, "Time Use before, during, and after"; Kroencke et al., "Well-Being"; Kuper et al., "Who Benefits."

13. Hall, *Relating through Technology*, 193.

14. Hamermesh, *Spending Time*, 80.

15. Rinderknecht et al., "Understanding the Growth."

16. Atalay, "Twenty-First Century of Solitude"; Fischer, *Still Connected*, 51–55.

17. Giacomo Vagni's 2022 study of U.K. time-use survey data showed that among couples with children, family time was linked to parents' higher subjective well-being. Specifically, time spent together was more enjoyable than time spent alone. Vagni also found that though mothers benefited from family time, their subjective well-being during family time tended to be lower than that of fathers because of inequities regarding housework. Vagni notes that the unfair division of household labor typifying many households resulted in mothers doing chores during family time, which made family time less enjoyable than it might otherwise have been if household work were more equitably distributed. Vagni, "From Me to You."

18. Atalay, "Twenty-First Century of Solitude"; Rinderknecht et al., "Solitary Leisure."

19. Hall and Liu, "Social Media Use."

20. Rinderknecht et al., "Understanding the Growth."

21. Atalay, "Twenty-First Century of Solitude"; Hall, Pennington, and Holmstrom, "Connecting through Technology."

22. Shirky, *Cognitive Surplus*, 4–29.

23. Hamermesh, *Spending Time*, 98.

24. Hall, "Price We Pay"; Hall and Liu, "Social Media Use."

25. Tay and Diener, "Needs and Subjective Well-Being."

26. Hawkley et al., "From Social Structural Factors."

27. Hall, *Relating through Technology*; Hamermesh, *Spending Time*, 77; Kuykendall, Boemerman, and Zhu, "Importance of Leisure."

28. Hamermesh, *Spending Time*, 145.

29. Hall, *Relating through Technology*, 190.

30. Hall et al., "Quality Conversation."

31. Hall, "There's No Substitute."

32. This tension between accelerating technological change, on the one hand, and the experience of inertia in our social life, on the other, is richly explored in the writing of the social theorist Hartmut Rosa in *Social Acceleration*, 22.

33. Vanden Abeele, Wolf, and Ling, "Mobile Media."

34. Vincent, *History of Solitude*, 37.

35. NCR, "How Frictionless Technology."

36. United States Bureau of Labor Statistics, "American Time Use Survey."

37. Sandstrom and Dunn, "Social Interactions."

38. Liming, *Hanging Out*, xix–xx.

39. Rinderknecht et al., "Understanding the Growth."

40. Fischer, *Still Connected*, 36; Ruddick, "End of Families."

41. Donovan et al., "Labor of Talking"; Hall et al., "Social Bandwidth."

42. Knapp et al., "Rhetoric of Goodbye."

43. Duck, *Meaningful Relationships*, 52.

44. Murthy, "We Have Become a Lonely Nation."

45. In Japan, some individuals are said to experience chronic and near total social isolation, or *hikikomori*, "to withdraw." Heavily reliant on technology—for both entertainment and communication—and having relatives, often parents, who shelter them, these individuals embody an extreme form of this social trend. Although it is unknown how many people are at this level of social isolation, some estimates were upwards of 700,000 in 2010. Kremer and Hammond, "Hikikomori."

46. Rinderknecht et al., "Understanding the Growth."

47. Allen et al., "Need to Belong."

48. There are also corollaries to be drawn with contemporary jobs and residences, which have caused many of us to lead a more sedentary lifestyle.

49. The jury is still out on the value of video chats; the evidence is mixed and inconsistent. Recent studies are complicated by pandemic-specific and remote-worker contexts, which probably function differently from purely social video calls. Hall, *Relating through Technology*, 103.

50. Epel, "Geroscience Agenda."

51. Ibid.

52. Brosschot, Verkuil, and Thayer, "Generalized Unsafety Theory."

53. Afifi, Callejas, and Harrison, "Resilience through Stress"; Bobba-Alves, Juster, and Picard, "Energetic Cost."

54. Afifi, Callejas, and Harrison, "Resilience through Stress"; Bobba-Alves, Juster, and Picard, "Energetic Cost."

55. Strazdins and Broom, "Mental Health Costs."

56. Epel, "Geroscience Agenda."

57. Afifi, Callejas, and Harrison, "Resilience through Stress."

58. Carlson et al., "Impact of the Baltimore Experience Corps"; Varma et al., "Experience Corps Baltimore."

59. Hawkley et al., "From Social Structural Factors."
60. Bobba-Alves, Juster, and Picard, "Energetic Cost."
61. Ibid.
62. Epel, "Geroscience Agenda."
63. Hawkley et al., "From Social Structural Factors."
64. Garrosa et al., "Energy Loss."
65. Hall, Mihailova, and Merolla, "Typicality and Volition."
66. Ibid.; Hall and Merolla, "Connecting Everyday Talk."
67. Snyder, "Hope Theory."

CHAPTER 6. WHEN SOCIETY ANTAGONIZES CONNECTION

1. Blakinger, *Corrections in Ink*, 39.
2. Ibid., 43.
3. Ibid., 43–44.
4. Goffman, *Asylums*, 4.
5. Ibid., 14, 21, 28, 42, 68.
6. Johansson, Borell, and Rosenberg, "Qualities of the Environment."
7. Berkman et al., "From Social Integration"; see also Blau's work on a theoretical perspective on the different levels of social structure and substructure in "Macrosociological Theory."
8. Small, *Someone to Talk To*, 159.
9. Ritzer and Goodman, in their text *Sociological Theory*, 69–70, provide a concise overview of work exploring links between agency and structure, a topic often associated with scholars such as Margaret Archer, Anthony Giddens, Pierre Bourdieu, and Jürgen Habermas.
10. Parks, *Personal Relationships*, 49.
11. Consider, for instance, George MacKerron and Susana Mourato's research for the "Mappiness Project," which indicates the affective benefits of natural environments. Alternatively, psychological research shows how natural environments can inspire a life-affirming sense of awe. MacKerron and Mourato, "Mappiness"; Anderson, Monroy, and Keltner, "Awe in Nature."
12. Imrie, " 'Lonely City' "; Klinenberg, *Palaces;* Mouratidis, "Rethinking How Built Environments."
13. Farber et al., "Social Interaction Potential"; King, *Social Chemistry*, 50–56.
14. Klein and Noenickx, "Can Gen Z."
15. Schinoff, Ashforth, and Corley, "Virtually (In)Separable."
16. Hawley, "Does Urban Density."

17. Menendian, Gambhir, and Gailes, "Roots of Structural Racism Project." It's important to note that defining and measuring regional-, city-, and community-level segregation is challenging, and different approaches have been taken. For a description of the various measures that exist and the one preferred by the Othering and Belonging Institute at UC Berkeley, please refer to their technical appendix: https://belonging.berkeley.edu/technical-appendix. Further, when researchers say that a city or community is segregated, that doesn't mean only one racial or ethnic group lives there or that residents are completely isolated from one another. Rather, it means that a residential community is less well-integrated across groups than the larger geographic areas surrounding it would lead one to expect. Thus, within more segregated residential areas and schools, cross-group interaction can occur, but its potential is restricted.

18. United States Government Accountability Office, "K–12 Education," 11.

19. In "School Choice," a striking study combining survey data and computer simulations, Kalinda Ukanwa, Aziza Jones, and Broderick Turner Jr. found that although parents often say that they value diversity in schools, they can still unwittingly perpetuate race-based school segregation owing to their differing (and often unconscious) preferences for school characteristics.

20. Cortright, "City Report"; Villalonga and Moreno, "Geography of Polarization."

21. Bishop with Cushing, *Big Sort,* 15.

22. Ibid., 298.

23. As Erza Klein points out in *Why We're Polarized,* 249–50, political polarization is not inherently bad. If one party holds a problematic viewpoint, such as an anti–civil rights stance, it's best that the other party vehemently oppose it. This is similar to the view that conflict in personal relationships can be important for identifying problems to be addressed. Polarization, however, becomes problematic when it's driven by incentives to treat others with disdain or, worse, violence. The same is true for other types of in-group solidarity, which can be more or less problematic depending on its causes and function. As scholars at UC Berkeley's Othering and Belonging Institute put it: "Certain forms of racial solidarity and community, such as an Irish festival or an Italian-American pride parade, religious services, holiday celebrations, or social gatherings are either innocuous or beneficial. But when segregation leads to the inequitable distribution of resources or access to life-enhancing goods or networks, then it is a source of great harm"; https://belonging.berkeley.edu/technical-appendix#footnote19_hjnr8or. Menendian, Gambhir, and Gailes, "Roots of Structural Racism Project."

24. There are also many nuances to the patterns we have described thus far. Residential segregation and ideological sorting are difficult things to measure and are intertwined with numerous factors, including race, ethnicity, education, and socioeconomic status. With regard to political sorting, critics of the big-sort hypothesis contend that ideological sorting, even if it's occurring across the country, has minimal

political consequences since neighbors rarely talk about politics, if they even talk at all (see Villalonga and Moreno, "Geography of Polarization"). Further, it could be argued that because people are living less and less of their lives in physical spaces and more and more of their lives in virtual ones, the influence of local communities on people's political views is minimized. But these critiques miss something important about the many functions of social interaction in communities and the realities of day-to-day life for many people in the United States. The vast majority of Americans do interact with their neighbors from time to time, and even if those interactions aren't about politics or policy, they serve important functions. What about that critique regarding Americans' mass migration to virtual spaces? The internet has changed many things about how we interact, and many people do spend a lot of time online. But that doesn't mean that online time necessarily displaces face-to-face social interaction. People can spend a lot of time online and interact face-to-face with their neighbors. Further, although it might seem that everyone is constantly glued to their screens, there are exceptions. Online time is restricted for many people because they lack or have inconsistent access to digital devices. The digital divide – another powerful structural force we could spend a lot of time discussing – has not closed for many Americans. Digital inequities persist. Many people, particularly those with low incomes, don't have reliable and stable internet access at home or through mobile devices (see Gonzales, "Contemporary US Digital Divide"; Vogel, "Digital Divide Persists"). We see, then, that face-to-face interaction, particularly in our communities, matters, and physical spaces (and the relationships developed within them) are essential factors influencing our daily moments of interaction. Villalonga and Moreno, "Geography of Polarization," 10–11; Hampton and Shin, "Disconnection More Problematic"; Read et al., "Making Stability Dependable."

25. Wasserman, "To Beat Trump."

26. Klein, *Why We're Polarized*, 42.

27. In fact, as we were finishing this book in the spring of 2023, the U.S. surgeon general, Dr. Vivek Murthy, released a report on the nation's "epidemic of loneliness and isolation" in which he emphasized some of the same points we've been making throughout this book about the benefits of social connection and our need to reinforce it. The report also underscored many of the same points (and reviewed some of the same research findings) we write about in this chapter about the economic and safety deficits caused by community-level disconnection.

28. Malawa, Gaarde, and Spellen, "Racism as a Root Cause Approach."

29. Banzhaf, Ma, and Timmins, "Environmental Justice."

30. Chetty et al., "Social Capital I"; Chetty et al., "Social Capital II." To conduct this analysis, Chetty's team analyzed data they scraped from the Facebook accounts of over 70 million users between the ages of twenty-five and forty-four.

31. Researchers of media, such as George Gerbner and his colleagues, used this same type of metaphor to describe the way media influence people's perceptions. In

their influential line of research (see "Growing Up"), they describe media effects as the accumulation of moment after moment of TV, movies, and social media that shapes, or "cultivates," how people view the world.

32. Not all neighbors are going to be trustworthy, of course, and some neighbors might simply prefer to keep to themselves. As we've discussed throughout the book, social interaction is an interdependent process, shaped by all parties involved. Trust and neighborhood belonging, moreover, are complex topics, and research on them reveals nuanced conclusions about the conditions under which they're most likely to emerge. W. Liu et al., "Bridging Mechanisms"; Stolle, Soroka, and Johnston, "When Does Diversity."

33. Aldrich, *Building Resilience*, 45–51.

34. Klinenberg, *Palaces*, 16.

35. Aldrich, "How Social Infrastructure." It's important to note that there are also drawbacks involved in the link between social capital and disaster recovery. As Aldrich argues, although social capital can help people in neighborhoods accrue resources following natural disasters, this can leave people without social capital at a distinct disadvantage. Likewise, Robert Putnam, in his influential book *Bowling Alone: The Collapse and Revival of American Community*, 21–22, argues for a nuanced understanding of social capital because, in addition to building important societally enhancing connections between people, it can also enable people in positions of power to benefit in ways that further marginalize and harm people in lower-power positions. Aldrich, *Building Resilience*, 43–44.

36. Klinenberg, *Palaces*, 18.

37. Aldrich, "How Social Infrastructure"; Klinenberg, *Palaces*.

38. Klinenberg, *Palaces*, 45.

39. Parker et al., "What Unites."

40. Murthy, "Our Epidemic of Loneliness."

41. Although we're discussing the benefits of connecting with diverse people, we're not saying that interacting with demographically similar people is somehow problematic. Research indicates that interacting with familiar others and in-group members can offer vital forms of support and solidarity, especially for people from minority or stigmatized groups. Debrosse, Thai, and Brieva, "When Skinfolk Are Kinfolk."

42. Israel, *Beyond Your Bubble*, 137.

43. Santoro and Broockman, "Promise and Pitfalls."

44. Antonoplis and John, "Who Has Different-Race Friends."

45. McGhee, *Sum of Us*, 62, 255–89.

46. Demsas, "What We Talk about."

47. Dinesen, Schaeffer, and Sønderskov, "Ethnic Diversity and Social Trust."

48. Stancato, Keltner, and Chen, "Gap between Us."

49. Glanville and Paxton, "How Do We Learn to Trust"; Laurence, Schmid, and Hewstone, "Ethnic Diversity"; Van Assche et al., "Intergroup Contact."

50. Van Assche et al., "Intergroup Contact."

51. Hässler et al., "Large-Scale Test."

52. Reimer and Sengupta, "Meta-Analysis of the 'Ironic' Effects." As Reimer and Sengupta discuss, intergroup contact might have some unexpected consequences when it comes to social change. Intergroup contact, for instance, might lead people from disadvantaged groups to feel more positively toward people from advantaged groups, while also reducing the motivation of people from disadvantaged groups to work toward social change; this latter outcome could plausibly undermine change efforts.

53. Barbee, Deal, and Gonzales, "Anti-Transgender Legislation"; Garcini et al., "No One Left Behind"; Lattanner and Hatzenbuehler, "Thwarted Belonging Needs"; Negi et al., " 'Solitude Absorbs' "; R. Smith, "Language of the Lost."

54. Sigman, "Handling the Discontinuous Aspects"; Sillars and Vangelisti, "Communication"; K. Tracy, *Everyday Talk.*

55. Blumer, *Symbolic Interactionism,* 1–20; Cooley, *Human Nature,* 147–53; Mead, *On Social Psychology,* 203–8.

56. Duck and Pittman, "Social and Personal"; Duck and Pond, "Friends, Romans, Countrymen"; Duck, *Meaningful Relationships,* 141–43.

57. Carl and Duck, "Do Things"; Duck, *Meaningful Relationships,* 32, 149.

58. Goffman, *Interaction Ritual,* 5.

59. Psychological research, especially work by William Swann and his colleagues on self-verification theory, shows that we often seek to verify our viewpoints in our interactions with others. See also scholarship on self-verification and belongingness processes, such as the work by Hillman and his colleagues. Swann, Stein-Seroussi, and Giesler, "People Self-Verify"; Hillman, Fowlie, and MacDonald, "Social Verification Theory."

60. Sigman, "Relationships and Communication."

61. Goffman, *Presentation of Self,* 2, 4.

62. S. Tracy and Trethewey, "Fracturing the Real-Self."

63. Books by Matthew O. Jackson and Marissa King provide numerous research-based insights about the nature and effects of homophily in social networks. Jackson, *Human Network,* 97–106; King, *Social Chemistry,* 88–91.

64. Able and Clarke, *Compassion Project,* 59, 139; see also Murthy, *Together.*

65. Able and Clarke, *Compassion Project,* 70–74.

66. Wilson, "Fighting Isolation."

67. Able and Clarke, *Compassion Project,* 79.

68. Ibid., 69.

69. Ibid., 12.

70. Rosenblum, "Do You Look."

71. Ibid.

72. Ibid.

CHAPTER 7. LIFE IN A SOCIAL BIOME

1. Quaglia, "How Your Microbiome"; Yong, *I Contain Multitudes*, 10.

2. Pennisi, "Meet the Psychobiome."

3. Foster, Rinaman, and Cryan, "Stress & the Gut-Brain Axis," 131; Norton, "Are Your Bacteria"; Rees, Bosch, and Douglas, "Microbiome Challenges"; Ward, "Microbiology."

4. Norton, "Are Your Bacteria."

5. Chang, Wei, and Hashimoto, "Brain–Gut–Microbiota"; Yue et al., "Microbiota-Gut–Brain"; Morais, Schreiber, and Mazmanian, "Gut Microbiota–Brain Axis"; Yong, *I Contain Multitudes*, 19–20.

6. Yong, *I Contain Multitudes*, 18.

7. Foster, Rinaman, and Cryan, "Stress & the Gut-Brain Axis."

8. Sillars and Vangelisti, "Communication."

9. Hall and Merolla, "Connecting Everyday Talk"; Merolla, Hall, and Bernhold, "Perseverative Cognition." The social biome concept was also inspired by the writing of many scholars (a number of whom we've cited throughout the book). Communication theorists such as Walter Carl and Steve Duck, for instance, advocated for a conceptualization of community as a "network of real and actively connected relationships." They further contended that "it is this matrix of relationships that serves as the grounding for our knowledge of the world and our place and value in it." Such ideas emphasize how our lives are lived out in moments of interaction within our various communities. Carl and Duck, "How to Do Things," 25. Other communication theorists, such as Stuart Sigman, have also written about the importance of conceptualizing phenomena, such as identity, as "a moment-by-moment creation of communication"; Sigman, *A Perspective on Social Communication*, 103. The research and writing of psychologists, such as Barbara Fredrickson, further highlight the complexity and well-being benefits of both receiving and enacting "micro-moments" of connection across relationship types; Fredrickson, *Love 2.0*, 30.

10. C. Brown and Fredrickson, "Characteristics and Consequences"; Fredrickson, *Love 2.0*, 17.

11. Carl and Duck, "How to Do Things."

12. Hall and Merolla, "Connecting Everyday Talk." The survey item we mentioned comes from the widely used life-satisfaction measure developed by Ed Diener, Robert A. Emmons, Randy J. Larsen, and Sharon Griffin; Diener et al., "The Satisfaction with Life Scale."

13. Lyubomirsky and Layous, "How Do Simple Positive Activities."

14. Another example is leisure time. Nearly half of Americans don't have enough of it. This lack is a barrier to relaxing and enjoying life. But having too much leisure time is no good, either; people tend to be unhappy when they have nothing to do. The good life seems to involve having between two and five hours of time each day to do as you please. After five hours, more leisure time seems less valuable. Sharif, Mogilner, and Hershfield, "Having Too Little."

15. Ren, Stavrova, and Loh, "Nonlinear Effect"; Stavrova and Ren, "Is More Always Better?"; Luo, Macdonald, and Hülür, "Not 'The More the Merrier.' "

16. Stavrova and Ren, "Is More Always Better?"

17. Hall, "Regulation of Social Interaction"; Helliwell and Huang, "Comparing the Happiness Effects"; Horst and Coffé, "How Friendship Network Characteristics."

18. Hampton, Lu, and Shin, "Digital Media"; Hobfoll, *Stress, Culture,* 208; Stavrova and Ren, "Is More Always Better?"

19. Hall, "Energy, Episode"; Sandstrom and Dunn, "Social Interactions"; Quoidbach et al., "Happiness and Social Behavior."

20. Baumeister and Robson, "Belongingness and the Modern Schoolchild."

21. Sandstrom and Dunn, "Social Interactions."

22. Epley and Schroeder, "Mistakenly Seeking Solitude."

23. Schroeder, Lyons, and Epley, "Hello, Stranger?"

24. Sandstrom and Boothby, "Why Do People Avoid Talking to Strangers"; Schroeder, Lyons, and Epley, "Hello, Stranger?" Also of note, personality features, introversion/extraversion in particular, don't appear to moderate these findings.

25. Algoe, "Find, Remind, and Bind."

26. Mehl et al., "Eavesdropping on Happiness," 540.

27. Milek et al., " 'Eavesdropping on Happiness' Revisited."

28. Quoidbach et al., "Happiness and Social Behavior."

29. Gunaydin et al., "Minimal Social Interactions."

30. It's especially important also to note that small talk and chitchat with strangers are not valued to the same extent around the world. Nilsson, "Why Swedes Don't Speak." Further, research on the benefits of "minimal social interactions" for enhanced well-being and belonging is limited outside the United States and Europe. (See, however, Itaru Ishiguro, "Minimal Social Interactions"; and Gunaydin et al., "Minimal Social Interactions," for examples of such work.)

31. Hall and Merolla, "Connecting Everyday Talk."

32. Hall et al., "Quality Conversation."

33. Hall, "Energy, Episode."

34. See also H. Liu, Xie, and Lou, "Everyday Social Interactions"; Sun, Harris, and Vazire, "Is Well-Being Associated."

35. Hall et al., "Quality Conversation."

36. Reis et al., "Daily Well-Being"; Wheeler, Reis, and Nezlek, "Loneliness."

37. Hall et al., "Quality Conversation"; Merolla, Otmar, and Salehuddin, "Past Relational Experiences"; Reis, Regan, and Lyubomirsky, "Interpersonal Chemistry."

38. Smith and Christakis, "Social Networks."

39. Andersson, "Dispositional Optimism."

40. Atir, Wald, and Epley, "Talking with Strangers."

41. Collins et al., "Relational Diversity"; Shor and Roelfs, "Social Contact Frequency"; Stavrova and Ren, "Is More Always Better."

42. Hirsch and Clark, "Multiple Paths?"

43. Hall and Merolla, "Connecting Everyday Talk"; Hall, Mihailova, and Merolla, "Typicality and Volition"; Merolla, Otmar, and Salehuddin, "Past Relational Experiences." Social scientific research of well-being suggests the benefits of choice are apparent no matter which path to well-being we're pursuing, whether it's gratitude, exercise, eating well, meditation, or connection. Sustainable changes are more likely to happen if (a) the activity is effective, (b) people invest energy, and (c) people are persistent (Lyubomirsky et al., "Becoming Happier"; Lyubomirsky and Layous, "How Do Simple Positive Activities"; Sheldon and Lyubomirsky, "Achieving Sustainable Gains"). The decision to act (and keep acting) seems to matter quite a bit in determining whether an intervention works.

44. Hall and Merolla, "Connecting Everyday Talk."

45. Uziel and Schmidt-Barad, "Choice Matters."

46. Tse, Lay, and Nakamura, "Autonomy Matters."

47. Friedman and Martin, *Longevity Project*, 168; Kuper et al., "Who Benefits."

48. There are, however, still very real challenges regarding stable and dependable access to digital technologies for many people. Read et al., "Making Stability Dependable."

49. Hall and Woszidlo, "Families Communicating through Technology"; Mendez Murillo and Kam, "Exploring How Culture"; Merolla, "Relational Maintenance and Noncopresence"; Valdez et al., "Enactment of Relational Maintenance."

50. Hall, *Relating through Technology*, 193.

51. Snap, "Friendship Report 2020."

52. Achterhof et al., "Adolescents' Real-Time"; Kroencke et al., "Well-Being."

53. Hall, Pennington, and Merolla, "Which Mediated Social Interactions."

54. Hall and Liu, "Social Media Use."

55. Burnholt et al., "Technological-Mediated Communication"; Hall, *Relating through Technology;* Hall, Pennington, and Holmstrom, "Connecting through Technology"; Teo et al., "Does Mode of Contact."

56. Hall, "Energy, Episode."

57. Methot et al., "Office Chitchat."

58. Bernstein et al., "Social Interactions."

59. Hall, "Energy, Episode"; Hall and Merolla, "Connecting Everyday Talk."

60. Binder, Roberts, and Sutcliffe, "Closeness, Loneliness, Support."

61. Hall et al., "Social Bandwidth."

62. Hall and Merolla, "Connecting Everyday Talk."

63. Nguyen, Ryan, and Deci, "Solitude as an Approach"; Uziel, "Language of Being Alone."

64. Garrosa et al., "Energy Loss."

65. Vincent, *History of Solitude*, 186.

66. Nguyen, Ryan, and Deci, "Solitude as an Approach."

67. Ross, Akgün, and Campbell, "Benefits of Solitude"; Tse, Lay, and Nakamura, "Autonomy Matters"; Uziel and Schmidt-Barad, "Choice Matters."

68. Campbell and Ross, "Re-Conceptualizing Solitude."

69. Jiang, Li, and Chung, "Living Alone."

70. United States Census Bureau, "Census Bureau Releases."

71. Murthy, *Together*, 240.

72. Atir, Wald, and Epley, "Talking with Strangers"; Schroeder, Lyons, and Epley, "Hello, Stranger?"

CHAPTER 8. HOPE IN OTHERS

1. Dickens et al., "Interventions"; Gardiner, Geldenhuys, and Gott, "Interventions to Reduce Social Isolation."

2. Reis et al., "Sociability Matters," 241–50.

3. Brenan, "Americans Less Optimistic"; Hickman et al., "Climate Anxiety."

4. Lauter, "Is Politics Making People Sick?"

5. Snyder, "Hypothesis," 4.

6. Eliott, "What Have We"; Snyder, Lopez, and Pedrotti, *Positive Psychology*.

7. Fremstedal, "Kierkegaard on Hope," 87; Snyder, "Hypothesis," 4.

8. Snyder, "Hope Theory"; Stotland, *Psychology of Hope*.

9. Snyder, Cheavens, and Michael, "Hope Theory," 105.

10. McDermott and Snyder, *Making Hope Happen*, 6.

11. Shimshock and Le, "Having the Will"; Snyder, "Hope Theory."

12. McDermott and Snyder, *Making Hope Happen*, 12–13.

13. Snyder, "Hope Theory."

14. Snyder and his colleagues, in "Hope Theory," contend that pathways and agency thinking are completely learned. It is plausible, however, that there's a genetic component to hope as well; see, for instance, research examining potential genetic bases for the related construct of optimism: Schulman, Keith, and Seligman, "Is Optimism Heritable?" In any case, learning through social interaction appears to be an essential part of hope development.

15. Curry et al., "Role of Hope."

16. Hackbarth et al., "Natural Disasters."

17. Peterson and Byron, "Exploring the Role of Hope."

18. Merolla, Bernhold, and Peterson, "Pathways to Connection." See also Andrew J. Howell and Denise J. Larsen, *Understanding Other-Oriented Hope,* for multidisciplinary insights into hope focused on other people.

19. Merolla, Otmar, and Neubauer, "Responsiveness."

20. McGeer, "Art of Good Hope," 125.

21. Ibid., 108.

22. Able and Clarke, *Compassion Project,* 144.

23. Snyder and Feldman, "Hope for the Many."

24. Hicks, *Dignity;* Jacobson, "Taxonomy of Dignity."

25. Jacobson, "Taxonomy of Dignity," 3.

26. McGeer, "Art of Good Hope." It's also important to acknowledge that the link we're discussing between hope and responsiveness doesn't obligate us to be responsive to others. Nor should it lead us to the conclusion that, in the interest of fostering hope in others, we should simply agree with people and blindly support any goals they have. That's not what responsiveness is all about. Responsiveness, as Reis and his colleagues discuss in "Sociability Matters," 252, supports rather than evades accountability in relationships. As we state in chapter 2, caring for, supporting, and validating someone can, and often must, occur while we're also challenging them, holding them accountable, and even persuading them to change their views. When people feel generally cared for and respected, they will feel less threatened and defensive when they're called out for bad behavior.

27. Hicks, *Dignity,* 6.

28. Watzlawick, *Ultra-Solutions,* 48.

29. Ibid., 51.

30. Brosschot, Verkuil, and Thayer, "Generalized Unsafety Theory"; Hari, *Stolen Focus,* 150–51, 176, 271.

31. Casas, Benuto, and Newlands, "Educational Experiences"; Kam et al., "Communicating Allyship"; Nienhusser and Oshio, "Postsecondary Education Access." These three articles explore various challenges undocumented students face in higher education and society in general. They also examine the complex roles of the Deferred Action for Childhood Arrivals (DACA) program in students' experiences, particularly in regard to higher education.

32. See also Christine S. Davis, *Communicating Hope,* on the communicative construction of hope in families, especially in mental health-care contexts, as well as Jaklin Eliott and Ian Olver, "Discursive Properties," on communicative aspects of hope among patients of an oncology care clinic.

33. Kam and Merolla, "Hope Communication." The data analyzed for this project were collected by Kam as part of her ongoing research line on understanding the challenges that immigrant families, especially those with undocumented family members, face, as well as families' sources of strength and thriving.

34. Importantly, these results were above and beyond differences related to a series of control variables, including students' high school GPAs and whether family members attended college.

35. Chetty et al., "Social Capital I"; Chetty et al., "Social Capital II."

36. Johann Hari, *Stolen Focus*, 151–55, offers an excellent discussion of the cruel optimism concept in regard to the difficulties of reducing stress in our lives that results from the powerful structural constraints that exist.

37. Merolla and Kam, "Parental Hope Communication."

38. Fredrickson and Joiner, "Reflections on Positive Emotions," 195.

39. Demiray, Mehl, and Martin, "Conversational Time Travel"; Killingsworth and Gilbert, "A Wandering Mind."

40. Finnbogadóttir and Berntsen, "Involuntary and Voluntary."

41. Stafford and Daly, "Conversational Memory."

42. Cooke-Jackson and Rubinsky, "Deeply Rooted"; Knapp, Stohl, and Reardon, " 'Memorable Messages' "; Otmar and Merolla, "Early Relational Exclusion."

43. Hicks, *Dignity*, 53; Iyadurai et al., "Intrusive Memories"; Visser, "Why Do Certain Moments."

44. Iyadurai et al., "Intrusive Memories."

45. Snyder, Cheavens, and Michael, "Hope Theory."

46. Baxter et al., "Exploring the Relationship"; Munoz, Pharris, and Hellman, "Linear Model."

47. McDermott and Snyder, *Making Hope Happen*.

48. Merolla, Beck, and Jones, "Memorable Messages."

BIBLIOGRAPHY

Able, Julian, and Lindsay Clarke. *The Compassion Project: A Case for Hope & Humankindness from the Town That Beat Loneliness.* London: Aster, 2020.

Achterhof, Robin, Olivia J. Kirtley, Maude Schneider, Noëmi Hagemann, Karlijn S. F. M. Hermans, Anu P. Hiekkaranta, Aleksandra Lecei, Ginette Lafit, and Inez Myin-Germeys. "Adolescents' Real-Time Social and Affective Experiences of Online and Face-to-Face Interactions." *Computers in Human Behavior* 129 (April 2022): 107159. https://doi.org/10.1016/j.chb.2021.107159.

Afifi, Tamara D., Michelle Acevedo Callejas, and Kathryn Harrison. "Resilience through Stress: The Theory of Resilience and Relational Load." In *The Oxford Handbook of the Physiology of Interpersonal Communication,* edited by Lindsey S. Aloia, Amanda Denes, and John P. Crowley, 210–34. New York: Oxford University Press, 2020. https://doi.org/10.1093/oxfordhb/978019067 9446.013.11.

Afifi, Tamara D., Nancy Collins, Kyle Rand, Chris Otmar, Allison Mazur, Norah E. Dunbar, Ken Fujiwara, Kathryn Harrison, and Rebecca Logsdon. "Using Virtual Reality to Improve the Quality of Life of Older Adults with Cognitive Impairments and Their Family Members Who Live at a Distance." *Health Communication* 38, no. 9 (2022): 1904–15. https://doi.org/10.1080/1041 0236.2022.2040170.

Afifi, Tamara D., Anne F. Merrill, and Shardé Davis. "The Theory of Resilience and Relational Load." *Personal Relationships* 23, no. 4 (December 2016): 663–83. https://doi.org/10.1111/pere.12159.

Ainsworth, Mary S. "Attachments beyond Infancy." *American Psychologist* 44, no. 4 (1989): 709–16. https://doi.org/10.1037/0003-066X.44.4.709.

Alberts, Jess K., Christina G. Yoshimura, Michael Rabby, and Rose Loschiavo. "Mapping the Topography of Couples' Daily Conversation." *Journal of Social and Personal Relationships* 22, no. 3 (June 2005): 299–322. https://doi.org/10.1177/0265407505050941.

Aldrich, Daniel P. *Building Resilience: Social Capital in Post-Disaster Recovery.* Chicago: University of Chicago Press, 2012.

——. "How Social Infrastructure Saves Lives: A Quantitative Analysis of Japan's 3/11 Disasters." *Japanese Journal of Political Science* 24, no. 1 (March 2023): 30–40. https://doi.org/10.1017/S1468109922000366.

Algoe, Sara B. "Find, Remind, and Bind: The Functions of Gratitude in Everyday Relationships." *Social and Personality Psychology Compass* 6, no. 6 (2012): 455–69. https://doi.org/10.1111/j.1751-9004.2012.00439.x.

Allen, Kelly-Ann, DeLeon L. Gray, Roy F. Baumeister, and Mark R. Leary. "The Need to Belong: A Deep Dive into the Origins, Implications, and Future of a Foundational Construct." *Educational Psychology Review* 34, no. 2 (June 2022): 1133–56. https://doi.org/10.1007/s10648-021-09633-6.

Anderson, Craig L., Maria Monroy, and Dacher Keltner. "Awe in Nature Heals: Evidence from Military Veterans, At-Risk Youth, and College Students." *Emotion* 18, no. 8 (2018): 1195–1202. https://doi.org/10.1037/emo0000442.

Andersson, Matthew A. "Dispositional Optimism and the Emergence of Social Network Diversity." *Sociological Quarterly* 53, no. 1 (2012): 92–115. https://doi.org/10.1111/j.1533-8525.2011.01227.x.

Antonoplis, Stephen, and Oliver P. John. "Who Has Different-Race Friends, and Does It Depend on Context? Openness (to Other), but Not Agreeableness, Predicts Lower Racial Homophily in Friendship Networks." *Journal of Personality and Social Psychology* 122, no. 5 (2022): 894–919. https://doi.org/10.1037/pspp0000413.

Arpin, Sarah N., Cynthia D. Mohr, and Debi Brannan. "Having Friends and Feeling Lonely: A Daily Process Examination of Transient Loneliness, Socialization, and Drinking Behavior." *Personality and Social Psychology Bulletin* 41, no. 5 (May 2015): 615–28. https://doi.org/10.1177/0146167215569722.

Arrigo, Bruce A., and Jennifer Leslie Bullock. "The Psychological Effects of Solitary Confinement on Prisoners in Supermax Units: Reviewing What We Know and Recommending What Should Change." *International Journal of Offender Therapy and Comparative Criminology* 52, no. 6 (December 2008): 622–40. https://doi.org/10.1177/0306624X07309720.

Atalay, Enghin. "Time Use before, during, and after the Pandemic." *Working Papers of the Federal Reserve Bank, Philadelphia,* WP432 (2023). https://www.philadelphiafed.org/-/media/frbp/assets/economy/articles/economic-in-

sights/2023/q4/eiq423-time-use-before-during-and-after-the-pandemic.
pdf.

———. "A Twenty-First Century of Solitude? Time Alone and Together in the United States." *Working Papers of the Federal Reserve Bank, Philadelphia*, WP22-11 (2022). https://www.philadelphiafed.org/-/media/frbp/assets/working-papers/2022/wp22-11.pdf.

Atir, Stav, Kristina A. Wald, and Nicholas Epley. "Talking with Strangers Is Surprisingly Informative." *Proceedings of the National Academy of Sciences* 119, no. 34 (August 2022): e2206992119. https://doi.org/10.1073/pnas.220 6992119.

Bahns, Angela J., Christian S. Crandall, Omri Gillath, and Kristopher J. Preacher. "Similarity in Relationships as Niche Construction: Choice, Stability, and Influence within Dyads in a Free Choice Environment." *Journal of Personality and Social Psychology* 112, no. 2 (2017): 329–55. https://doi.org/10.1037/pspp0000088.

Banzhaf, Spencer, Lala Ma, and Christopher Timmins. "Environmental Justice: The Economics of Race, Place, and Pollution." *Journal of Economic Perspectives* 33, no. 1 (February 2019): 185–208. https://doi.org/10.1257/jep.33.1.185.

Barbee, Harry, Cameron Deal, and Gilbert Gonzales. "Anti-Transgender Legislation—A Public Health Concern for Transgender Youth." *JAMA Pediatrics* 176, no. 2 (February 2022): 125–26. https://doi.org/10.1001/jamapediatrics.2021.4483.

Barge, J. Kevin. "Hope, Communication, and Community Building." *Southern Communication Journal* 69, no. 1 (December 2003): 63–81. https://doi.org/10.1080/10417940309373279.

Barzeva, Stefania A., Jennifer S. Richards, René Veenstra, Wim H. J. Meeus, and Albertine J. Oldehinkel. "Quality over Quantity: A Transactional Model of Social Withdrawal and Friendship Development in Late Adolescence." *Social Development* 31, no. 1 (February 2022): 126–46. https://doi.org/10.1111/sode.12530.

Baumeister, Roy F., and Mark R. Leary. "The Need to Belong: Desire for Interpersonal Attachments as a Fundamental Human Motivation." *Psychological Bulletin* 117, no. 3 (1995): 497–529. https://doi.org/10.1037/0033-2909.117.3.497.

Baumeister, Roy F., and Davina A. Robson. "Belongingness and the Modern Schoolchild: On Loneliness, Socioemotional Health, Self-Esteem, Evolutionary Mismatch, Online Sociality, and the Numbness of Rejection." *Australian Journal of Psychology* 73, no. 1 (January 2021): 103–11. https://doi.org/10.1080/00 049530.2021.1877573.

BIBLIOGRAPHY

Bavelas, Janet B., Linda Coates, and Trudy Johnson. "Listeners as Co-Narrators." *Journal of Personality and Social Psychology* 79, no. 6 (2000): 941–52. https://doi.org/10.1037/0022-3514.79.6.941.

Baxter, Leslie A. "Dialectical Contradictions in Relationship Development." *Journal of Social and Personal Relationships* 7, no. 1 (February 1990): 69–88. https://doi.org/10.1177/0265407590071004.

———. "Interpersonal Communication as Dialogue: A Response to the 'Social Approaches' Forum." *Communication Theory* 2, no. 4 (November 1992): 330–37. https://doi.org/10.1111/j.1468-2885.1992.tb00048.x.

Baxter, Leslie A., and Barbara M. Montgomery. *Relating: Dialogues and Dialectics.* New York: Guilford, 1996.

Baxter, Michael A., Eden J. Hemming, Heather C. McIntosh, and Chan M. Hellman. "Exploring the Relationship between Adverse Childhood Experiences and Hope." *Journal of Child Sexual Abuse* 26, no. 8 (2017): 948–56. https://doi.org/10.1080/10538712.2017.1365319.

Berkman, Lisa F., Thomas Glass, Ian Brissette, and Teresa E. Seeman. "From Social Integration to Health: Durkheim in the New Millennium." *Social Science & Medicine* 51, no. 6 (September 2000): 843–57. https://doi.org/10.1016/S0277-9536(00)00065-4.

Bernstein, Michael J., Andreas B. Neubauer, Jacob A. Benfield, Lindsey Potter, and Joshua M. Smyth. "Within-Person Effects of Inclusion and Exclusion on Well-Being in Daily Life." *Personal Relationships* 28, no. 4 (2021): 940–60. https://doi.org/10.1111/pere.12399.

Bernstein, Michael J., Matthew J. Zawadzki, Vanessa Juth, Jacob A. Benfield, and Joshua M. Smyth. "Social Interactions in Daily Life: Within-Person Associations between Momentary Social Experiences and Psychological and Physical Health Indicators." *Journal of Social and Personal Relationships* 35, no. 3 (March 2018): 372–94. https://doi.org/10.1177/0265407517691366.

Binder, Jens F., Sam G. B. Roberts, and Alistair G. Sutcliffe. "Closeness, Loneliness, Support: Core Ties and Significant Ties in Personal Communities." *Social Networks* 34, no. 2 (May 2012): 206–14. https://doi.org/10.1016/j.socnet.2011.12.001.

Bishop, Bill, with Robert G. Cushing. *The Big Sort: Why the Clustering of Like-Minded America Is Tearing Us Apart.* Boston: Houghton Mifflin, 2008.

Blakinger, Keri. *Corrections in Ink: A Memoir.* New York: St. Martin's Press, 2022.

Blau, Peter M. "A Macrosociological Theory of Social Structure." *American Journal of Sociology* 83, no. 1 (1977): 26–54.

Blumer, Herbert. *Symbolic Interactionism: Perspective and Method.* Berkeley: University of California Press, 1969.

Bobba-Alves, Natalia, Robert-Paul Juster, and Martin Picard. "The Energetic Cost of Allostasis and Allostatic Load." *Psychoneuroendocrinology* 146 (2022): 105951. https://doi.org/10.1016/j.psyneuen.2022.105951.

Bodie, Graham D., Kellie St. Cyr, Michelle Pence, Michael Rold, and James Honeycutt. "Listening Competence in Initial Interactions I: Distinguishing between What Listening Is and What Listeners Do." *International Journal of Listening* 26, no. 1 (January 2012): 1–28. https://doi.org/10.1080/10904018.2012.639645.

Boland, Julie E., Pedro Fonseca, Ilana Mermelstein, and Myles Williamson. "Zoom Disrupts the Rhythm of Conversation." *Journal of Experimental Psychology: General* 151, no. 6 (June 2022): 1272–82. https://doi.org/10.1037/xge0001150.

Boothby, Erica J., Gus Cooney, Gillian M. Sandstrom, and Margaret S. Clark. "The Liking Gap in Conversations: Do People Like Us More Than We Think?" *Psychological Science* 29, no. 11 (November 2018): 1742–56. https://doi.org/10.1177/0956797618783714.

Bowker, Anne. "Predicting Friendship Stability during Early Adolescence." *Journal of Early Adolescence* 24, no. 2 (2004): 85–112. https://doi.org/10.1177/0272431603262666.

Brenan, Megan. "Americans Less Optimistic about Next Generation's Future." Gallup Organization, October 25, 2022. https://news.gallup.com/poll/403760/americans-less-optimistic-next-generation-future.aspx.

Brosschot, Jos F., Bart Verkuil, and Julian F. Thayer. "Generalized Unsafety Theory of Stress: Unsafe Environments and Conditions, and the Default Stress Response." *International Journal of Environmental Research and Public Health* 15, no. 3 (March 2018). https://www.ncbi.nlm.nih.gov/pmc/articles/PMC5877009/.

Brown, Brené. "Listening to Shame." *TED: Ideas Worth Spreading,* March 2012. https://www.ted.com/talks/brene_brown_listening_to_shame.

Brown, Casey L., and Barbara L. Fredrickson. "Characteristics and Consequences of Co-Experienced Positive Affect: Understanding the Origins of Social Skills, Social Bonds, and Caring, Healthy Communities." *Current Opinion in Behavioral Sciences* 39 (June 2021): 58–63. https://doi.org/10.1016/j.cobeha.2021.02.002.

Bryson, Bill. *A Short History of Nearly Everything.* New York: Crown, 2004.

Burger, Jerry M. "Individual Differences in Preference for Solitude." *Journal of Research in Personality* 29, no. 1 (1995): 85–108. https://doi.org/10.1006/jrpe.1995.1005.

Burnholt, V., G. Windle, M. Gott, and D. J. Morgan. "Technology-Mediated Communication in Familial Relationships: Moderated-Mediation Models of Isolation and Loneliness." *Gerontologist* 60, no. 7 (2020): 1202–12. https://doi.org/10.1093/geront/gnaa040.

Burns, Holly. "How to Nurse an Oversharing Hangover." *New York Times,* September 16, 2022, sec. Well. https://www.nytimes.com/2022/09/16/ well/mind/vulnerability-hangover-shame-spiral.html.

Cacioppo, John T., and Stephanie Cacioppo. "Loneliness in the Modern Age: An Evolutionary Theory of Loneliness (ETL)." In *Advances in Experimental Social Psychology,* vol. 58, edited by James M. Olson, 127–97. San Diego: Elsevier Academic Press, 2018.

Cacioppo, John T., Stephanie Cacioppo, Steven W. Cole, John P. Capitanio, Luc Goossens, and Dorret I. Boomsma. "Loneliness across Phylogeny and a Call for Comparative Studies and Animal Models." *Perspectives on Psychological Science* 10, no. 2 (March 2015): 202–12. https://doi.org/10.1177/174569161 4564876.

Cacioppo, John T., and Louise C. Hawkley. "Loneliness." In *Handbook of Individual Differences in Social Behavior,* edited by Mark R. Leary and Rick H. Hoyle, 227–40. New York: Guilford, 2009.

Cacioppo, John T., and William Patrick. *Loneliness: Human Nature and the Need for Social Connection.* New York: W. W. Norton, 2008.

Cacioppo, Stephanie, Munirah Bangee, Stephen Balogh, Carlos Cardenas-Iniguez, Pamela Qualter, and John T. Cacioppo. 2016. "Loneliness and Implicit Attention to Social Threat: A High-Performance Electrical Neuroimaging Study." *Cognitive Neuroscience* 7 (1–4): 138–59. https://doi.org/10.1080/17 588928.2015.1070136.

Cameron, C. Daryl, Cendri A. Hutcherson, Amanda M. Ferguson, Julian A. Scheffer, Eliana Hadjiandreou, and Michael Inzlicht. "Empathy Is Hard Work: People Choose to Avoid Empathy Because of Its Cognitive Costs." *Journal of Experimental Psychology: General* 148, no. 6 (2019): 962–76. https://doi. org/10.1037/xge0000595.

Campa, Mary I. "Developmental Trends and Bonding Milestones: From Parents to Partners." In *Human Bonding: The Science of Affectional Ties,* edited by Cindy Hazan and Mary I. Campa, 74–100. New York: Guilford, 2013.

Campbell, Scott W., and Morgan Q. Ross. "Re-Conceptualizing Solitude in the Digital Era: From 'Being Alone' to 'Noncommunication.'" *Communication Theory* 32, no. 3 (August 2022): 387–406. https://doi.org/10.1093/ct/ qtab021.

Camus, Albert. *Lyrical and Critical Essays.* Edited by Philip Thody. Translated by Ellen Conroy Kennedy. 1968; reprint, New York: Vintage, 1970.

Carl, Walter J., and Steve Duck. "How to Do Things with Relationships . . . and How Relationships Do Things with Us." *Annals of the International Communication Association* 28, no. 1 (January 2004): 1–35. https://doi.org/10.1080/238089 85.2004.11679031.

Carlson, Michelle C., Julie H. Kuo, Yi-Fang Chuang, Vijay R. Varma, Greg Harris, Marilyn S. Albert, Kirk I. Erickson, et al. "Impact of the Baltimore Experience Corps Trial on Cortical and Hippocampal Volumes." *Alzheimer's & Dementia* 11, no. 11 (2015): 1340–48. https://doi.org/10.1016/j.jalz.2014.12.005.

Carmichael, Cheryl L., Harry T. Reis, and Paul R. Duberstein. "In Your 20s It's Quantity, in Your 30s It's Quality: The Prognostic Value of Social Activity across 30 Years of Adulthood." *Psychology and Aging* 30, no. 1 (2015): 95–105. https://doi.org/10.1037/pag0000014.

Carter, C. S., and E. B. Keverne. "The Neurobiology of Social Affiliation and Pair Bonding." In *Hormones, Brain and Behavior,* edited by Donald W. Pfaff, Arthur P. Arnold, Susan E. Fahrbach, Anne M. Etgen, and Robert T. Rubin, 299–337. San Diego: Academic Press, 2002. https://doi.org/10.1016/B978-012532104-4/50006-8.

Casas, Jena B., Lorraine T. Benuto, and Rory Newlands. "The Educational Experiences of DACA Recipients." *Journal of Latinos and Education* 20, no. 2 (April 2021): 120–35. https://doi.org/10.1080/15348431.2019.1568250.

Caughlin, John P. "A Multiple Goals Theory of Personal Relationships: Conceptual Integration and Program Overview." *Journal of Social and Personal Relationships* 27, no. 6 (September 2010): 824–48. https://doi.org/10.1177/0265407510373262.

Cegala, Donald J. "Affective and Cognitive Manifestations of Interaction Involvement during Unstructured and Competitive Interactions." *Communication Monographs* 51, no. 4 (December 1984): 320–38. https://doi.org/10.1080/03637758409390205.

Chang, Lijia, Yan Wei, and Kenji Hashimoto. "Brain–Gut–Microbiota Axis in Depression: A Historical Overview and Future Directions." *Brain Research Bulletin* 182 (May 2022): 44–56. https://doi.org/10.1016/j.brainresbull.2022.02.004.

Chetty, Raj, Matthew O. Jackson, Theresa Kuchler, Johannes Stroebel, Nathaniel Hendren, Robert B. Fluegge, Sara Gong, et al. "Social Capital I: Measurement and Associations with Economic Mobility." *Nature* 608, no. 7921 (August 2022): 108–21. https://doi.org/10.1038/s41586-022-04996-4.

——. "Social Capital II: Determinants of Economic Connectedness." *Nature* 608, no. 7921 (August 2022): 122–34. https://doi.org/10.1038/s41586-022-04997-3.

Cheung, Elaine O., Wendi L. Gardner, and Jason F. Anderson. "Emotionships: Examining People's Emotion-Regulation Relationships and Their Consequences for Well-Being." *Social Psychological and Personality Science* 6, no. 4 (2015): 407–14. https://doi.org/10.1177/1948550614564223.

Clark, Herbert H., and Jean E. Fox Tree. "Using *Uh* and *Um* in Spontaneous Speaking." *Cognition* 84, no. 1 (May 2002): 73–111. https://doi.org/10.1016/S0010-0277(02)00017-3.

Clark, Margaret S., Judson Mills, and Martha C. Powell. "Keeping Track of Needs in Communal and Exchange Relationships." *Journal of Personality and Social Psychology* 51, no. 2 (1986): 333–38. https://doi.org/10.1037/0022-3514.51.2.333.

Cohn, Michael A., and Barbara L. Fredrickson. "Beyond the Moment, beyond the Self: Shared Ground between Selective Investment Theory and the Broaden-and-Build Theory of Positive Emotions." *Psychological Inquiry* 17, no. 1 (2006): 39–44.

Collins, Hanne K., Serena F. Hagerty, Jordi Quoidbach, Michael I. Norton, and Alison Wood Brooks. "Relational Diversity in Social Portfolios Predicts Well-Being." *Proceedings of the National Academy of Sciences* 119, no. 43 (October 2022): e2120668119. https://doi.org/10.1073/pnas.2120668119.

Collins, Nancy L., and Lynn Carol Miller. "Self-Disclosure and Liking: A Meta-Analytic Review." *Psychological Bulletin* 116, no. 3 (1994): 457–75. https://doi.org/10.1037/0033-2909.116.3.457.

Collins, Randall. "Emotional Energy as the Common Denominator of Rational Action." *Rationality and Society* 5, no. 2 (1993): 203–30. https://doi.org/10.1177/1043463193005002005.

Cooke-Jackson, Angela, and Valerie Rubinsky. "Deeply Rooted in Memories: Toward a Comprehensive Overview of 30 Years of Memorable Message Literature." *Health Communication* 33, no. 4 (April 2018): 409–22. https://doi.org/10.1080/10410236.2016.1278491.

Cooley, Charles Horton. *Human Nature and the Social Order.* New York: Charles Scribner's Sons, 1902.

Cortright, Joe. "City Report: Less in Common." *City Observatory* [Portland, Ore.], June 6, 2015. https://cityobservatory.org/less-in-common/.

Coupland, Justine, Nikolas Coupland, and Jeffrey D. Robinson. " 'How Are You?': Negotiating Phatic Communion." *Language in Society* 21, no. 2 (June 1992): 207–30. https://doi.org/10.1017/S0047404500015268.

Crasta, Dev, Ronald D. Rogge, Michael R. Maniaci, and Harry T. Reis. "Toward an Optimized Measure of Perceived Partner Responsiveness: Development and Validation of the Perceived Responsiveness and Insensitivity Scale." *Psychological Assessment* 33, no. 4 (2021): 338–55. https://doi.org/10.1037/pas0000986.

Cummins, Eleanor. "We're All Bad Neighbors Now." *New Republic,* June 6, 2023. https://newrepublic.com/article/173045/were-bad-neighbors-now.

Curry, Lewis A., C. R. Snyder, David L. Cook, Brent C. Ruby, and Michael Rehm. "Role of Hope in Academic and Sport Achievement." *Journal of Personality and Social Psychology* 73, no. 6 (1997): 1257–67. https://doi.org/10.1037/0022-3514.73.6.1257.

Dailey, René M. "Confirmation in Personal Relationships." *Current Opinion in Psychology* 52 (August 2023): 101593. https://doi.org/10.1016/j.copsyc.2023.101593.

Dainton, Marianne, and Elaine D. Zelley. *Applying Communication Theory for Professional Life: A Practical Introduction.* 4th ed. Los Angeles: Sage, 2019.

Davis, Christine. *Communicating Hope: An Ethnography of a Children's Mental Health Care Team.* Walnut Creek, Calif.: Left Coast Press, 2013.

Davis, Daniel Alan Cochece. "Development and Initial Tests of a Human Energy Management Theory of Communication." PhD dissertation, University of Southern California, 1997. https://www.proquest.com/docview/304369999/abstract/C04FEB6400EB4FF3PQ/1.

Davis, Shardé M. "When Sistahs Support Sistahs: A Process of Supportive Communication about Racial Microaggressions among Black Women." *Communication Monographs* 86, no. 2 (April 2019): 133–57. https://doi.org/10.1080/03637751.2018.1548769.

Debrosse, Régine, Sabrina Thai, and Tess Brieva. "When Skinfolk Are Kinfolk: Higher Perceived Support and Acceptance Characterize Close Same-Race (vs. Interracial) Relationships for People of Color." *Journal of Social Issues* 79, no. 1 (March 2023): 21–49. https://doi.org/10.1111/josi.12534.

Demiray, Burcu, Matthias R. Mehl, and Mike Martin. "Conversational Time Travel: Evidence of a Retrospective Bias in Real Life Conversations." *Frontiers in Psychology* 9 (2018): 2160.

Demsas, Jerusalem. "What We Talk about When We Talk about Gentrification." *Vox,* September 5, 2021. https://www.vox.com/22629826/gentrification-definition-housing-racism-segregation-cities.

Denworth, Lydia. *Friendship: The Evolution, Biology, and Extraordinary Power of Life's Fundamental Bond.* New York: W. W. Norton, 2020.

Dickens, Andy P., Suzanne H. Richards, Colin J. Greaves, and John L. Campbell. "Interventions Targeting Social Isolation in Older People: A Systematic Review." *BMC Public Health* 11, no. 1 (August 2011): 1–22. https://doi.org/10.1186/1471-2458-11-647.

Diener, Ed, Robert A. Emmons, Randy J. Larsen, and Sharon Griffin. "The Satisfaction with Life Scale." *Journal of Personality Assessment* 49, no. 1 (February 1985): 71–75. https://doi.org/10.1207/s15327752jpa4901_13.

Dinesen, Peter Thisted, Merlin Schaeffer, and Kim Mannemar Sønderskov. "Ethnic Diversity and Social Trust: A Narrative and Meta-Analytical Review." *Annual*

Review of Political Science 23, no. 1 (2020): 441–65. https://doi.org/10.1146/annurev-polisci-052918-020708.

Dissing, Agnete Skovlund, Naja Hulvej Rod, Thomas A. Gerds, and Rikke Lund. "Smartphone Interactions and Mental Well-Being in Young Adults: A Longitudinal Study Based on Objective High-Resolution Smartphone Data." *Scandinavian Journal of Public Health* 49, no. 3 (May 2021): 325–32. https://doi.org/10.1177/1403494820920418.

Dominguez, Jess, Shelby Bowman, Jeffrey A. Hall, and Andy Merolla. "Working Hard to Make a Good Impression: The Relational Consequences of Effortful Self-Presentation." *Communication Research Reports* 37, no. 5 (October 2020): 276–85. https://doi.org/10.1080/08824096.2020.1846511.

Donovan, Erin E., Renee Alducin, Kayleigh Spaulding, Joon Kim, Hussain Alkhafaji, Chloe Gonzales, Braidyn Lazenby, Anusha Naeem, and Faiza Sarwar. "The Labor of Talking to Stay Healthy and Socially Connected: Communication Work during the COVID-19 Pandemic." *SSM – Qualitative Research in Health* 2 (December 2022): 100102. https://doi.org/10.1016/j.ssmqr.2022.100102.

Douglas, William. "Expectations about Initial Interaction: An Examination of the Effects of Global Uncertainty." *Human Communication Research* 17, no. 3 (March 1991): 355–84. https://doi.org/10.1111/j.1468-2958.1991.tb00237.x.

Du, Danyang, Daantje Derks, and Arnold B. Bakker. "Daily Spillover from Family to Work: A Test of the Work-Home Resources Model." *Journal of Occupational Health Psychology* 23, no. 2 (April 2018): 237–47. https://doi.org/10.1037/ocp0000073.

Duck, Steve. "Diaries and Logs." In *Studying Interpersonal Interaction*, edited by Barbara Montgomery and Steve Duck, 141–61. New York: Guilford, 1991.

——. *Meaningful Relationships: Talking, Sense, and Relating.* Thousand Oaks, Calif.: Sage, 1994.

Duck, Steve, and Garth Pittman. "Social and Personal Relationships." In *Handbook of Interpersonal Communication*, edited by Mark Knapp and Gerald Miller, 2nd ed., 676–95. Thousand Oaks, Calif.: Sage, 1994.

Duck, Steve, and Kris Pond. "Friends, Romans, Countrymen, Lend Me Your Retrospections: Rhetoric and Reality in Personal Relationships." In *Close Relationships*, edited by Clyde Hendrick, 6–16. Newbury Park, Calif.: Sage, 1989.

Dunbar, Robin. *Friends: Understanding the Power of Our Most Important Relationships.* London: Little, Brown, 2021.

BIBLIOGRAPHY

Dunn, Elizabeth W., and Iris Lok. "Can Sociability Be Increased?" In *The Psychology of Sociability: Understanding Human Attachment*, edited by Joseph Forgas, William Crano, and Klaus Fiedler, 98–115. New York: Routledge, 2022. https://doi.org/10.4324/978100328582-8.

Economist. "America's New Exceptionalism." *Economist*, July 7, 2022. https://www.economist.com/leaders/2022/07/07/americas-new-exceptionalism.

Edwards, Autumn, and Gregory J. Shepherd. "Theories of Communication, Human Nature, and the World: Associations and Implications." *Communication Studies* 55, no. 2 (June 2004): 197–208. https://doi.org/10.1080/105109 70409388614.

Eliott, Jaklin A. "What Have We Done with Hope? A Brief History." In *Interdisciplinary Perspectives on Hope*, edited by Jaklin A. Eliott, 3–45. Hauppauge, N.Y.: Nova Science, 2005.

Eliott, Jaklin, and Ian Olver. "The Discursive Properties of 'Hope': A Qualitative Analysis of Cancer Patients' Speech." *Qualitative Health Research* 12, no. 2 (February 2002): 173–93. https://doi.org/10.1177/104973230201200204.

Enfield, N. J. *How We Talk: The Inner Workings of Conversation*. New York: Basic Books, 2017.

Entringer, Theresa M., and Samuel D. Gosling. "Loneliness during a Nationwide Lockdown and the Moderating Effect of Extroversion." *Social Psychological and Personality Science* 13, no. 3 (April 2022): 769–80. https://doi.org/10.1177/ 19485506211037871.

Epel, Elissa S. "The Geroscience Agenda: Toxic Stress, Hormetic Stress, and the Rate of Aging." *Ageing Research Reviews* 63 (November 2020): 101167. https://doi.org/10.1016/j.arr.2020.101167.

Epley, Nicholas, and Juliana Schroeder. "Mistakenly Seeking Solitude." *Journal of Experimental Psychology: General* 143, no. 5 (2014): 1980–99. https://doi. org/10.1037/a0037323.

Eramian, Laura, Peter Mallory, and Morgan Herbert. "Friendship, Intimacy, and the Contradictions of Therapy Culture." *Cultural Sociology* (2023): 17499755231157440. https://doi.org/10.1177/17499755231157440.

Farber, Steven, Tijs Neutens, Juan-Antonio Carrasco, and Carolina Rojas. "Social Interaction Potential and the Spatial Distribution of Face-to-Face Social Interactions." *Environment and Planning B: Planning and Design* 41, no. 6 (December 2014): 960–76. https://doi.org/10.1068/b120034p.

Fardghassemi, Sam, and Hélène Joffe. "The Causes of Loneliness: The Perspective of Young Adults in London's Most Deprived Areas." *PLOS ONE* 17, no. 4 (April 2022): e0264638. https://doi.org/10.1371/journal.pone. 0264638.

BIBLIOGRAPHY

Feeney, Brooke C., and Nancy L. Collins. "A New Look at Social Support: A Theoretical Perspective on Thriving through Relationships." *Personality and Social Psychology Review* 19, no. 2 (May 2015): 113–47. https://doi.org/10.1177/1088868314544222.

Ferguson, Merideth. "You Cannot Leave It at the Office: Spillover and Crossover of Coworker Incivility." *Journal of Organizational Behavior* 33, no. 4 (May 2012): 571–88. https://doi.org/10.1002/job.774.

Fernández, Aurelio, Charo Sádaba, Javier Garcia-Manglano, and Mariek Vanden Abeele. "Why We Socially Interact? The Need, the Ability, and the Desire." Session on interpersonal communication, International Communication Association meeting, Toronto, Ont, May 25–29, 2023..

Finkel, Michael. *The Stranger in the Woods: The Extraordinary Story of the Last True Hermit.* New York: Knopf, 2017.

——. "The Strange Tale of the North Pond Hermit." *GQ,* August 5, 2014. https://www.gq.com/story/the-last-true-hermit.

Finnbogadóttir, Hildur, and Dorthe Berntsen. "Involuntary and Voluntary Mental Time Travel in High and Low Worriers." *Memory* 19, no. 6 (August 2011): 625–40. https://doi.org/10.1080/09658211.2011.595722.

Fischer, Claude S. *Still Connected: Family and Friends in America since 1970.* New York: Russell Sage Foundation, 2011.

Fiske, Susan T., and Shelley E. Taylor. *Social Cognition: From Brains to Culture.* 4th ed. Thousand Oaks, Calif.: Sage, 2021.

Floyd, Kory, Corey A. Pavlich, Dana R. Dinsmore, and Colter D. Ray. "The Physiology of Affectionate Communication." In *The Oxford Handbook of the Physiology of Interpersonal Communication,* edited by Lindsey S. Aloia, Amanda Denes, and John P. Crowley, 31–47. New York: Oxford University Press, 2020. https://doi.org/10.1093/oxfordhb/9780190679446.013.4.

Folk, Dunigan, Karynna Okabe-Miyamoto, Elizabeth Dunn, and Sonja Lyubomirsky. "Did Social Connection Decline during the First Wave of COVID-19? The Role of Extraversion." Edited by Brent Donnellan. *Collabra: Psychology* 6, no. 1 (2020): 37. https://doi.org/10.1525/collabra.365.

Foster, Jane A., Linda Rinaman, and John F. Cryan. "Stress & the Gut-Brain Axis: Regulation by the Microbiome." *Neurobiology of Stress* 7 (December 2017): 124–36. https://doi.org/10.1016/j.ynstr.2017.03.001.

Fredrickson, Barbara L. *Love 2.0: How Our Supreme Emotion Affects Everything We Feel, Think, Do, and Become.* New York: Avery, 2013.

Fredrickson, Barbara L., and Thomas Joiner. "Reflections on Positive Emotions and Upward Spirals." *Perspectives on Psychological Science* 13, no. 2 (March 2018): 194–99. https://doi.org/10.1177/1745691617692106.

Fremstedal, R. "Kierkegaard on Hope as Essential to Selfhood." In *The Moral Psychology of Hope*, edited by C. Blöser and T. Stahl, 75–92. Lanham, Md.: Rowman & Littlefield, 2020.

Freres, Martin. "Financial Costs of Workplace Conflict." *Journal of the International Ombudsman Association* 6, no. 2 (July 2013): 83–94.

Friedman, Howard S., and Leslie R. Martin. *The Longevity Project: Surprising Discoveries for Health and Long Life from the Landmark Eight-Decade Study.* New York: Hudson Street Press, 2011.

Frisby, Brandi N., Robert J. Sidelinger, and Melanie Booth-Butterfield. "No Harm, No Foul: A Social Exchange Perspective on Individual and Relational Outcomes Associated with Relational Baggage." *Western Journal of Communication* 79, no. 5 (October 2015): 555–72. https://doi.org/10.1080/10570314.2015.107 5585.

Gable, Shelly L., and Alisa Bedrov. "Social Isolation and Social Support in Good Times and Bad Times." *Current Opinion in Psychology* 44 (April 2022): 89–93. https://doi.org/10.1016/j.copsyc.2021.08.027.

Gallois, Cindy, Bernadette M. Watson, and Howard Giles. "Intergroup Communication: Identities and Effective Interactions." *Journal of Communication* 68, no. 2 (April 2018): 309–17. https://doi.org/10.1093/joc/jqx016.

Garcini, Luz M., Kimberly Nguyen, Autumn Lucas-Marinelli, Oswaldo Moreno, and Pamela L. Cruz. " 'No One Left Behind': A Social Determinant of Health Lens to the Wellbeing of Undocumented Immigrants." *Current Opinion in Psychology* 47 (October 2022): 101455. https://doi.org/10.1016/j. copsyc.2022.101455.

Gardiner, Clare, Gideon Geldenhuys, and Merryn Gott. "Interventions to Reduce Social Isolation and Loneliness among Older People: An Integrative Review." *Health & Social Care in the Community* 26, no. 2 (2018): 147–57. https://doi. org/10.1111/hsc.12367.

Garrosa, Eva, Luis Manuel Blanco-Donoso, Jennifer E. Moreno-Jiménez, Eugenia McGrath, Helena D. Cooper-Thomas, and Felix Ladstätter. "Energy Loss after Daily Role Stress and Work Incivility: Caring for Oneself with Emotional Wellness." *Journal of Happiness Studies* 23, no. 8 (2022): 3929–59. https:// doi.org/10.1007/s10902-022-00570-x.

Gasiorek, Jessica. "Theoretical Perspectives on Interpersonal Adjustments in Language and Communication." In *Communication Accommodation Theory: Negotiating Personal Relationships and Social Identities across Contexts,* edited by Howard Giles, 13–35. Cambridge: Cambridge University Press, 2016.

Gerassi, John, ed. *Talking with Sartre: Conversations and Debates.* New Haven: Yale University Press, 2009.

BIBLIOGRAPHY

Gerbner, George, Larry Gross, Michael Morgan, Nancy Signorielli, and James Shanahan. "Growing Up with Television: Cultivation Processes." In *Media Effects: Advances in Theory and Research,* edited by Dolf Zillman, 2nd ed. Hillsdale, N.J.: Lawrence Erlbaum, 2002.

Gilligan, M., J. J. Suitor, and K. Pillemer. "Estrangement between Mothers and Adult Children: The Role of Norms and Values." *Journal of Marriage and Family* 77, no. 4 (2015): 908–20. https://doi.org/10.1111/jomf.12207.

Glanville, Jennifer L., and Pamela Paxton. "How Do We Learn to Trust? A Confirmatory Tetrad Analysis of the Sources of Generalized Trust." *Social Psychology Quarterly* 70, no. 3 (September 2007): 230–42. https://doi.org/10.1177/019027250707000303.

Goffman, Erving. *Asylums: Essays on the Social Situation of Mental Patients and Other Inmates.* Garden City, N.Y.: Anchor Books, 1961.

——. *Interaction Ritual: Essays on Face-to-Face Behavior.* Garden City, N.Y.: Anchor Books, 1967.

——. *The Presentation of Self in Everyday Life.* Garden City, N.Y.: Anchor Books, 1959.

Gonzales, Amy. "The Contemporary US Digital Divide: From Initial Access to Technology Maintenance." *Information, Communication & Society* 19, no. 2 (February 2016): 234–48. https://doi.org/10.1080/1369118X.2015.1050438.

Goo, Sara Kehaulani. "The Skills Americans Say Kids Need to Succeed in Life." Pew Research Center, February 19, 2015. https://www.pewresearch.org/short-reads/2015/02/19/skills-for-success/.

Gottman, John M. *The Marriage Clinic: A Scientifically Based Marital Therapy.* New York: W. W. Norton, 1999.

——. *The Science of Trust: Emotional Attunement for Couples.* New York: W. W. Norton, 2011.

Gottman, John M., Janice Driver, and Amber Tabares. "Repair during Marital Conflict in Newlyweds: How Couples Move from Attack-Defend to Collaboration." *Journal of Family Psychotherapy* 26, no. 2 (2015): 85–108. https://doi.org/10.1080/08975353.2015.1038962.

Gottman, John M., and Nan Silver. *The Seven Principles for Making Marriage Work: A Practical Guide from the Country's Foremost Relationship Expert.* New York: Three Rivers Press, 1999.

Gouldner, Alvin W. "The Norm of Reciprocity: A Preliminary Statement." *American Sociological Review* 25, no. 2 (April 1960): 161. https://doi.org/10.2307/2092623.

Grammer, Karl, Wulf Schiefenhövel, Margret Schleidt, Beatrice Lorenz, and Irenäus Eibl-Eibesfeldt. "Patterns on the Face: The Eyebrow Flash in

Crosscultural Comparison." *Ethology* 77, no. 4 (1988): 279–99. https://doi.org/10.1111/j.1439-0310.1988.tb00211.x.

Granovetter, Mark S. "The Strength of Weak Ties." *American Journal of Sociology* 78, no. 6 (1973): 1360–80.

Gunaydin, Gul, Hazal Oztekin, Deniz Hazal Karabulut, and Selin Salman-Engin. "Minimal Social Interactions with Strangers Predict Greater Subjective Well-Being." *Journal of Happiness Studies* 22, no. 4 (April 2021): 1839–53. https://doi.org/10.1007/s10902-020-00298-6.

Hackbarth, Maria, Thomas Pavkov, Joseph Wetchler, and Michael Flannery. "Natural Disasters: An Assessment of Family Resiliency Following Hurricane Katrina." *Journal of Marital and Family Therapy* 38, no. 2 (April 2012): 340–51. https://doi.org/10.1111/j.1752-0606.2011.00227.x.

Hall, Jeffrey A. "Energy, Episode, and Relationship: A Test of Communicate Bond Belong Theory." *Communication Quarterly* 66, no. 4 (August 2018): 380–402. https://doi.org/10.1080/01463373.2017.1411377.

———. "Friendship Standards: The Dimensions of Ideal Expectations." *Journal of Social and Personal Relationships* 29, no. 7 (November 2012): 884–907. https://doi.org/10.1177/0265407512448274.

———. "How Many Hours Does It Take to Make a Friend?" *Journal of Social and Personal Relationships* 36, no. 4 (April 2019): 1278–96. https://doi.org/10.1177/0265407518761225.

———. "The Price We Pay for Being Less Social." *Wall Street Journal*, August 11, 2022, sec. Life. https://www.wsj.com/articles/price-we-pay-for-being-less-social-11660068416.

———. "The Regulation of Social Interaction in Everyday Life: A Replication and Extension of O'Connor and Rosenblood (1996)." *Journal of Social and Personal Relationships* 34, no. 5 (August 2017): 699–716. https://doi.org/10.1177/0265407516654580.

———. *Relating through Technology*. Cambridge: Cambridge University Press, 2020. https://doi.org/10.1017/9781108629935.

———. "There's No Substitute for Meeting in Person. Here's Why." *Wall Street Journal*, March 9, 2023, sec. Life. https://www.wsj.com/articles/meeting-in-person-technology-4daa955c.

Hall, Jeffrey A., and Daniel Cochece Davis. "Proposing the Communicate Bond Belong Theory: Evolutionary Intersections with Episodic Interpersonal Communication." *Communication Theory* 27, no. 1 (2017): 21–47. https://doi.org/10.1111/comt.12106.

Hall, Jeffrey A., Jess Dominguez, Andy J. Merolla, and Christopher D. Otmar. "Social Bandwidth: When and Why Are Social Interactions Energy Intensive?"

Journal of Social and Personal Relationships 40, no. 8 (2023): 2614–36. https://doi.org/10.1177/02654075231154937.

Hall, Jeffrey A., Jess Dominguez, and Teodora Mihailova. "Interpersonal Media and Face-to-Face Communication: Relationship with Life Satisfaction and Loneliness." *Journal of Happiness Studies* 24, no. 1 (January 2023): 331–50. https://doi.org/10.1007/s10902-022-00581-8.

Hall, Jeffrey A., Amanda J. Holmstrom, Natalie Pennington, Evan K. Perrault, and Daniel Totzkay. "Quality Conversation Can Increase Daily Well-Being." *Communication Research* (2023): 00936502221139363. https://doi.org/10.1177/00936502221139363.

Hall, Jeffrey A., and Dong Liu. "Social Media Use, Social Displacement, and Well-Being." *Current Opinion in Psychology* 46 (August 2022): 101339. https://doi.org/10.1016/j.copsyc.2022.101339.

Hall, Jeffrey A., and Andy J. Merolla. "Connecting Everyday Talk and Time Alone to Global Well-Being." *Human Communication Research* 46, no. 1 (January 2020): 86–111. https://doi.org/10.1093/hcr/hqz014.

Hall, Jeffrey A., Teodora Mihailova, and Andy J. Merolla. "Typicality and Volition as Fundamental Features of Everyday Relational Communication." *Personal Relationships* 28, no. 3 (2021): 607–26. https://doi.org/10.1111/pere.12387.

Hall, Jeffrey A., Natalie Pennington, and Amanda Holmstrom. "Connecting through Technology during COVID-19." *Human Communication & Technology* 2, no. 1 (2021). https://doi.org/10.17161/hct.v3i1.15026.

Hall, Jeffrey A., Natalie Pennington, and Allyn Lueders. "Impression Management and Formation on Facebook: A Lens Model Approach." *New Media & Society* 16, no. 6 (September 2014): 958–82. https://doi.org/10.1177/1461444813495166.

Hall, Jeffrey A., Natalie Pennington, and Andy J. Merolla. "Which Mediated Social Interactions Satisfy the Need to Belong?" *Journal of Computer-Mediated Communication* 28, no. 1 (January 2023): 1–12. https://doi.org/10.1093/jcmc/zmac026.

Hall, Jeffrey A., and Alesia Woszidlo. "Families Communicating through Technology." In *The Routledge Handbook of Family Communication*, edited by Anita Vangelisti, 3rd ed. New York: Routledge, 2021. https://doi.org/10.4324/9781003043423.

Hamermesh, Daniel S. *Spending Time: The Most Valuable Resource.* New York: Oxford University Press, 2019.

Hampton, Keith N., Weixu Lu, and Inyoung Shin. "Digital Media and Stress: The Cost of Caring 2.0." *Information, Communication & Society* 19, no. 9 (September 2016): 1267–86. https://doi.org/10.1080/1369118X.2016.1186714.

Hampton, Keith N., and Inyoung Shin. "Disconnection More Problematic for Adolescent Self-Esteem Than Heavy Social Media Use: Evidence from Access Inequalities and Restrictive Media Parenting in Rural America." *Social Science Computer Review* 41, no. 2 (April 2023): 626–47. https://doi.org/10.1177/08944393221117466.

Hank, Karsten, and Anja Steinbach. "Sibling Estrangement in Adulthood." *Journal of Social and Personal Relationships* 40, no. 4 (April 2023): 1277–87. https://doi.org/10.1177/02654075221127863.

Hari, Johann. *Stolen Focus: Why You Can't Pay Attention — and How to Think Deeply Again.* New York: Crown, 2022.

Harris, Kelci, and Simine Vazire. "On Friendship Development and the Big Five Personality Traits." *Social and Personality Psychology Compass* 10, no. 11 (2016): 647–67. https://doi.org/10.1111/spc3.12287.

Harvard Health Publishing. "Calories Burned in 30 Minutes of Leisure and Routine Activities," March 8, 2021. https://www.health.harvard.edu/diet-and-weight-loss/calories-burned-in-30-minutes-for-people-of-three-different-weights.

Hässler, Tabea, Johannes Ullrich, Michelle Bernardino, Nurit Shnabel, Colette Van Laar, Daniel Valdenegro, Simone Sebben, et al. "A Large-Scale Test of the Link between Intergroup Contact and Support for Social Change." *Nature Human Behaviour* 4, no. 4 (April 2020): 380–86. https://doi.org/10.1038/s41562-019-0815-z.

Hawkley, Louise C., and John T. Cacioppo. "Social Connectedness and Health." In *Human Bonding: The Science of Affectional Ties,* edited by Cindy Hazan and Mary I. Campa, 343–64. New York: Guilford, 2013.

Hawkley, Louise C., Mary Elizabeth Hughes, Linda J. Waite, Christopher M. Masi, Ronald A. Thisted, and John T. Cacioppo. "From Social Structural Factors to Perceptions of Relationship Quality and Loneliness: The Chicago Health, Aging, and Social Relations Study." *Journals of Gerontology: Series B* 63, no. 6 (November 2008): S375–84. https://doi.org/10.1093/geronb/63.6.S375.

Hawkley, Louise C., Kristen Wroblewski, Till Kaiser, Maike Luhmann, and L. Philip Schumm. "Are U.S. Older Adults Getting Lonelier? Age, Period, and Cohort Differences." *Psychology and Aging* 34, no. 8 (2019): 1144–57. https://doi.org/10.1037/pag0000365.

Hawley, Zackary B. "Does Urban Density Promote Social Interaction? Evidence from Instrumental Variable Estimation." *Review of Regional Studies* 42, no. 3 (November 2012): 223–48. https://doi.org/10.52324/001c.8101.

Hawn, Allison. "The Civility Cudgel: The Myth of Civility in Communication." *Howard Journal of Communications* 31, no. 2 (March 2020): 218–30. https://doi.org/10.1080/10646175.2020.1731882.

Helliwell, John F., and Haifang Huang. "Comparing the Happiness Effects of Real and On-Line Friends." *PLOS ONE* 8, no. 9 (September 2013): e72754. https://doi.org/10.1371/journal.pone.0072754.

Hickman, Caroline, Elizabeth Marks, Panu Pihkala, Susan Clayton, R. Eric Lewandowski, Elouise E. Mayall, Britt Wray, Catriona Mellor, and Lise van Susteren. "Climate Anxiety in Children and Young People and Their Beliefs about Government Responses to Climate Change: A Global Survey." *Lancet Planetary Health* 5, no. 12 (December 2021): e863–73. https://doi.org/10.1016/S2542-5196(21)00278-3.

Hicks, Donna. *Dignity: Its Essential Role in Resolving Conflict.* New Haven: Yale University Press, 2011.

High, Andrew C., and James Price Dillard. "A Review and Meta-Analysis of Person-Centered Messages and Social Support Outcomes." *Communication Studies* 63, no. 1 (January 2012): 99–118. https://doi.org/10.1080/10510974.2011.598208.

Hill, Craig A. "Affiliation Motivation: People Who Need People . . . but in Different Ways." *Journal of Personality and Social Psychology* 52, no. 5 (1987): 1008–18. https://doi.org/10.1037/0022-3514.52.5.1008.

Hillman, James G., Devin I. Fowlie, and Tara K. MacDonald. "Social Verification Theory: A New Way to Conceptualize Validation, Dissonance, and Belonging." *Personality and Social Psychology Review* 27, no. 3 (2023): 309–31. https://doi.org/10.1177/10888683221138384.

Hippel, William von, and Nicholas M. A. Smith. "Evolutionary Origins and Consequences of Human Sociability." In *The Psychology of Sociability: Understanding Human Attachment,* edited by Joseph P. Forgas, William Crano, and Klaus Fiedler, 22–35. New York: Routledge, 2022. https://doi.org/10.4324/9781003258582-3.

Hirsch, Jennifer L., and Margaret S. Clark. "Multiple Paths to Belonging That We Should Study Together." *Perspectives on Psychological Science* 14, no. 2 (March 2019): 238–55. https://doi.org/10.1177/1745691618803629.

Hoang, Peter, James A. King, Sarah Moore, Kim Moore, Krista Reich, Harman Sidhu, Chin Vern Tan, Colin Whaley, and Jacqueline McMillan. "Interventions Associated with Reduced Loneliness and Social Isolation in Older Adults: A Systematic Review and Meta-Analysis." *JAMA Network Open* 5, no. 10 (October 2022): e2236676. https://doi.org/10.1001/jamanetworkopen.2022.36676.

Hobfoll, Stevan E. *Stress, Culture, and Community: The Psychology and Philosophy of Stress.* New York: Plenum, 1998.

Hochschild, Arlie Russell. *The Managed Heart: Commercialization of Human Feeling.* 3rd ed. Berkeley: University of California Press, 2012.

BIBLIOGRAPHY

Hofmann, Wilhelm, Kathleen D. Vohs, and Roy F. Baumeister. "What People Desire, Feel Conflicted about, and Try to Resist in Everyday Life." *Psychological Science* 23, no. 6 (June 2012): 582–88. https://doi.org/10.1177/0956797612437426.

Holt-Lunstad, Julianne. "The Major Health Implications of Social Connection." *Current Directions in Psychological Science* 30, no. 3 (June 2021): 251–59. https://doi.org/10.1177/0963721421999630.

Holt-Lunstad, Julianne, Theodore F. Robles, and David A. Sbarra. "Advancing Social Connection as a Public Health Priority in the United States." *American Psychologist* 72, no. 6 (September 2017): 517–30. https://doi.org/10.1037/amp0000103.

Holt-Lunstad, Julianne, Timothy B. Smith, Mark Baker, Tyler Harris, and David Stephenson. "Loneliness and Social Isolation as Risk Factors for Mortality: A Meta-Analytic Review." *Perspectives on Psychological Science* 10, no. 2 (March 2015): 227–37. https://doi.org/10.1177/1745691614568352.

Holt-Lunstad, Julianne, Timothy B. Smith, and J. Bradley Layton. "Social Relationships and Mortality Risk: A Meta-Analytic Review." *PLOS Medicine* 7, no. 7 (July 2010): e1000316. https://doi.org/10.1371/journal.pmed.1000316.

Honeycutt, James M. "Imagined Interactions and Inner Speech." *Imagination, Cognition and Personality* 39, no. 4 (June 2020): 386–96. https://doi.org/10.1177/0276236619869163.

Horst, Mariska van der, and Hilde Coffé. "How Friendship Network Characteristics Influence Subjective Well-Being." *Social Indicators Research* 107, no. 3 (July 2012): 509–29. https://doi.org/10.1007/s11205-011-9861-2.

House, James S., Karl R. Landis, and Debra Umberson. "Social Relationships and Health." *Science* 241, no. 4865 (1988): 540–45. https://doi.org/10.1126/science.3399889.

Howell, Andrew J., and Denise J. Larsen. *Understanding Other-Oriented Hope: An Integral Concept within Hope Studies.* Cham, Switzerland: Springer International, 2015. https://doi.org/10.1007/978-3-319-15007-9.

Hruschka, Daniel J. *Friendship: Development, Ecology, and Evolution of a Relationship.* Berkeley: University of California Press, 2010.

Hutten, Elody, Ellen M. M. Jongen, KlaasJan Hajema, Robert A. C. Ruiter, Femke Hamers, and Arjan E. R. Bos. "Risk Factors of Loneliness across the Life Span." *Journal of Social and Personal Relationships* 39, no. 5 (May 2022): 1482–1507. https://doi.org/10.1177/02654075211059193.

Imrie, Rob. " 'The Lonely City': Urban Infrastructure and the Problem of Loneliness." In *Narratives of Loneliness: Multidisciplinary Perspectives from the*

21st Century, edited by Olivia Sagan and Eric D. Miller, 140–52. New York: Routledge, 2018.

Ishiguro, Itaru. "Minimal Social Interactions and Subjective Well-Being in the Japanese Context: Examination of Mediation Processes Using a National Representative Sample." *Social Sciences & Humanities Open* 8, no. 1 (2023): 100713. https://doi.org/10.1016/j.ssaho.2023.100713.

Israel, Tania. *Beyond Your Bubble: How to Connect across the Political Divide, Skills and Strategies for Conversations That Work*. Washington, D.C.: American Psychological Association, 2020.

Itzchakov, Guy, and Harry T. Reis. "Perceived Responsiveness Increases Tolerance of Attitude Ambivalence and Enhances Intentions to Behave in an Open-Minded Manner." *Personality and Social Psychology Bulletin* 47, no. 3 (March 2021): 468–85. https://doi.org/10.1177/0146167220929218.

Itzchakov, Guy, Netta Weinstein, Eli Vinokur, and Avinoam Yomtovian. "Communicating for Workplace Connection: A Longitudinal Study of the Outcomes of Listening Training on Teachers' Autonomy, Psychological Safety, and Relational Climate." *Psychology in the Schools* 60, no. 4 (April 2023): 1279–98. https://doi.org/10.1002/pits.22835.

Iyadurai, Lalitha, Renée M. Visser, Alex Lau-Zhu, Kate Porcheret, Antje Horsch, Emily A. Holmes, and Ella L. James. "Intrusive Memories of Trauma: A Target for Research Bridging Cognitive Science and Its Clinical Application." *Clinical Psychology Review* 69 (April 2019): 67–82. https://doi.org/10.1016/j.cpr.2018.08.005.

Jackson, Matthew O. *The Human Network: How Your Social Position Determines Your Power, Beliefs, and Behavior*. New York: Pantheon Books, 2019.

Jacobson, Nora. "A Taxonomy of Dignity: A Grounded Theory Study." *BMC International Health and Human Rights* 9, no. 3 (February 24, 2009). https://doi.org/10.1186/1472-698X-9-3.

Jacoby, Sally, and Elinor Ochs. "Co-Construction: An Introduction." *Research on Language and Social Interaction* 28, no. 3 (July 1995): 171–83. https://doi.org/10.1207/s15327973rlsi2803_1.

Jacques-Hamilton, Rowan, Jessie Sun, and Luke D. Smillie. "Costs and Benefits of Acting Extraverted: A Randomized Controlled Trial." *Journal of Experimental Psychology: General* 148, no. 9 (2019): 1538–56. https://doi.org/10.1037/xge0000516.

Jarman, Hannah K., Siân A. McLean, Susan J. Paxton, Chris G. Sibley, and Mathew D. Marques. "Examination of the Temporal Sequence between Social Media Use and Well-Being in a Representative Sample of Adults." *Social Psychiatry and Psychiatric Epidemiology* 58 (September 2022): 1247–58. https://doi.org/10.1007/s00127-022-02363-2.

—

Jiang, Yanping, Mengting Li, and Tammy Chung. "Living Alone and All-Cause Mortality in Community-Dwelling Older Adults: The Moderating Role of Perceived Neighborhood Cohesion." *Social Science & Medicine* 317 (January 2023): 115568. https://doi.org/10.1016/j.socscimed.2022.115568.

Johansson, Karin, Lena Borell, and Lena Rosenberg. "Qualities of the Environment That Support a Sense of Home and Belonging in Nursing Homes for Older People." *Ageing & Society* 42, no. 1 (January 2022): 157–78. https://doi.org/10.1017/S0144686X20000896.

Johnson, Matthew D., Nancy L. Galambos, and Jared R. Anderson. "Skip the Dishes? Not So Fast! Sex and Housework Revisited." *Journal of Family Psychology* 30, no. 2 (2016): 203–13. https://doi.org/10.1037/fam0000161.

Joshanloo, Mohsen, M. Joseph Sirgy, and Joonha Park. "Directionality of the Relationship between Social Well-Being and Subjective Well-Being: Evidence from a 20-Year Longitudinal Study." *Quality of Life Research* 27, no. 8 (August 2018): 2137–45. https://doi.org/10.1007/s11136-018-1865-9.

Kahneman, Daniel. "Daniel Kahneman on Cutting through the Noise." *Conversations with Tyler.* Interview by Tyler Cowen. https://medium.com/conversations-with-tyler/tyler-cowen-daniel-kahneman-economics-bias-noise-167275de691f.

Kam, Jennifer A., Monica Cornejo, Roselia Mendez Murillo, and Tamara D. Afifi. "Communicating Allyship According to College Students with Deferred Action for Childhood Arrivals." *Journal of Social and Personal Relationships* 39, no. 6 (June 2022): 1623–47. https://doi.org/10.1177/02654075211061715.

Kam, Jennifer A., and Andy J. Merolla. "Hope Communication as a Predictor of Documented and Undocumented Latina/o High School Students' College Intentions across an Academic Year." *Communication Monographs* 85, no. 3 (July 2018): 399–422. https://doi.org/10.1080/03637751.2018.1463101.

Kang, Cecilia. "The Humble Phone Call Has Made a Comeback." *New York Times,* April 9, 2020. https://www.nytimes.com/2020/04/09/technology/phone-calls-voice-virus.html.

Kant, Immanuel. "Civilization and Enlightenment: 'Idea for a Universal History from a Cosmopolitan Point of View.'" Translated by Lewis White Beck. In *Classical Readings in Culture and Civilization,* edited by Stephen Mennell and John Rundell, 39–47. 1784; reprint London: Routledge, 1998.

Kashdan, Todd B., and John E. Roberts. "Social Anxiety, Depressive Symptoms, and Post-Event Rumination: Affective Consequences and Social Contextual Influences." *Journal of Anxiety Disorders* 21, no. 3 (January 2007): 284–301. https://doi.org/10.1016/j.janxdis.2006.05.009.

Killingsworth, Matthew A., and Daniel T. Gilbert. "A Wandering Mind Is an Unhappy Mind." *Science* 330, no. 6006 (November 2010): 932. https://doi.org/10.1126/science.1192439.

Kim, Ildo, and Nicholas A. Palomares. "The Role of a Bystander in Targets' Perceptions of Teasing among Friends: Are You Really Teasing Me?" *International Journal of Communication* 16 (August 2022): 19.

King, Marissa. *Social Chemistry: Decoding the Patterns of Human Connection*. New York: Dutton, 2021.

Klein, Ezra. *Why We're Polarized*. New York: Avid Reader Press, 2020.

Klein, Jessica, and Casey Noenickx. "Can Gen Z Make Friends in the Pandemic Era?" BBC, February 17, 2023. https://www.bbc.com/worklife/article/20230201-can-gen-z-make-friends-in-the-pandemic-era.

Klinenberg, Eric. *Palaces for the People: How Social Infrastructure Can Help Fight Inequality, Polarization, and the Decline of Civic Life*. New York: Crown, 2018.

Kluger, Avraham N., and Guy Itzchakov. "The Power of Listening at Work." *Annual Review of Organizational Psychology and Organizational Behavior* 9, no. 1 (January 2022): 121–46. https://doi.org/10.1146/annurev-orgpsych-012420-091013.

Knapp, Mark L., Judith A. Hall, and Terrance G. Horgan. *Nonverbal Communication in Human Interaction*. 8th ed. Boston: Wadsworth, Cengage Learning, 2014.

Knapp, Mark L., Roderick P. Hart, Gustav W. Friedrich, and Gary M. Shulman. "The Rhetoric of Goodbye: Verbal and Nonverbal Correlates of Human Leave-Taking." *Speech Monographs* 40, no. 3 (August 1973): 182–98. https://doi.org/10.1080/03637757309375796.

Knapp, Mark L., Cynthia Stohl, and Kathleen K. Reardon. " 'Memorable' Messages." *Journal of Communication* 31, no. 4 (December 1981): 27–41. https://doi.org/10.1111/j.1460-2466.1981.tb00448.x.

Korobov, Neill. "A Discursive Approach to Young Adult Romantic Couples Use of Active Listening to Manage Conflict during Natural Everyday Conversations." *International Journal of Listening* 37, no. 3 (2023): 227–41. https://doi.org/10.1080/10904018.2022.2082970.

Kottke, Jason. 2014. "The Last True Hermit." Kottke.org (blog). 2014. https://kottke.org/tag/Christopher%20Knight.

Kremer, William, and Claudia Hammond. "Hikikomori: Why Are So Many Japanese Men Refusing to Leave Their Rooms?" *BBC News,* July 4, 2013, sec. Magazine. https://www.bbc.com/news/magazine-23182523.

Kroencke, Lara, Gabriella M. Harari, Mitja D. Back, and Jenny Wagner. "Well-Being in Social Interactions: Examining Personality-Situation Dynamics in Face-to-Face and Computer-Mediated Communication." *Journal of Personality and Social Psychology* 124, no. 2 (2023): 437–60. https://doi.org/10.1037/pspp0000422.

Kumar, Amit, and Nicholas Epley. "Undersociality Is Unwise." *Journal of Consumer Psychology* 33, no. 1 (January 2023): 199–212. https://doi.org/10.1002/jcpy.1336.

Kun, Andrew, Raffaella Sadun, Orit Shaer, and Thomaz Teodorovicz. "Where Did the Commute Time Go?" *Harvard Business Review,* December 10, 2020. https://hbr.org/2020/12/where-did-the-commute-time-go.

Kuper, Niclas, Lara Kroencke, Gabriella M. Harari, and Jaap J. A. Denissen. "Who Benefits from Which Activity? On the Relations between Personality Traits, Leisure Activities, and Well-Being." *Journal of Personality and Social Psychology* 125, no. 1 (2023): 141–72. https://doi.org/10.1037/pspp0000438.

Kuykendall, Lauren, Louis Boemerman, and Ze Zhu. "The Importance of Leisure for Subjective Well-Being." In *Handbook of Well-Being,* edited by Ed Diener, Shigehiro Oishi, and Louis Tay. Salt Lake City: DEF, 2018. https://nobas-cholar.com/chapters/31/download.pdf.

Lapowsky, Issie, and Gili Benita. "Where Did All Your Zoom Friends Go?" *New York Times,* March 18, 2023, sec. Business. https://www.nytimes.com/2023/03/18/business/zoom-friends-socializing.html.

Lattanner, Micah R., and Mark L. Hatzenbuehler. "Thwarted Belonging Needs: A Mechanism Prospectively Linking Multiple Levels of Stigma and Interpersonal Outcomes among Sexual Minorities." *Journal of Social Issues* 79, no. 1 (2023): 410–45. https://doi.org/10.1111/josi.12564.

Laurence, James, Katharina Schmid, and Miles Hewstone. "Ethnic Diversity, Inter-Group Attitudes and Countervailing Pathways of Positive and Negative Inter-Group Contact: An Analysis across Workplaces and Neighbourhoods." *Social Indicators Research* 136, no. 2 (April 2018): 719–49. https://doi.org/10.1007/s11205-017-1570-z.

Lauter, David. "Is Politics Making People Sick? A Lot of Young People Say So," *Los Angeles Times,* April 29, 2022. https://www.latimes.com/politics/newsletter/2022-04-29/politics-bad-for-mental-health-young-people-say-essential-politics.

Lavrusheva, Olga. "The Concept of Vitality: Review of the Vitality-Related Research Domain." *New Ideas in Psychology* 56 (January 2020): 100752. https://doi.org/10.1016/j.newideapsych.2019.100752.

Leary, Mark R. *The Curse of the Self: Self-Awareness, Egotism, and the Quality of Human Life.* Oxford: Oxford University Press, 2004.

Leary, Mark R., and Deborah L. Downs. "Interpersonal Functions of the Self-Esteem Motive: The Self-Esteem System as a Sociometer." In *Efficacy, Agency, and Self-Esteem,* edited by Michael H. Kernis, 123–44. New York: Plenum, 1995.

Leikas, Sointu, and Ville-Juhani Ilmarinen. "Happy Now, Tired Later? Extraverted and Conscientious Behavior Are Related to Immediate Mood Gains, but to Later Fatigue." *Journal of Personality* 85, no. 5 (2017): 603–15. https://doi.org/10.1111/jopy.12264.

Lemay, Edward P., and Margaret S. Clark. "How the Head Liberates the Heart: Projection of Communal Responsiveness Guides Relationship Promotion." *Journal of Personality and Social Psychology* 94, no. 4 (2008): 647–71. https://doi.org/10.1037/0022-3514.94.4.647.

Lieberman, Matthew D. *Social: Why Our Brains Are Wired to Connect.* New York: Crown, 2013.

Liming, Sheila. *Hanging Out: The Radical Power of Killing Time.* Brooklyn: Melville House, 2023.

Lin, Lisa, Mallory J. Feldman, Ashley Tudder, Abriana M. Gresham, Brett J. Peters, and David Dodell-Feder. "Friends in Sync? Examining the Relationship between the Degree of Nonverbal Synchrony, Friendship Satisfaction and Support." *Journal of Nonverbal Behavior* 47 (September 2023): 361–84. https://doi.org/10.1007/s10919-023-00431-y.

Lipetz, Liora, Avraham N. Kluger, and Graham D. Bodie. "Listening Is Listening Is Listening: Employees' Perception of Listening as a Holistic Phenomenon." *International Journal of Listening* 34, no. 2 (May 2020): 71–96. https://doi.or g/10.1080/10904018.2018.1497489.

Liu, Huiying, Qian Wen Xie, and Vivian W. Q. Lou. "Everyday Social Interactions and Intra-Individual Variability in Affect: A Systematic Review and Meta-Analysis of Ecological Momentary Assessment Studies." *Motivation and Emotion* 43, no. 2 (April 2019): 339–53. https://doi.org/10.1007/s11031-018-9735-x.

Liu, Wenlin, Minhee Son, Andrea Wenzel, Zheng An, Nan Zhao Martin, Seungahn Nah, and Sandra Ball-Rokeach. "Bridging Mechanisms in Multiethnic Communities: Place-Based Communication, Neighborhood Belonging, and Intergroup Relations." *Journal of International and Intercultural Communication* 11, no. 1 (2018): 58–80. https://doi.org/10.1080/17513057.2017.1384 506.

Luhmann, Maike, and Louise C. Hawkley. "Age Differences in Loneliness from Late Adolescence to Oldest Old Age." *Developmental Psychology* 52, no. 6 (2016): 943–59. https://doi.org/10.1037/dev0000117.

Luo, Minxia, Birthe Macdonald, and Gizem Hülür. "Not 'The More the Merrier': Diminishing Returns to Daily Face-to-Face Social Interaction Frequency for Well-Being in Older Age." *Journals of Gerontology: Series B* 77, no. 8 (August 2022): 1431–41. https://doi.org/10.1093/geronb/gbac010.

Luo, Minxia, Theresa Pauly, Christina Röcke, and Gizem Hülür. "Alternating Time Spent on Social Interactions and Solitude in Healthy Older Adults." *British Journal of Psychology* 113, no. 4 (2022): 987–1008. https://doi.org/10.1111/bjop.12586.

———

Lyubomirsky, Sonja, Rene Dickerhoof, Julia K. Boehm, and Kennon M. Sheldon. "Becoming Happier Takes Both a Will and a Proper Way: An Experimental Longitudinal Intervention to Boost Well-Being." *Emotion* 11, no. 2 (April 2011): 391–402. https://doi.org/10.1037/a0022575.

Lyubomirsky, Sonja, and Kristin Layous. "How Do Simple Positive Activities Increase Well-Being?" *Current Directions in Psychological Science* 22, no. 1 (February 2013): 57–62. https://doi.org/10.1177/0963721412469809.

Macdonald, Birthe, Minxia Luo, and Gizem Hülür. "Daily Social Interactions and Well-Being in Older Adults: The Role of Interaction Modality." *Journal of Social and Personal Relationships* 38, no. 12 (December 2021): 3566–89. https://doi.org/10.1177/02654075211052536.

MacGeorge, Erina L., Bo Feng, and Lisa M. Guntzviller. "Advice: Expanding the Communication Paradigm." *Annals of the International Communication Association* 40, no. 1 (January 2016): 213–43. https://doi.org/10.1080/23808985.2015.11735261.

MacKerron, George, and Susana Mourato. "Mappiness: Natural Environments and in-the-Moment Happiness." In *Handbook of Wellbeing, Happiness and the Environment,* edited by David Maddison, Katrin Rehdanz, and Heinz Welsch, 266–82. Northampton, Mass.: Edward Elgar, 2020.

Madlock, P. E., and M. Booth-Butterfield. "The Influence of Relational Maintenance Strategies among Coworkers." *Journal of Business Communication* 49, no. 1 (January 2012): 21–47. https://doi.org/10.1177/0021943611425237.

Malawa, Zea, Jenna Gaarde, and Solaire Spellen. "Racism as a Root Cause Approach: A New Framework." *Pediatrics* 147, no. 1 (January 2021): e2020015602. https://doi.org/10.1542/peds.2020-015602.

Malinowski, Bronislaw. "The Problem of Meaning in Primitive Languages." In *The Meaning of Meaning,* edited by C. K. Ogden and I. A. Richards, 296–336. New York: Harcourt & Brace, 1923.

Manusov, Valerie. "Interpersonal Communication." In *The Handbook of Listening,* edited by Debra L. Worthington and Graham D. Bodie, 103–19. Hoboken, N.J.: John Wiley & Sons, 2020.

Martela, Frank, and Kennon M. Sheldon. "Clarifying the Concept of Well-Being: Psychological Need Satisfaction as the Common Core Connecting Eudaimonic and Subjective Well-Being." *Review of General Psychology* 23, no. 4 (December 2019): 458–74. https://doi.org/10.1177/1089268019880886.

Marzoratti, Analia, and Tanya M. Evans. "Measurement of Interpersonal Physiological Synchrony in Dyads: A Review of Timing Parameters Used in the Literature." *Cognitive, Affective, & Behavioral Neuroscience* 22, no. 6 (December 2022): 1215–30. https://doi.org/10.3758/s13415-022-01011-1.

BIBLIOGRAPHY

Matthews, Gillian A., and Kay M. Tye. "Neural Mechanisms of Social Homeostasis." *Annals of the New York Academy of Sciences* 1457, no. 1 (December 2019): 5–25. https://doi.org/10.1111/nyas.14016.

McCullough, Michael E. *Beyond Revenge: The Evolution of the Forgiveness Instinct.* San Francisco: Jossey-Bass, 2008.

McDermott, Diane, and C. R. Snyder. *Making Hope Happen: A Workbook for Turning Possibilities into Reality.* Oakland, Calif.: New Harbinger, 1999.

McGeer, Victoria. "The Art of Good Hope." *Annals of the American Academy of Political and Social Science* 592, no. 1 (March 2004): 100–127. https://doi.org/10.1177/0002716203261781.

McGhee, Heather. *The Sum of Us: What Racism Costs Everyone and How We Can Prosper Together.* New York: One World, 2021.

Mead, George Herbert. *On Social Psychology: Selected Papers.* Edited by Anselm Strauss. Rev. ed. Chicago: University of Chicago Press, 1964.

Mehl, Matthias R., Simine Vazire, Shannon E. Holleran, and C. Shelby Clark. "Eavesdropping on Happiness: Well-Being Is Related to Having Less Small Talk and More Substantive Conversations." *Psychological Science* 21, no. 4 (2010): 539–41. https://doi.org/10.1177/0956797610362675.

Mehl, Matthias R., Simine Vazire, Nairán Ramírez-Esparza, Richard B. Slatcher, and James W. Pennebaker. "Are Women Really More Talkative Than Men?" *Science* 317, no. 5834 (July 2007): 82. https://doi.org/10.1126/science.1139940.

Mendez Murillo, Roselia, and Jennifer A Kam. "Exploring How Cultural and Structural Elements Relate to Communal Coping for Separated Latina/o/x Immigrant Families." *Journal of Communication* 73, no. 2 (April 2023): 150–62. https://doi.org/10.1093/joc/jqac048.

Menendian, Stephen, Samir Gambhir, and Arthur Gailes. "The Roots of Structural Racism Project." UC Berkeley Othering and Belonging Institute, 2021. https://belonging.berkeley.edu/roots-structural-racism.

Merolla, Andy J. "Forgiveness Following Conflict: What It Is, Why It Happens, and How It's Done." In *Communicating Interpersonal Conflict in Close Relationships: Contexts, Challenges, and Opportunities,* edited by Jennifer A. Samp, 227–49. New York: Routledge, 2017.

———. "Relational Maintenance and Noncopresence Reconsidered: Conceptualizing Geographic Separation in Close Relationships." *Communication Theory* 20, no. 2 (2010): 169–93. https://doi.org/10.1111/j.1468-2885.2010.01359.x.

Merolla, Andy J., Gary A. Beck, and Alice Jones. "Memorable Messages as Sources of Hope." *Communication Quarterly* 65, no. 4 (August 2017): 456–80. https://doi.org/10.1080/01463373.2017.1288149.

Merolla, Andy J., Quinten Bernhold, and Christina Peterson. "Pathways to Connection: An Intensive Longitudinal Examination of State and Dispositional Hope, Day Quality, and Everyday Interpersonal Interaction." *Journal of Social and Personal Relationships* 38, no. 7 (July 2021): 1961–86. https://doi.org/10.1177/02654075211001933.

Merolla, Andy J., Jeffrey A. Hall, and Quinten Bernhold. "Perseverative Cognition, Distracted Communication, and Well-Being in Everyday Social Interaction." *Personal Relationships* 26, no. 3 (2019): 507–28. https://doi.org/10.1111/pere.12286.

Merolla, Andy J., and Jennifer A. Kam. "Parental Hope Communication and Parent-Adolescent Constructive Conflict Management: A Multilevel Longitudinal Analysis." *Journal of Family Communication* 18, no. 1 (2018): 32–50. https://doi.org/10.1080/15267431.2017.1385461.

Merolla, Andy J., Andreas B. Neubauer, and Christopher D. Otmar. "Responsiveness, Social Connection, Hope, and Life Satisfaction in Everyday Social Interaction: An Experience Sampling Study." *Journal of Happiness Studies* 25, no. 7 (2024). https://doi.org/10.1007/s10902-024-00710-5.

Merolla, Andy J., Christopher D. Otmar, and Abdullah S. Salehuddin. "Past Relational Experiences and Social Interaction: Direct, Moderated, and Mediated Associations between Relational Difficulty, Communication, and Perception in Two Samples." *Communication Research* (April 2023): 00936502231162232. https://doi.org/10.1177/00936502231162232.

Methot, Jessica R., Emily H. Rosado-Solomon, Patrick E. Downes, and Allison S. Gabriel. "Office Chitchat as a Social Ritual: The Uplifting yet Distracting Effects of Daily Small Talk at Work." *Academy of Management Journal* 64, no. 5 (October 2021): 1445–71. https://doi.org/10.5465/amj.2018.1474.

Mikulincer, Mario, and Philip R. Shaver. "An Attachment Perspective on Human Sociability: Interpersonal Goals, Mental Representations, and Information Processing." In *The Psychology of Sociability: Understanding Human Attachment*, edited by Joseph P. Forgas, William Crano, and Klaus Fiedler, 219–38. New York: Routledge, 2022.

Milek, Anne, Emily A. Butler, Allison M. Tackman, Deanna M. Kaplan, Charles L. Raison, David A. Sbarra, Simine Vazire, and Matthias R. Mehl. " 'Eavesdropping on Happiness' Revisited: A Pooled, Multisample Replication of the Association between Life Satisfaction and Observed Daily Conversation Quantity and Quality." *Psychological Science* 29, no. 9 (September 2018): 1451–62. https://doi.org/10.1177/0956797618774252.

Miller, Katherine I., Jennifer Considine, and Johny Garner. " 'Let Me Tell You about My Job': Exploring the Terrain of Emotion in the Workplace." *Management Communication Quarterly* 20, no. 3 (February 2007): 231–60. https://doi.org/10.1177/0893318906293589.

Miritello, Giovanna, Esteban Moro, Rubén Lara, Rocío Martínez-López, John Belchamber, Sam G. B. Roberts, and Robin I. M. Dunbar. "Time as a Limited Resource: Communication Strategy in Mobile Phone Networks." *Social Networks* 35, no. 1 (January 2013): 89–95. https://doi.org/10.1016/j.socnet.2013.01.003.

Montgomery, Lucy Maud. *Anne of Green Gables.* 1908; reprint, Amazon Classics, 2017. Kindle.

Morais, Livia H., Henry L. Schreiber, and Sarkis K. Mazmanian. "The Gut Microbiota–Brain Axis in Behaviour and Brain Disorders." *Nature Reviews Microbiology* 19, no. 4 (April 2021): 241–55. https://doi.org/10.1038/s41579-020-00460-0.

Morrison, Rachel L. "Negative Relationships in the Workplace: Associations with Organisational Commitment, Cohesion, Job Satisfaction and Intention to Turnover." *Journal of Management & Organization* 14, no. 4 (2008): 330–44. https://doi.org/10.5172/jmo.837.14.4.330.

Mouratidis, Kostas. "Rethinking How Built Environments Influence Subjective Well-Being: A New Conceptual Framework." *Journal of Urbanism: International Research on Placemaking and Urban Sustainability* 11, no. 1 (January 2018): 24–40. https://doi.org/10.1080/17549175.2017.1310749.

Mueller, Swantje, Nilam Ram, David E. Conroy, Aaron L. Pincus, Denis Gerstorf, and Jenny Wagner. "Happy Like a Fish in Water? The Role of Personality–Situation Fit for Momentary Happiness in Social Interactions across the Adult Lifespan." *European Journal of Personality* 33, no. 3 (2019): 298–316. https://doi.org/10.1002/per.2198.

Munoz, Ricky T., Angela B. Pharris, and Chan M. Hellman. "A Linear Model of Adverse Childhood Experiences (ACEs) as Drivers of Lower Hope Mediated by Lower Attachment Security in an Adult Sample." *Journal of Family Violence* 37, no. 4 (May 2022): 671–79. https://doi.org/10.1007/s10896-021-00282-5.

Murray, Henry A. "Needs, Viscerogenic and Psychogenic." In *Milestones in Motivation: Contribution to the Psychology of Drive and Purpose,* edited by Wallace A. Russell, 364–71. New York: Appleton-Century-Crofts, 1970.

Murthy, Vivek. "Our Epidemic of Loneliness and Isolation: The U.S. Surgeon General's Advisory on the Healing Effects of Social Connection and Community." Office of the United States Surgeon General, 2023.

———. *Together: The Healing Power of Human Connection in a Sometimes Lonely World.* New York: Harper Wave, 2020.

———. "We Have Become a Lonely Nation. It's Time to Fix That." *New York Times,* April 30, 2023, sec. Opinion. https://www.nytimes.com/2023/04/30/opinion/loneliness-epidemic-america.html.

BIBLIOGRAPHY

National Academies of Sciences, Engineering, and Medicine. *Social Isolation and Loneliness in Older Adults: Opportunities for the Health Care System.* Washington, D.C.: National Academies Press, 2020. https://doi.org/10.17226/25663.

NCR. "How Frictionless Technology Made Its Way from Silicon Valley to Main Street." NCR, December 10, 2020. https://www.ncr.com/blogs/how-frictionless-technology-made-its-way-from-silicon-valley-to-main-street.

Neff, Kristin, and Oliver Davidson. "Self-Compassion: Embracing Suffering with Kindness." In *Mindfulness in Positive Psychology: The Science of Meditation and Wellbeing,* edited by Itai Ivtzan and Tim Lomas, 37–50. New York: Routledge, 2016.

Negi, Nalini Junko, Jennifer L. Siegel, Priya B. Sharma, and Gabriel Fiallos. " 'The Solitude Absorbs and It Oppresses': 'Illegality' and Its Implications on Latino Immigrant Day Laborers' Social Isolation, Loneliness and Health." *Social Science & Medicine* 273 (March 2021): 113737. https://doi.org/10.1016/j.socscimed.2021.113737.

Nguyen, Thuy-vy T., Richard M. Ryan, and Edward L. Deci. "Solitude as an Approach to Affective Self-Regulation." *Personality and Social Psychology Bulletin* 44, no. 1 (January 2018): 92–106. https://doi.org/10.1177/0146167217733073.

Nienhusser, H. Kenny, and Toko Oshio. "Postsecondary Education Access (Im)Possibilities for Undocu/DACAmented Youth Living with the Potential Elimination of DACA." *Educational Studies* 56, no. 4 (July 2020): 366–88. https://doi.org/10.1080/00131946.2020.1757448.

Nilsson, Björn. "Why Swedes Don't Speak to Strangers." BBC, November 27, 2023. https://www.bbc.com/travel/article/20201203-why-swedes-dont-speak-to-strangers.

Norton, Elizabeth. "Are Your Bacteria Jet-Lagged?" *Science,* October 17, 2014. https://www.science.org/content/article/are-your-bacteria-jet-lagged.

O'Connor, Shawn C., and Lorne K. Rosenblood. "Affiliation Motivation in Everyday Experience: A Theoretical Comparison." *Journal of Personality and Social Psychology* 70, no. 3 (1996): 513–22. https://doi.org/10.1037/0022-3514.70.3.513.

Ogolsky, Brian G., and Jill R. Bowers. "A Meta-Analytic Review of Relationship Maintenance and Its Correlates." *Journal of Social and Personal Relationships* 30, no. 3 (May 2013): 343–67. https://doi.org/10.1177/0265407512463338.

O'Keefe, Barbara J. "The Logic of Message Design: Individual Differences in Reasoning about Communication." *Communication Monographs* 55, no. 1 (1988): 80–103. https://doi.org/10.1080/03637758809376159.

O'Keefe, Barbara J., Bruce L. Lambert, and Carol A. Lambert. "Conflict and Communication in a Research and Development Unit." In *Case Studies in*

BIBLIOGRAPHY

Organizational Communication 2: Perspectives on Contemporary Work Life, edited by Beverley Davenport Sypher. New York: Guilford, 1997.

Otmar, Christopher D., and Andy J. Merolla. "Early Relational Exclusion and Present-Day Minority Stress, Social Anxiety, and Coping Responses among Sexual Minority Men." *Journal of Social and Personal Relationships* 41, no. 1 (2024): 46–68. https://doi.org/10.1177/02654075231206414.

Overall, Nickola C., and James K. McNulty. "What Type of Communication during Conflict Is Beneficial for Intimate Relationships?" *Current Opinion in Psychology* 13 (February 2017): 1–5. https://doi.org/10.1016/j.copsyc.2016.03.002.

Parker, Kim, Juliana Horowitz, Anna Brown, Richard Fry, D'vera Cohn, and Ruth Igielnik. "What Unites and Divides Urban, Suburban and Rural Communities." Pew Research Center, May 22, 2018. https://www.pewresearch.org/social-trends/2018/05/22/what-unites-and-divides-urban-suburban-and-rural-communities/.

Parks, Malcolm R. *Personal Relationships and Personal Networks.* Mahwah, N.J.: Lawrence Erlbaum, 2007.

Pasupathi, Monisha, and Ben Rich. "Inattentive Listening Undermines Self-Verification in Personal Storytelling." *Journal of Personality* 73, no. 4 (August 2005): 1051–86. https://doi.org/10.1111/j.1467-6494.2005.00338.x.

Pennisi, Elizabeth. "Meet the Psychobiome." *Science* 368, no. 6491 (May 2020): 570–73. https://doi.org/10.1126/science.368.6491.570.

Peterson, Suzanne J., and Kristin Byron. "Exploring the Role of Hope in Job Performance: Results from Four Studies." *Journal of Organizational Behavior* 29, no. 6 (August 2008): 785–803. https://doi.org/10.1002/job.492.

Petrusich, Amanda. "Nick Cave on the Fragility of Life." *New Yorker,* March 23, 2023. https://www.newyorker.com/culture/the-new-yorker-interview/nick-cave-on-the-fragility-of-life.

Philipsen, Gerry. "A Theory of Speech Codes." In *Developing Communication Theories,* edited by Gerry Philipsen and Terrance L. Albrecht, 119–56. Albany: State University of New York Press, 1997.

Pinquart, Martin, and Silvia Sorensen. "Risk Factor for Loneliness in Adulthood and Old Age: A Meta-Analysis." In *Advances in Psychology Research,* edited by Serge P. Shohov, 19:111–43. Hauppauge, N.Y.: Nova Science, 2003.

Prentice, Mike, Marc Halusic, and Kennon M. Sheldon. "Integrating Theories of Psychological Needs-as-Requirements and Psychological Needs-as-Motives: A Two Process Model." *Social and Personality Psychology Compass* 8, no. 2 (2014): 73–85. https://doi.org/10.1111/spc3.12088.

Prislin, Radmila, and William D. Crano. "Sociability: A Foundational Construct in Social Psychology." In *The Psychology of Sociability: Understanding Human*

Attachment, edited by Joseph P. Forgas, William D. Crano, and Klaus Fiedler, 3–56. New York: Routledge, 2022.

Putnam, Robert D. *Bowling Alone: The Collapse and Revival of American Community.* New York: Simon & Schuster, 2000.

Quaglia, Sofia. "How Your Microbiome Can Improve Your Health." BBC, November 15, 2021. https://www.bbc.com/future/article/20211115-how-your-microbiome-can-improve-your-health.

Quoidbach, Jordi, Maxime Taquet, Martin Desseilles, Yves-Alexandre de Montjoye, and James J. Gross. "Happiness and Social Behavior." *Psychological Science* 30, no. 8 (August 2019): 1111–22. https://doi.org/10.1177/0956797619849666.

Radtke, Kristen. *Seek You: A Journey through American Loneliness.* New York: Pantheon, 2021.

Raichle, Marcus E., and Debra A. Gusnard. "Appraising the Brain's Energy Budget." *Proceedings of the National Academy of Sciences* 99, no. 16 (August 2002): 10237–39. https://doi.org/10.1073/pnas.172399499.

Ramstead, Maxwell James Désormeau, Paul Benjamin Badcock, and Karl John Friston. "Answering Schrödinger's Question: A Free-Energy Formulation." *Physics of Life Reviews* 24 (March 2018): 1–16. https://doi.org/10.1016/j.plrev.2017.09.001.

Read, Glenna L., Harry Yaojun Yan, Philip B. Anderson, Laura P. B. Partain, Zachary Vaughn, Antonina Semivolos, Yeweon Kim, and Amy L. Gonzales. "Making Stability Dependable: Stable Cellphone Access Leads to Better Health Outcomes for Those Experiencing Poverty." *Information, Communication & Society* 25, no. 14 (October 2022): 2122–39. https://doi.org/10.1080/1369118X.2021.1928263.

Rees, Tobias, Thomas Bosch, and Angela E. Douglas. "How the Microbiome Challenges Our Concept of Self." *PLOS Biology* 16, no. 2 (February 2018): e2005358. https://doi.org/10.1371/journal.pbio.2005358.

Refresh Leadership. "83% of Companies Say 'Willingness to Learn' Essential for Job Applicants." *Refresh Leadership Blog,* July 28, 2021. https://www.refreshleadership.com/index.php/2021/07/83-companies-willingness-learn-essential-job-applicants/#:~:text=Specifically%2C%20more%20than%208%20in,very%20important%20when%20considering%20applicants.

Regan, Annie, and Sonja Lyubomirsky. "Inducing Sociability: Insights from Well-Being Science." In *The Psychology of Sociability: Understanding Human Attachment,* edited by Joseph P. Forgas, William Crano, and Klaus Fiedler, 79–97. New York: Routledge, 2022. https://doi.org/10.4324/9781003258582-7.

Reimer, Nils Karl, and Nikhil Kumar Sengupta. "Meta-Analysis of the 'Ironic' Effects of Intergroup Contact." *Journal of Personality and Social Psychology* 124, no. 2 (February 2023): 362–80. https://doi.org/10.1037/pspi0000404.

Reinhardt, Joann P., Kathrin Boerner, and Amy Horowitz. "Good to Have but Not to Use: Differential Impact of Perceived and Received Support on Well-Being." *Journal of Social and Personal Relationships* 23, no. 1 (2006): 117–29. https://doi.org/10.1177/0265407506060182.

Reis, Harry T., Margaret S. Clark, and John G. Holmes. "Perceived Partner Responsiveness as an Organizing Construct in the Study of Intimacy and Closeness." In *Handbook of Closeness and Intimacy,* edited by Debra J. Mashek and Arthur Aron, 201–25. Mahwah, N.J.: Lawrence Erlbaum, 2004.

Reis, Harry T., Guy Itzchakov, Karisa Y. Lee, and Yan Ruan. "Sociability Matters: Downstream Consequences of Perceived Partner Responsiveness in Social Life." In *The Psychology of Sociability: Understanding Human Attachment,* edited by Joseph P. Forgas, William Crano, and Klaus Fiedler, 239–57. New York: Routledge, 2022.

Reis, Harry T., Annie Regan, and Sonja Lyubomirsky. "Interpersonal Chemistry: What Is It, How Does It Emerge, and How Does It Operate?" *Perspectives on Psychological Science* 17, no. 2 (2022): 530–58. https://doi.org/10.1177/1745691621994241.

Reis, Harry T., Kennon M. Sheldon, Shelly L. Gable, Joseph Roscoe, and Richard M. Ryan. "Daily Well-Being: The Role of Autonomy, Competence, and Relatedness." *Personality and Social Psychology Bulletin* 26, no. 4 (April 2000): 419–35. https://doi.org/10.1177/0146167200266002.

Reissmann, Andreas, Ewelina Stollberg, Joachim Hauser, Ivo Kaunzinger, and Klaus W. Lange. "The Role of State Feelings of Loneliness in the Situational Regulation of Social Affiliative Behavior: Exploring the Regulatory Relations within a Multilevel Framework." *PLOS ONE* 16, no. 6 (June 2021): e0252775. https://doi.org/10.1371/journal.pone.0252775.

Ren, Dongning, and Anthony M. Evans. "Leaving the Loners Alone: Dispositional Preference for Solitude Evokes Ostracism." *Personality and Social Psychology Bulletin* 47, no. 8 (August 2021): 1294–1308. https://doi.org/10.1177/0146167220968612.

Ren, Dongning, Olga Stavrova, and Wen Wei Loh. "Nonlinear Effect of Social Interaction Quantity on Psychological Well-Being: Diminishing Returns or Inverted U?" *Journal of Personality and Social Psychology* 122, no. 6 (2022): 1056–74. https://doi.org/10.1037/pspi0000373.

Ren, Xinhua Steve. "Marital Status and Quality of Relationships: The Impact on Health Perception." *Social Science & Medicine* 44, no. 2 (January 1997): 241–49. https://doi.org/10.1016/S0277-9536(96)00158-X.

Riggio, Ronald E., and Alan Crawley. "Nonverbal Skills in Relationships: Too Little or Too Much May Be a Bad Thing." In *Nonverbal Communication in Close Relationships: What Words Don't Tell Us,* edited by Robert J. Sternberg and

Aleksandra Kostić, 341–61. Cham, Switzerland: Palgrave Macmillan, 2022. https://doi.org/10.1007/978-3-030-94492-6_13.

Rinderknecht, R. Gordon, Daniela V. Negraia, Sophie Lohmann, and Emilio Zagheni. "Understanding the Growth of Solitary Leisure in the U.S., 1965–2018." Rostock, Germany: Max Planck Institute for Demographic Research, 2023. https://doi.org/10.4054/MPIDR-WP-2023-025.

Ritzer, George, and Douglas J. Goodman. *Sociological Theory.* 6th edition. Boston: McGraw-Hill, 2004.

Rosa, Hartmut. *Social Acceleration: A New Theory of Modernity.* Translated by Jonathan Trejo-Mathys. New York: Columbia University Press, 2013. https://doi.org/10.7312/rosa14834.

Rosenblum, Cassady. " 'Do You Look After Your Neighbors as Close as Your Crop or Herd?' " *New York Times,* October 6, 2022, sec. Opinion. https://www.nytimes.com/2022/10/06/opinion/colorado-farmer-suicides.html.

Ross, Morgan Quinn, Eliz Akgün, and Scott W. Campbell. "Benefits of Solitude for Connected Individuals in the United States but Not China: Situating Solitude in Communicate Bond Belong Theory." *Computers in Human Behavior* 144 (July 2023): 107731. https://doi.org/10.1016/j.chb.2023.107731.

Routledge, Clay, Tim Wildschut, Constantine Sedikides, and Jacob Juhl. "Nostalgia as a Resource for Psychological Health and Well-Being: Nostalgia and Psychological Health." *Social and Personality Psychology Compass* 7, no. 11 (2013): 808–18. https://doi.org/10.1111/spc3.12070.

Ruddick, Graham. "End of Families Gathering Round the TV as Binge Watching Grows." *Guardian,* August 2, 2017, sec. Television & Radio. https://www.theguardian.com/tv-and-radio/2017/aug/03/end-of-families-gathering-round-the-tv-as-binge-watching-grows.

Ruesch, Jurgen, and Gregory Bateson. *Communication: The Social Matrix of Psychiatry.* New York: W. W. Norton, 1951.

Ryan, Richard M., and Christina Frederick. "On Energy, Personality, and Health: Subjective Vitality as a Dynamic Reflection of Well-Being." *Journal of Personality* 65, no. 3 (September 1997): 529–65. https://doi.org/10.1111/j.1467-6494.1997.tb00326.x.

Sandstrom, Gillian M., and Erica J. Boothby. "Why Do People Avoid Talking to Strangers? A Mini Meta-Analysis of Predicted Fears and Actual Experiences Talking to a Stranger." *Self and Identity* 20, no. 1 (January 2021): 47–71. https://doi.org/10.1080/15298868.2020.1816568.

Sandstrom, Gillian M., and Elizabeth W. Dunn. "Social Interactions and Well-Being: The Surprising Power of Weak Ties." *Personality and Social Psychology Bulletin* 40, no. 7 (July 2014): 910–22. https://doi.org/10.1177/0146167214529799.

Santoro, Erik, and David E. Broockman. "The Promise and Pitfalls of Cross-Partisan Conversations for Reducing Affective Polarization: Evidence from Randomized Experiments." *Science Advances* 8, no. 25 (June 2022): eabn5515. https://doi.org/10.1126/sciadv.abn5515.

Sasaki, Eri, and Nickola C. Overall. "Constructive Conflict Resolution Requires Tailored Responsiveness to Specific Needs." *Current Opinion in Psychology* 52 (August 2023): 101638. https://doi.org/10.1016/j.copsyc.2023.101638.

Scharp, Kristina M., and Elizabeth Dorrance Hall. "Family Marginalization, Alienation, and Estrangement: Questioning the Nonvoluntary Status of Family Relationships." *Annals of the International Communication Association* 41, no. 1 (January 2017): 28–45. https://doi.org/10.1080/23808985.2017.1285680.

Schinoff, Beth S., Blake E. Ashforth, and Kevin G. Corley. "Virtually (In)Separable: The Centrality of Relational Cadence in the Formation of Virtual Multiplex Relationships." *Academy of Management Journal* 63, no. 5 (October 2020): 1395–1424. https://doi.org/10.5465/amj.2018.0466.

Schmidt, W. D., P. J. O'Connor, J. B. Cochrane, and M. Cantwell. "Resting Metabolic Rate Is Influenced by Anxiety in College Men." *Journal of Applied Physiology* 80, no. 2 (February 1, 1996): 638–42. https://doi.org/10.1152/jappl.1996.80.2.638.

Schroeder, Juliana, Donald Lyons, and Nicholas Epley. "Hello, Stranger? Pleasant Conversations Are Preceded by Concerns about Starting One." *Journal of Experimental Psychology: General* 151, no. 5 (2022): 1141–53. https://doi.org/10.1037/xge0001118.

Schulman, Peter, Donald Keith, and Martin E. P. Seligman. "Is Optimism Heritable? A Study of Twins." *Behaviour Research and Therapy* 31, no. 6 (July 1993): 569–74. https://doi.org/10.1016/0005-7967(93)90108-7.

Scott, Allison M. "A Longitudinal Examination of Enacted Goal Attention in End-of-Life Communication in Families." *Communication Research* 50, no. 8 (2023): 1044–75. https://doi.org/10.1177/00936502211058040.

Segal, Steven P., Carol Silverman, and Tanya Temkin. "Social Networks and Psychological Disability among Housed and Homeless Users of Self-Help Agencies." *Social Work in Health Care* 25, no. 3 (October 1997): 49–61. https://doi.org/10.1300/J010v25n03_05.

Selye, Hans. *Stress without Distress*. Philadelphia: Lippincott, 1974.

Sharif, Marissa A., Cassie Mogilner, and Hal E. Hershfield. "Having Too Little or Too Much Time Is Linked to Lower Subjective Well-Being." *Journal of Personality and Social Psychology* 121, no. 4 (2021): 933–47. https://doi.org/10.1037/pspp0000391.

Sheldon, Kennon M., and Alexander Gunz. "Psychological Needs as Basic Motives, Not Just Experiential Requirements." *Journal of Personality* 77, no. 5 (2009): 1467–92. https://doi.org/10.1111/j.1467-6494.2009.00589.x.

Sheldon, Kennon M., and Sonja Lyubomirsky. "Achieving Sustainable Gains in Happiness: Change Your Actions, Not Your Circumstances." *Journal of Happiness Studies* 7, no. 1 (March 2006): 55–86. https://doi.org/10.1007/s10902-005-0868-8.

———. "Revisiting the Sustainable Happiness Model and Pie Chart: Can Happiness Be Successfully Pursued?" *Journal of Positive Psychology* 16, no. 2 (March 2021): 145–54. https://doi.org/10.1080/17439760.2019.1689421.

Sheldon, Kennon M., and Julia Schüler. "Wanting, Having, and Needing: Integrating Motive Disposition Theory and Self-Determination Theory." *Journal of Personality and Social Psychology* 101, no. 5 (2011): 1106–23. https://doi.org/10.1037/a0024952.

Shimshock, Claire J., and Bonnie M. Le. "Having the Will, Finding the Ways, and Wishes for the Future: A Model of Relational Hope and Well-Being." *Social and Personality Psychology Compass* 16, no. 8 (2022): e12697. https://doi.org/10.1111/spc3.12697.

Shin, Oejin, Sojung Park, Takashi Amano, Eunsun Kwon, and BoRin Kim. "Nature of Retirement and Loneliness: The Moderating Roles of Social Support." *Journal of Applied Gerontology* 39, no. 12 (December 2020): 1292–1302. https://doi.org/10.1177/0733464819886262.

Shirky, Clay. *Cognitive Surplus: Creativity and Generosity in a Connected Age.* New York: Penguin, 2010.

Shor, Eran, and David J. Roelfs. "Social Contact Frequency and All-Cause Mortality: A Meta-Analysis and Meta-Regression." *Social Science & Medicine* 128 (March 2015): 76–86. https://doi.org/10.1016/j.socscimed.2015.01.010.

Shor, Eran, David J. Roelfs, and Tamar Yogev. "The Strength of Family Ties: A Meta-Analysis and Meta-Regression of Self-Reported Social Support and Mortality." *Social Networks* 35, no. 4 (October 2013): 626–38. https://doi.org/10.1016/j.socnet.2013.08.004.

Sigman, Stuart J. "Handling the Discontinuous Aspects of Continuous Social Relationships: Toward Research on the Persistence of Social Forms." *Communication Theory* 1, no. 2 (May 1991): 106–27. https://doi.org/10.1111/j.1468-2885.1991.tb00008.x.

———. *A Perspective on Social Communication.* Lexington, Mass.: Lexington Books, 1987.

———. "Relationships and Communication: A Social Communication and Strongly Consequential View." In *The Meaning of "Relationship" in Interpersonal*

Communication, edited by Richard L. Conville and L. Edna Rogers, 47–68. Westport, Conn.: Praeger, 1998.

Sillars, Alan L., and Anita L. Vangelisti. "Communication: Basic Properties and Their Relevance to Relationship Research." In *Cambridge Handbook of Personal Relationships,* edited by Anita L. Vangelisti and Daniel Perlman, 331–51. Cambridge: Cambridge University Press, 2006.

Small, Mario Luis. *Someone to Talk To.* New York: Oxford University Press, 2017.

Smith, Kirsten P., and Nicholas A. Christakis. "Social Networks and Health." *Annual Review of Sociology* 34, no. 1 (2008): 405–29. https://doi.org/10.1146/annurev.soc.34.040507.134601.

Smith, Rachel A. "Language of the Lost: An Explication of Stigma Communication." *Communication Theory* 17, no. 4 (November 2007): 462–85. https://doi.org/10.1111/j.1468-2885.2007.00307.x.

Snap. "The Friendship Report 2020. Insights on How to Maintain Friendships, Navigate Endships, and Stay Connected in COVID-19." Snap, October 28, 2020. https://images.ctfassets.net/inb32lme5009/5MJXbvGtFXFXbdofsi Ybp/f24adc95cfad109994ebb8f9467bc842/Snap_Inc._The_Friendship_ Report_2020_-Global-.pdf.

Snyder, C. R. "Hope Theory: Rainbows in the Mind." *Psychological Inquiry* 13, no. 4 (2002): 249–75. https://doi.org/10.1207/S15327965PLI1304_01.

———. "Hypothesis: There Is Hope." In *Handbook of Hope: Theory, Measures, and Applications,* edited by C. R. Snyder, 3–21. San Diego: Academic Press, 2000.

Snyder, C. R., Jennifer S. Cheavens, and Scott T. Michael. "Hope Theory: History and Elaborated Model." In *Interdisciplinary Perspectives on Hope,* edited by Jaklin A. Eliott, 101–18. Hauppauge, N.Y.: Nova Science, 2005.

Snyder, C. R., Jennifer Cheavens, and Susie C. Sympson. "Hope: An Individual Motive for Social Commerce." *Group Dynamics: Theory, Research, and Practice* 1, no. 2 (1997): 107–18. https://doi.org/10.1037/1089-2699.1.2.107.

Snyder, C. R., and David B. Feldman. "Hope for the Many: An Empowering Social Agenda." In *Handbook of Hope: Theory, Measures, and Applications,* edited by C. R. Snyder, 389–412. San Diego: Academic Press, 2000.

Snyder, C. R., Shane J. Lopez, and Jennifer Teramoto Pedrotti. *Positive Psychology: The Scientific and Practical Explorations of Human Strengths,* 2nd ed. Thousand Oaks, Calif.: Sage, 2011.

Soliz, Jordan, Howard Giles, and Jessica Gasiorek. "Communication Accommodation Theory: Converging toward an Understanding of Communication Adaptation in Interpersonal Relationships." In *Engaging Theories in Interpersonal Communication: Multiple Perspectives,* edited by Dawn O. Braithwaite and Paul Schrodt, 3rd ed., 130–42. New York: Routledge, 2022.

Solomon, Denise Haunani, Miriam Brinberg, Graham D. Bodie, Susanne Jones, and Nilam Ram. "A Dynamic Dyadic Systems Approach to Interpersonal Communication." *Journal of Communication* 71, no. 6 (December 2021): 1001–26. https://doi.org/10.1093/joc/jqab035.

Sonnentag, Sabine, Dana Unger, and Inga J. Nägel. "Workplace Conflict and Employee Well-Being: The Moderating Role of Detachment from Work during Off-Job Time." *International Journal of Conflict Management* 24, no. 2 (2013): 166–83. https://doi.org/10.1108/10444061311316780.

Spithoven, A. W. M., S. Cacioppo, L. Goossens, and J. T. Cacioppo. "Genetic Contributions to Loneliness and Their Relevance to the Evolutionary Theory of Loneliness." *Perspectives on Psychological Science* 14, no. 3 (May 2019): 376–96. https://doi.org/10.1177/1745691618812684.

Spitzberg, Brian H. "What Is Good Communication?" *JACA: Journal of the Association for Communication Administration* 29, no. 1 (2000): 103–19.

Stadler, Gertraud, Kenzie A. Snyder, Andrea B. Horn, Patrick E. Shrout, and Niall P. Bolger. "Close Relationships and Health in Daily Life: A Review and Empirical Data on Intimacy and Somatic Symptoms." *Psychosomatic Medicine* 74, no. 4 (May 2012): 398–409. https://doi.org/10.1097/PSY.0b013e31825473b8.

Stafford, Laura. "Communication and Relationship Maintenance." In *Relationship Maintenance: Theory, Process, and Context,* edited by Brian G. Ogolsky and J. Kale Monk, 109–33. Cambridge: Cambridge University Press, 2019. https://doi.org/10.1017/9781108304320.007.

Stafford, Laura, and John A. Daly. "Conversational Memory: The Effects of Recall Mode and Memory Expectancies on Remembrances of Natural Conversations." *Human Communication Research* 10, no. 3 (March 1984): 379–402. https://doi.org/10.1111/j.1468-2958.1984.tb00024.x.

Stamps, David L., Lyric Mandell, and Renee Lucas. "Relational Maintenance, Collectivism, and Coping Strategies among Black Populations during COVID-19." *Journal of Social and Personal Relationships* 38, no. 8 (August 2021): 2376–96. https://doi.org/10.1177/02654075211025093.

Stancato, Daniel M., Dacher Keltner, and Serena Chen. "The Gap between Us: Income Inequality Reduces Social Affiliation in Dyadic Interactions." *Personality and Social Psychology Bulletin* (April 2023): 014616722311642. https://doi.org/10.1177/01461672231164213.

Stavrova, Olga, and Dongning Ren. "Is More Always Better? Examining the Nonlinear Association of Social Contact Frequency with Physical Health and Longevity." *Social Psychological and Personality Science* 12, no. 6 (August 2021): 1058–70. https://doi.org/10.1177/1948550620961589.

Stewart, John, and Jody Koenig Kellas. "Co-Constructing Uniqueness: An Interpersonal Process Promoting Dialogue." *Atlantic Journal of Communication* 28, no. 1 (January 2020): 5–21. https://doi.org/10.1080/15456870 .2020.1684289.

Stijovic, Ana, Paul A. G. Forbes, Livia Tomova, Nadine Skoluda, Anja C. Feneberg, Giulio Piperno, Ekaterina Pronizius, Urs M. Nater, Claus Lamm, and Giorgia Silani. "Homeostatic Regulation of Energetic Arousal during Acute Social Isolation: Evidence from the Lab and the Field." *Psychological Science* 34, no. 5 (May 2023): 537–51. https://doi.org/10.1177/09567976231156413.

Stolle, Dietlind, Stuart Soroka, and Richard Johnston. "When Does Diversity Erode Trust? Neighborhood Diversity, Interpersonal Trust and the Mediating Effect of Social Interactions." *Political Studies* 56, no. 1 (March 2008): 57–75. https://doi.org/10.1111/j.1467-9248.2007.00717.x.

Stotland, Ezra. *The Psychology of Hope: An Integration of Experimental, Clinical, and Social Approaches.* San Francisco: Jossey-Bass, 1969.

Strazdins, Lyndall, and Dorothy H. Broom. "The Mental Health Costs and Benefits of Giving Social Support." *International Journal of Stress Management* 14, no. 4 (November 2007): 370–85. https://doi.org/10.1037/1072-5245.14. 4.370.

Stulberg, Brad. "For People to Really Know Us, We Need to Show Up." *New York Times,* May 20, 2023, sec. Opinion. https://www.nytimes.com/2023/05/20/ opinion/the-case-for-obligation.html.

Sun, Jessie, Kelci Harris, and Simine Vazire. "Is Well-Being Associated with the Quantity and Quality of Social Interactions?" *Journal of Personality and Social Psychology* 119, no. 6 (2020): 1478–96. https://doi.org/10.1037/pspp0 000272.

Swann, William B., Alan Stein-Seroussi, and R. Brian Giesler. "Why People Self-Verify." *Journal of Personality and Social Psychology* 62, no. 3 (1992): 392–401. https://doi.org/10.1037/0022-3514.62.3.392.

Tay, Louis, and Ed Diener. "Needs and Subjective Well-Being around the World." *Journal of Personality and Social Psychology* 101, no. 2 (2011): 354–65. https:// doi.org/10.1037/a0023779.

Teo, Alan R., HwaJung Choi, Sarah B. Andrea, Marcia Valenstein, Jason T. Newsom, Steven K. Dobscha, and Kara Zivin. "Does Mode of Contact with Different Types of Social Relationships Predict Depression in Older Adults? Evidence from a Nationally Representative Survey." *Journal of the American Geriatrics Society* 63, no. 10 (2015): 2014–22. https://doi.org/10.1111/ jgs.13667.

Tergesen, Anne. "Your 401(k) Isn't Enough: To Invest for Retirement, Build Friendships and Hobbies." *Wall Street Journal,* December 29, 2022, sec.

Markets. https://www.wsj.com/articles/your-401-k-isnt-enough-to-invest-for-retirement-build-friendships-and-hobbies-11672269861.

Tomova, Livia, Kimberly L. Wang, Todd Thompson, Gillian A. Matthews, Atsushi Takahashi, Kay M. Tye, and Rebecca Saxe. "Acute Social Isolation Evokes Midbrain Craving Responses Similar to Hunger." *Nature Neuroscience* 23, no. 12 (December 2020): 1597–1605. https://doi.org/10.1038/s41593-020-00742-z.

Tonković, Željka, Dražen Cepić, and Ivan Puzek. "Loneliness and Social Networks in Europe: ISSP Data from 13 European Countries." *Revija za Sociologiju* 51, no. 3 (December 2021): 381–407. https://doi.org/10.5613/rzs.51.3.3.

Tracy, Karen. *Everyday Talk: Building and Reflecting Identities.* New York: Guilford Press, 2002.

Tracy, Sarah J. "Let's Talk: Conversation as a Defining Moment for the Communication Discipline." *Health Communication* 35, no. 7 (June 2020): 910–16. https://doi.org/10.1080/10410236.2019.1593081.

———. "Locking Up Emotion: Moving beyond Dissonance for Understanding Emotion Labor Discomfort." *Communication Monographs* 72, no. 3 (September 2005): 261–83. https://doi.org/10.1080/03637750500206474.

Tracy, Sarah J., and Angela Trethewey. "Fracturing the Real-Self↔Fake-Self Dichotomy: Moving toward 'Crystallized' Organizational Discourses and Identities." *Communication Theory* 15, no. 2 (2005): 168–95. https://doi.org/10.1111/j.1468-2885.2005.tb00331.x.

Treisman, Rachel. "A Spanish Athlete Spent 500 Days Alone in a Cave — for Science." NPR, April 17, 2023, sec. Europe. https://www.npr.org/2023/04/17/1170388759/500-days-cave-beatriz-flamini-spain.

Tse, Dwight C. K., Jennifer C. Lay, and Jeanne Nakamura. "Autonomy Matters: Experiential and Individual Differences in Chosen and Unchosen Solitary Activities from Three Experience Sampling Studies." *Social Psychological and Personality Science* 13, no. 5 (July 2022): 946–56. https://doi.org/10.1177/19485506211048066.

Twenge, Jean M., Brian H. Spitzberg, and W. Keith Campbell. "Less In-Person Social Interaction with Peers among U.S. Adolescents in the 21st Century and Links to Loneliness." *Journal of Social and Personal Relationships* 36, no. 6 (June 2019): 1892–1913. https://doi.org/10.1177/0265407519836170.

Ukanwa, Kalinda, Aziza C. Jones, and Broderick L. Turner. "School Choice Increases Racial Segregation Even When Parents Do Not Care about Race." *Proceedings of the National Academy of Sciences* 119, no. 35 (August 2022): e2117979119. https://doi.org/10.1073/pnas.2117979119.

United States Bureau of Labor Statistics. "American Time Use Survey," 2021. https://www.bls.gov/tus/.

BIBLIOGRAPHY

United State Census Bureau. "Census Bureau Releases New Estimates on America's Families and Living Arrangements," November 21, 2021. https://www.census.gov/newsroom/press-releases/2021/families-and-living-arrangements.html.

United States Government Accountability Office. "K–12 Education: Student Population Has Significantly Diversified, but Many Schools Remain Divided along Racial, Ethnic, and Economic Lines," 2022. https://www.gao.gov/products/gao-22-104737.

Uziel, Liad. "Individual Differences in the Social Facilitation Effect: A Review and Meta-Analysis." *Journal of Research in Personality* 41, no. 3 (June 2007): 579–601. https://doi.org/10.1016/j.jrp.2006.06.008.

———. "The Language of Being Alone and Being with Others." *Social Psychology* 52, no. 1 (2021): 13–22. https://doi.org/10.1027/1864-9335/a000430.

Uziel, Liad, and Tomer Schmidt-Barad. "Choice Matters More with Others: Choosing to Be with Other People Is More Consequential to Well-Being Than Choosing to Be Alone." *Journal of Happiness Studies* 23, no. 6 (August 2022): 2469–89. https://doi.org/10.1007/s10902-022-00506-5.

Vagni, Giacomo. "From Me to You: Time Together and Subjective Well-Being in the UK." *Sociology* 56, no. 2 (April 2022): 262–79. https://doi.org/10.1177/00380385211033147.

Vaillant, George E. *Triumphs of Experience: The Men of the Harvard Grant Study*. Cambridge: Belknap Press of Harvard University Press, 2015.

Valdez, Carmen R., Karen Schlag, Anita L. Vangelisti, and Brian Padilla. "The Enactment of Relational Maintenance When Guatemalan Parents Are Forcibly Separated from Their Families Due to Deportation." *Journal of Applied Communication Research* 52, no. 1 (May 2023): 72–90. https://doi.org/10.1080/00909882.2023.2206460.

Van Assche, Jasper, Hermann Swart, Katharina Schmid, Kristof Dhont, Ananthi Al Ramiah, Oliver Christ, Mathias Kauff, et al. "Intergroup Contact Is Reliably Associated with Reduced Prejudice, Even in the Face of Group Threat and Discrimination." *American Psychologist* 78, no. 6 (September 2023): 761–74. https://doi.org/10.1037/amp0001144.

Vanden Abeele, Mariek, Ralf De Wolf, and Rich Ling. "Mobile Media and Social Space: How Anytime, Anyplace Connectivity Structures Everyday Life." *Media and Communication* 6, no. 2 (May 2018): 5–14. https://doi.org/10.17645/mac.v6i2.1399.

Vangelisti, Anita L., and Nicholas Brody. "The Physiology of Social Pain: Examining, Problematizing, and Contextualizing the Experience of Social Pain." In *Handbook of the Physiology of Interpersonal Communication*, edited by

Lindsey S. Aloia, Amanda Denes, and John P. Crowley, 48–68. Oxford: Oxford University Press, 2021.

Vangelisti, Anita L., Mark L. Knapp, and John A. Daly. "Conversational Narcissism." *Communication Monographs* 57, no. 4 (December 1990): 251–74. https://doi.org/10.1080/03637759009376202.

Varma, Vijay R., Michelle C. Carlson, Jeanine M. Parisi, Elizabeth K. Tanner, Sylvia McGill, Linda P. Fried, Linda H. Song, and Tara L. Gruenewald. "Experience Corps Baltimore: Exploring the Stressors and Rewards of High-Intensity Civic Engagement." *Gerontologist* 55, no. 6 (December 2015): 1038–49. https://doi.org/10.1093/geront/gnu011.

Victor, Christina R., and Keming Yang. "The Prevalence of Loneliness among Adults: A Case Study of the United Kingdom." *Journal of Psychology* 146, no. 1–2 (January 2012): 85–104. https://doi.org/10.1080/00223980.2011.6 13875.

Villalonga, Patrick J., and Dario Moreno. "The Geography of Polarization." In *A Divided Union: Structural Challenges to Bipartisanship in America,* edited by Dario Moreno, Eduardo Gamarra, Patrick E. Murphy, and David Jolly, 6–23. New York: Routledge, 2021.

Vincent, David. *A History of Solitude.* Cambridge, U.K.: Polity, 2020.

Visser, Renée M. "Why Do Certain Moments Haunt Us? Conceptualizing Intrusive Memories as Conditioned Responses." *Biological Psychiatry: Cognitive Neuroscience and Neuroimaging* 5, no. 4 (April 2020): 375–76. https://doi.org/10.1016/j.bpsc.2020.02.007.

Vogel, Emily. "Digital Divide Persists Even as Americans with Lower Incomes Make Gains in Tech Adoption." Pew Research Center, 2021.

Wang, Fan, Yu Gao, Zhen Han, Yue Yu, Zhiping Long, Xianchen Jiang, Yi Wu, et al. "A Systematic Review and Meta-Analysis of 90 Cohort Studies of Social Isolation, Loneliness and Mortality." *Nature Human Behaviour* 7 (August 2023): 1307–19. https://doi.org/10.1038/s41562-023-01617-6.

Wang, Zheng, John M. Tchernev, and Tyler Solloway. "A Dynamic Longitudinal Examination of Social Media Use, Needs, and Gratifications among College Students." *Computers in Human Behavior* 28, no. 5 (September 2012): 1829–39. https://doi.org/10.1016/j.chb.2012.05.001.

Ward, Alie. "Microbiology (Gut Biome) with Dr. Elaine Hsiao." Ologies with Alie Ward, n.d. https://www.alieward.com/ologies/microbiology-gut-biome.

Wasserman, David. "To Beat Trump, Democrats May Need to Break Out of the 'Whole Foods' Bubble." *New York Times,* February 27, 2020, sec. The Upshot. https://www.nytimes.com/interactive/2020/02/27/upshot/democrats-may-need-to-break-out-of-the-whole-foods-bubble.html.

Watzlawick, Paul. *Ultra-Solutions, or, How to Fail Most Successfully.* New York: W. W. Norton, 1988.

Watzlawick, Paul, Janet Helmick Beavin, and Don D. Jackson. *Pragmatics of Human Communication: A Study of Interactional Patterns, Pathologies, and Paradoxes.* New York: W. W. Norton, 1967.

Weger, Harry, Gina Castle Bell, Elizabeth M. Minei, and Melissa C. Robinson. "The Relative Effectiveness of Active Listening in Initial Interactions." *International Journal of Listening* 28, no. 1 (January 2014): 13–31. https://doi.org/10.108 0/10904018.2013.813234.

Wells, Jenna L., Claudia M. Haase, Emily S. Rothwell, Kendyl G. Naugle, Marcela C. Otero, Casey L. Brown, Jocelyn Lai, et al. "Positivity Resonance in Long-Term Married Couples: Multimodal Characteristics and Consequences for Health and Longevity." *Journal of Personality and Social Psychology* 123, no. 5 (2022): 983–1003. https://doi.org/10.1037/pspi0000385.

Wheeler, Ladd, and John Nezlek. "Sex Differences in Social Participation." *Journal of Personality and Social Psychology* 35, no. 10 (October 1977): 742–54. https://doi.org/10.1037/0022-3514.35.10.742.

Wheeler, Ladd, Harry Reis, and John B. Nezlek. "Loneliness, Social Interaction, and Sex Roles." *Journal of Personality and Social Psychology* 45 (1983): 943–53. https://doi.org/10.1037/0022-3514.45.4.943.

Whillans, Ashley V., and Elizabeth W. Dunn. "Valuing Time over Money Is Associated with Greater Social Connection." *Journal of Social and Personal Relationships* 36, no. 8 (2019): 2549–65. https://doi.org/10.1177/026540 7518791322.

Wilmot, William W. "Communication Spirals, Paradoxes, and Conundrums." In *Bridges Not Walls: A Book about Interpersonal Communication,* edited by John Stewart, 7th ed., 320–34. Boston: McGraw-Hill, 1999.

——. "Metacommunication: A Re-Examination and Extension." *Annals of the International Communication Association* 4, no. 1 (December 1980): 61–69. https://doi.org/10.1080/23808985.1980.11923794.

Wilson, Patrick B., Jaison L. Wynne, Alex M. Ehlert, and Zachary Mowfy. "Life Stress and Background Anxiety Are Not Associated with Resting Metabolic Rate in Healthy Adults." *Applied Physiology, Nutrition, and Metabolism* 45, no. 8 (August 2020): 812–16. https://doi.org/10.1139/apnm-2019-0875.

Wilson, Peter. "Fighting Isolation in a Time of Crisis." *New York Times,* December 15, 2021, sec. Business. https://www.nytimes.com/2021/12/15/business/england-city-fights-isolation.html.

Wilt, Joshua, and William Revelle. "The Big Five, Everyday Contexts and Activities, and Affective Experience." *Personality and Individual Differences* 136 (January 2019): 140–47. https://doi.org/10.1016/j.paid.2017.12.032.

———. "Extraversion." In *Handbook of Individual Differences in Social Behavior*, edited by Mark R. Leary and Rick H. Hoyle, 27–45. New York: Guilford, 2009.

Winkielman, Piotr, and Andrzej Nowak. "Beyond the Features: The Role of Consistency in Impressions of Trust." *Social Psychological Bulletin* 17 (September 2022): 1–20. https://doi.org/10.32872/spb.9233.

Wolf, Wouter, Amanda Nafe, and Michael Tomasello. "The Development of the Liking Gap: Children Older Than 5 Years Think That Partners Evaluate Them Less Positively Than They Evaluate Their Partners." *Psychological Science* 32, no. 5 (May 2021): 789–98. https://doi.org/10.1177/0956797620980754.

World Health Organization. "Skills for Health: Skills-Based Health Education Including Life Skills: An Important Component of a Child-Friendly/Health-Promoting School." World Health Organization, 2003. https://apps.who.int/iris/bitstream/handle/10665/42818/924159103X.pdf.

Yong, Ed. *I Contain Multitudes: The Microbes within Us and a Grander View of Life*. New York: Ecco, 2016.

Yue, Qiang, Mingfei Cai, Bo Xiao, Qiong Zhan, and Chang Zeng. "The Microbiota–Gut–Brain Axis and Epilepsy." *Cellular and Molecular Neurobiology* 42, no. 2 (March 2022): 439–53. https://doi.org/10.1007/s10571-021-01130-2.

Zelenski, John M., Maya S. Santoro, and Deanna C. Whelan. "Would Introverts Be Better Off If They Acted More Like Extraverts? Exploring Emotional and Cognitive Consequences of Counterdispositional Behavior." *Emotion* 12, no. 2 (2012): 290–303. https://doi.org/10.1037/a0025169.

Zerwas, Felicia K., and Brett Q. Ford. "The Paradox of Pursuing Happiness." *Current Opinion in Behavioral Sciences* 39 (June 2021): 106–12. https://doi.org/10.1016/j.cobeha.2021.03.006.

Zhaoyang, Ruixue, Martin J. Sliwinski, Lynn M. Martire, and Joshua M. Smyth. "Social Interactions and Physical Symptoms in Daily Life: Quality Matters for Older Adults, Quantity Matters for Younger Adults." *Psychology & Health* 34, no. 7 (July 2019): 867–85. https://doi.org/10.1080/08870446.2019.1579908.

Zhou, Xinyue, Constantine Sedikides, Tiantian Mo, Wanyue Li, Emily K. Hong, and Tim Wildschut. "The Restorative Power of Nostalgia: Thwarting Loneliness by Raising Happiness during the COVID-19 Pandemic." *Social Psychological and Personality Science* 13, no. 4 (May 2022): 803–15. https://doi.org/10.1177/19485506211041830.

Zhou, Xinyue, Constantine Sedikides, Tim Wildschut, and Ding-Guo Gao. "Counteracting Loneliness: On the Restorative Function of Nostalgia." *Psychological Science* 19, no. 10 (October 2008): 1023–29. https://doi.org/10.1111/j.1467-9280.2008.02194.x.

———

ACKNOWLEDGMENTS

This book was a collaboration in the truest sense between Andy and Jeff. Over the two years they worked on it, they challenged each other to bring their ideas to life. They also supported one another, mostly at a distance, through countless phone calls, texts, and video chats, through the early uncertainties of the pandemic, the trials and tribulations of caring for young children during stay-at-home orders, and family illnesses and surgeries. Through it all, they learned just how central they were to one another's social biomes, creating the very moments of connection they wrote about.

Andy offers special thanks to Jennifer and Kai — his two greatest sources of hope — for the love, support, joy, and meaning they bring to his life each day. He also thanks his parents for their endless love and encouragement throughout his educational journey and his cross-country moves. He thanks Keith for his constant support and friendship. He's also grateful to all the friends who checked in about how the book was coming along and offered feedback.

Jeff thanks the University of Kansas and Department of Communication Studies for granting him a sabbatical leave and funding a trip to UCSB, both of which helped make this book possible. He thanks Amber, Graham, and Rowan for daily love and support. And, of course, he thanks his friends who listened to this book being built idea by idea, shaping its direction and focus along the way.

Andy and Jeff's research informed ideas in this book, and that research often involved the contributions of many talented researchers and assistants. Gratitude is expressed to all the people who contributed to Andy and Jeff's research that was cited in the book, with special thanks to the following collaborators: Gary Beck, Quinten Bernhold, Daniel Cochece Davis, Jess Dominguez, Afsoon Hansia, Amanda Holmstrom, Jennifer Kam, Teodora Mihailova, Christopher Otmar, Natalie Pennington, Abdullah Salehuddin, and Shuangyue Zhang. Andy and Jeff also thank Jonathan Bowman and Jennifer Kam for reading and providing helpful comments on some of the chapter drafts, as well as Christopher Otmar for his helpful assistance with references. And they thank all the scholars whose ideas they drew from and were inspired by in the book. It's Andy and Jeff's hope that they did these scholars' work justice.

Andy and Jeff also express their gratitude to their agent, Linda Konner, who believed in the book from the start and guided them through the proposal and contract phase. Andy and Jeff also offer a heartfelt thanks to Jean Thomson Black and Elizabeth Sylvia at Yale University Press for working with them, answering their questions, carefully reviewing their ideas, offering invaluable feedback on argumentation and formatting, and doing so with kindness and grace. Massive thanks are also extended to Liz DeWolf for her expert and heartening editorial work that helped bring the ideas in the book together.

ACKNOWLEDGMENTS

They thank Ann Twombly for her astute and insightful copyediting. Andy and Jeff also extend gratitude to Mary Pasti for her excellent and supportive copyediting assistance. They also thank the peer reviewers of the book's proposal and final draft for their time and extremely helpful suggestions and comments.

INDEX

INDEX

Hamermesh, Daniel, 82
Hari, Johann, 192 n.36
Hartnoll, Jenny, 120
Hawkley, Louise, 72
hedonic flexibility principle, 65
Hesiod, 149–50
Hicks, Donna, 154, 160
hikikomori, 181 n.45
Hill, Craig, 164 n.16
Hippel, William von, 3
Holt-Lunstad, Julianne, 1, 12
homeostatic social system, 59, 62,
    178 n.77
homophily, 119
hope, 3, 148–61; communal, 153; goals
    and, 150–51; responsive, 152–55
hope communication, 158–60
hope theory, 150–51
hormesis, 42, 53, 62, 95–97
hormetic social stress, 42–43, 78
human dignity: lack of as contagion,
    155–57; responsive hope and,
    152–54
humor, 76–77

inertia, social, viii, 79, 100
institutionally mediated interactions,
    104
interactions, social: constraints on,
    103–22; cross-class, 110; diversity in,
    115–16, 134–36; dividends of,
    113–17; energy costs of, 47, 49, 53;
    moments of, 126–28, 160–61;
    painful, 13–14; place and, 106–9;
    positive intergroup, 116; quality of,
    vii, 8, 9, 12–15, 63, 133–34;
    quantity of, 8–9, 133; social nutrition
    and, 8–9; space and, 106–9;
    structural constraints on, 104, 105,
    106–13; voluntariness of, 47, 50–51.
    See also connection; conversation

intergroup contact, 116, 186 n.52
interiority: age of, vii, 59; historical trends
    of, 81, 88–91; increase in, 79–81, 87;
    as isolation, 74–76; normalization of,
    75, 91–95; sociability and, 61–63;
    states of, 64; unwanted, 70–72. *See
    also* solitude
introversion, 66–69, 73
isolation, 5, 58; health concerns with, 80;
    interiority becoming, 74–76;
    normalization of, 75. *See also* loneliness
Israel, Tania, 113–14; *Beyond Your Bubble*,
    114

Jacobson, Nora, 154
John, Oliver, 114
Joiner, Thomas, 159–60
Jones, Aziza, 183 n.19

Kahneman, Daniel, 56
Kam, Jennifer, 157, 159
Kant, Immanuel: "Idea for a Universal
    History from a Cosmopolitan Point of
    View," 69, 70
Katrina, Hurricane, 151
King, Marissa, 172 n.78
Kingston, Helen, 119, 120
Klein, Ezra: *Why We're Polarized*, 109, 183
    n.23
Klinenberg, Eric: *Palaces for the People*,
    112–13
Knight, Christopher Thomas, 58,
    174 n.1

ladder of communication, 139–40
Lake Turkana, Kenya, 5
Leary, Mark, 4, 5–6, 11, 176 n.47
leisure time, 68, 80, 84, 93, 187–88 n.14
liking gap, 38
Liming, Sheila: *Hanging Out*, 57
listening behaviors, 22–28

INDEX

loneliness, 35, 144; chronic, 72, 73; definition of, 70–71, 72; evolutionary theory of, 72; health concerns with, 80; heritable component, 177 n.70; in periods of life, 75; self-perpetuating, 72–74. *See also* interiority; solitude

MacKerron, George, 182 n.11
McDermott, Diane, 150
McGeer, Victoria: "The Art of Good Hope," 153
McGhee, Heather: *The Sum of Us,* 115
McNulty, James, 167 n.10
Mead, George Herbert, 117
meaning, 27; co-construction of, 20
media, cultivation, 184–85 n.31; use of, 84–85, 90–91
Mehl, Matthias, 131, 164 n.14
memorable messages, 161
Menendian, Stephen, 108
Merolla, Andy, 3, 38, 50, 152, 157, 159
message design logics, 29, 170 n.43
messaging. *See* texting
microbiome, 124–25
microcultures, relational, 21
moments of social interaction, ix, 126–28, 160–61; emotions in, 126–27; episodes in, 126, 127; people in, 126, 127; routine in, 126, 127; structure in, 126, 127–28
Mourato, Susan, 182 n.11
Murthy, Vivek, 93, 184 n.27

needs, 2–3; belonging, 4–6, 10–12, 93, 164 n.17
Neubauer, Andreas, 152
Nezlek, John, 7
nostalgia, 77–78
nutrition, social, 8–9

O2, 114–15, 119
obligation, vii, 5–6, 27, 42–43, 57, 78, 89, 91, 93, 99
O'Connor, Shawn, 8, 62
O'Keefe, Barbara, 28–29, 169–70 n.43
Olver, Ian, 191 n.32
oneliness, 60
Otmar, Christopher, 152
Overall, Nickola, 167 n.10

Parks, Malcolm, 105
pathways thinking, 101, 150–54, 157–58, 190 n.14
perceived partner responsiveness, 31, 152
phatic communication, 9
Prentice, Mike, 8
Putnam, Robert: *Bowling Alone,* 185 n.35

Quoidbach, Jordi, 65

racial segregation, 107–8, 109–10, 183 n.17–23
Radtke, Kirsten: *Seek You,* 70
redlining, 107–8
Reis, Harry, 7, 31, 165 n.32
relational maintenance behaviors, 26, 32, 169 n.41
relationships: benefits in, 15–17; difficulties in, 19–20; energy for building, 52–54; health and, 1, 12–15, 80; interdependence of, 63; protecting, 97–99
reminiscence therapy, 77–78
responsive hope, 153
responsiveness, 31–32, 33, 34, 152, 191 n.26; clashing values and, 36–37; perceived partner, 31, 152
rhetorical vision, 117–19, 128, 134
Robson, Davina, 18–19
Rocky Ford, Colorado, 121–22

244

INDEX

Rosa, Hartmut: *Social Acceleration*, 181 n.32

Rosenblood, Lorne, 8, 62

Rosenblum, Cassady, 121–22

routines, social, 99–102, 126, 127

Santoro, Erik, 114

Sartre, Jean-Paul: *No Exit*, 77

segregation: costs of, 109–13; ideological, 108–9; racial, 107–8, 109–10

self-care, 60–61

self-verification theory, 186 n.59

Shirky, Clay, 85

Sigman, Stuart, 187 n.9

Silver, Nan, 25

Small, Mario, 104

Smith, Nicholas, 3

Snyder, C. R., 3, 150

sociability, 78; choosing, 12, 50–51, 136–38; connected, 63–66; disconnected, 63–66; interiority and, 61–63; solitude and, 59–61; states of, 64; unsocial, 69–70, 78

social anxiety, 45

social biome, ix, 123, 125–47; communication with strangers, 48, 64–65, 130–33, 188 n.30; diversity of moments, 115–16, 134–36; elements in, 128–47; ladder of communication in, 11, 138–40; quality of interactions, 8–9, 12–15, 133–34; restorative solitude, 142–47; sociability, choosing, 12, 136–38; social energy ratio and, 140–42

social calories, 6–10

social contact, 165 n.35. *See also* interactions, social

social-contextual perspective, 105

social energy, 44–45; factors in expenditure of, 47–52; gaining, 46–47; needed to build a relationship, 52–53; routines and, 99–102; spending, 46–52

social energy ratio, 140–42

social inertia, viii, 79, 100

social interaction diaries, 7–8

social media, vii, 11, 51, 76, 139

social nutrition, 8. *See also* social calories

social stress. *See* stress, social

social support, 21–22, 168 n.17

sociometer, 4

solidarity dividends, 115

solitude, 59, 73; connection and, 58–78; increase in, 79–81; restorative, 142–47; sociability and, 59–61; voluntariness of, 71–72

Spitzberg, Brian, 167 n.10

strangers, communication with, 48, 64–65, 130–33, 188 n.30; weak ties, 6

stress, social, x, 41, 53–55, 138; hormetic, 42–43, 78; managing, 14, 96

Stulberg, Brad, 27

Swann, William, 186 n.59

symbolic interaction, 117

technology: as barrier to socialization, 88–91; energy, 47, 51; frictionless, 89; mobile, 90, 139–40

telephone calls, 11, 51, 74, 140

texting, vii, 11, 51, 140

Thayer, Julian, 14

time: in life, 85–86; social, 84, 86; usage of, 79–85

total institutions, 103–4

Turner, Broderick, Jr., 183 n.19

TV, 82–84, 90, 98

Ukanwa, Kalinda, 183 n.19

unsocial sociability, 69–70, 78

upward spirals of positivity, 13, 159

U.S. Department of Labor: American Time Use Survey, 81–82, 83, 86, 179 n.11

U.S. Government Accountability Office, 108

INDEX